MR. BOJANGLES

The Biography of BILL ROBINSON

★

Jim Haskins and N. R. Mitgang

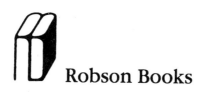

Robson Books

First published in Great Britain in 2001 by Robson Books,
10 Blenheim Court, Brewery Road, London N7 9NY

A member of the Chrysalis Group plc

First published in the USA by William Morrow and Company Inc.,
New York

British Library Cataloguing in Publication Data
A catalogue record for this title is available from the
British Library

ISBN 1 86105 423 8

Printed in Great Britain by Bell & Bain Ltd., Glasgow

To the memory of Eunice Riedel

—JIM HASKINS

To the memory of a great father, Jack Mitgang, a man who nurtured me with hopes and dreams.

—N. R. MITGANG

CONTENTS

INTRODUCTION

(The following is an open letter from Rosetta LeNoire (founder and artistic director of the AMAS Repertory Theatre; star of stage, screen, and television) to her godfather, Bill "Bojangles" Robinson.)

10/30/87

Dear Uncle Bo:

It has always been my theory that as long as people remember you in their conversations or in any manner after you leave this world, you are never gone or considered dead. Now that your biography has been written and you have been installed in the Hall of Fame for Dancers and Choreographers in Saratoga, New York, along with the great, late Mr. Fred Astaire, you will be dancing from decade to decade and accentuating your positive contributions to dance with your various dance steps, your special way of telling jokes, and your special way with humor will continue.

Uncle Bo, you have always been and will always be one of the most accomplished, creative, famous, and talented dancers. Your generosity to everyone, regardless of sex, race, creed, or color, will never be topped. I mean that in the full sense of the word. You just loved people. Your generosity on all levels to everyone will never be topped.

There has never been before, or since, as glamorous

and exciting an opening night on Broadway as the night *The Hot Mikado* premiered at the Broadhurst Theater, starring the Mayor of Harlem, the Mikado himself, tap dancer *extraordinaire,* Mr. Bill "Bojangles" Robinson with your cast of 125 black Japanese—all from Harlem. Thank God I was one of them—one of the Three Little Maids, Peep-Bo. Frances Davis, better known as Frances Brock, played Pitti-Sing and Gwendolyn Reyde played Yum-Yum. It is still to this day the highest point and one of my most theatrical and warmest opening-night memories.

I smile every time I think of how clean you were about yourself and your surroundings. You also insisted that all of our dressing rooms be kept in absolute neatness and cleanliness. You had chair covers made for all of us with three sets of shoe pockets in the back. On the left were pockets lined with shammy to contain our toothpaste, toothbrushes, washcloths, and soap. There was a pocket to the right of the chair covers for our brushes and combs. Our dressing tables not only had the lined oilcloth, but individual little paper doilies for makeup. And we could not leave our dressing room unless our tables were absolutely clean and organized. There could be no spilled powder, no rouge lying around, no opened lipstick. And that had to be done before the stage manager or production manager called, "Places," which meant go onstage as the overture started.

Uncle Bo, when I sum up your life, I can believe in miracles that only God can make. You were in some ways looked down upon as an Uncle Tom by your own race. And yet you opened doors for so many of every race. For me, you will remain as you were alive—an uncle, godfather, friend, and model. In the true sense, a wonderful model for all people. You know, I can remember you constantly saying, "Believe in yourself. You can accomplish a great deal with whatever you've got if you believe in yourself and always believe in God."

Uncle Bo, I'm thanking you not only for myself, but for all of us. And wherever you are, I know, quoting you, that *you've never been so happy since you been colored.*

God bless you and thanks again.

Love and prayers,
Rosetta

P.S. Next time you see my piano teacher, Eubie Blake, say, "His daffodil sends love and kisses."

MR.
BOJANGLES

1

"Everything Is Copasetic!"

On the death of Bill "Bojangles" Robinson, his friends decided that it was only fitting that his body lie in state in Harlem, where he had been the official "locality mayor" for some fifteen years and unofficial mayor for years before that. Originally, the plan was to have his body on view at Abyssinian Baptist Church, 132 West 138th Street, where the funeral would be held. But it was decided that even that huge church would be too small for the crowds expected, and so Bill's body was moved to the 369th Regiment Armory, Fifth Avenue at 142nd Street, not quite Harlem but close enough. Unfortunately, the last-minute change was not well publicized, and when Bill's body was brought to the armory at 4:00 P.M. on Saturday, November 27, 1949, only fifty persons were waiting outside. Word soon got around, however, and the crowds that had gathered at the church made their way east to the armory. For the next two days, the people of Harlem and others from around the world filed past the body, taking a last look at a man who had become a legend. Many among the thirty-two thousand people who visited the armory could not remember a time when the name Bojangles had not been a household word, when their parents and neighbors had not gossiped about his latest show, or gambling exploit, or award, or relationship with whites, speaking in that proprietary manner blacks used when talking about the few of their number who had managed to burrow out from under the layers of anonymity and degradation that the centuries had laid upon them.

So this was the famous Bojangles. Dressed in a dark blue suit, white shirt, and a figured gray tie, an American flag covering the lower half of the casket, he seemed too small physically to have borne all that fame and responsibility with such seeming effortlessness, too ordinary-looking to have counted presidents, governors, mayors, and the biggest names in the show business and sports worlds among his friends. But the mourners and the curious who filed by the casket were not looking at the spirit of Bill Robinson. They could not see the smile, hear the taps, feel the energy, or marvel at the personality that had taken that slim body so far and enabled Bill to do so much for so many.

At the funeral, Bill's friends and acquaintances tried to recapture that spirit. Few people wept. Instead, in quiet tones appropriate to the occasion, they shared with one another their favorite anecdotes about Bill. These anecdotes were as varied as the people who took part in the service or managed to witness it from inside the church, which could hold only three thousand of the thirteen thousand who attended. Jimmy Durante, Bob Hope, Louis B. Mayer, Darryl Zanuck, Jackie Robinson, Joe DiMaggio, Lee Shubert, Duke Ellington, Alfred Lunt, Irving Berlin, Cole Porter, Joe Louis, Milton Berle, and Don Newcombe were among the honorary pallbearers. Danny Kaye, Sugar Ray Robinson, W. C. Handy, Eddie "Rochester" Anderson, Ethel Merman, Arthur Treacher, James Barton, and a galaxy of other show business and sports stars sat side by side with Mayor Paul O'Dwyer, Manhattan Borough President Hugo Rogers, Chief Magistrate Edgar Bromberger, Parole Commissioner Samuel J. Battle, Manhattan Borough President-elect Robert F. Wagner, Jr., and Tammany Hall leader Carmine DeSapio. Robert Merrill of the Metropolitan Opera sang "The Lord's Prayer"; the New York Fire Department Glee Club sang "Softly and Tenderly." The presence of so many luminaries overshadowed the small group that comprised Bill's immediate family—his younger brother, Percy, blind now, who had come up from North Carolina, his ex-wife, Fannie, and his young widow, Elaine, and her family, whom Bill had adopted as his own—and those who had been almost like family to him: Marty Forkins, his manager for almost thirty-five years, Mrs. Rae Samuels Forkins—"The Blue Streak of Vaudeville"—and George W. Cooper, his vaudeville partner in the early years of the century.

Ed Sullivan was in charge of the funeral arrangements. Introduced by Noble Sissle, he read from a selection of telegrams, then said, "I suppose that in any analysis of show business it would be agreed that Bill Robinson hit the lightest taps, but despite the softness of his taps, no performer and very few Americans ever touched the heart of this city, and this nation, with greater impact, than Bojangles. As he was playing out his last one-week stand at the Harkness Pavilion on the bare and lonely stage of an oxygen tent, there was an amazing thing . . . people all over this country were praying for his recovery. Over ten thousand letters and cards came to the hospital. They came from little towns that some of us had never seen before. I remember one card from a little town, Pikestone, Minnesota, that enclosed a prayer for Bill's recovery. And some of the cards and letters were simply addressed, 'Bojangles, N.Y.,' because they knew they would be delivered. And yesterday in the bitter cold and snow, over twenty thousand people stood in line all day long outside the armory to pay their last tribute to a giant of his profession, a giant of his race, and a giant of kindliness.

"I know that all of the show people who are here today would tell you this, that Bojangles would be deeply pleased at this. He would be very proud that Mayor O'Dwyer ripped his entire day's schedule apart to be here to deliver the eulogy. He would be very thrilled to know that the kids, the schoolchildren of Harlem, were granted a half day off so they could take part in these services. I could just see Bill's eyes shining and snapping. . . . It would have been a great consolation for him to know that the fellows who were particularly close to him, New York's finest, from the time he passed, this long line of blue were guarding him in death, and at this very moment, this strong line of blue is stretching out to the cemetery in Brooklyn, covering the complete route because this was Bojangles. I know he would be happy to know that the flags of Harlem and Broadway are at half-mast in his honor, because just as Babe Ruth never forgot the orphanage from which he came, Bill Robinson never forgot the grandmother who had raised him, and that grandmother had been a slave. And so every honor that he received throughout his lifetime, he accepted as an honor to his mother and father, to his grandmother, and particularly to those of his race.

"And this last, vast tribute is another laid as Bill would want it laid, right in the hearts of his people. I am quite sure that Bill, I know that he was conscious that he had lived a very full and a very rich life. He told me one night when he was down at our apartment—he used to drop in occasionally—he said, 'You know, it's really been a great life for me. Within my lifetime, I've seen the miracle of a Dr. Ralph Bunche. I've seen and heard the world cheering Joe Louis. And I've seen Jackie Robinson not only break down the barriers of big-league baseball, but within three years go on to win The Most Valuable Player award as a player and as a gentleman.' I am quite sure that if Bill were here today he would say that everything was *copasetic*."[1]

Reverend Adam Clayton Powell, Jr., member of the U.S. House of Representatives and pastor of Abyssinian Baptist Church, spoke next. "We have gathered together at this afternoon hour to pay this last tribute of respect to one who we knew and loved, and who knew and loved us. And by our attendance here in this house of

God, and in the streets of our community, we indicate to his family and loved ones, our sympathy.

"As the minister of this church and as the minister of Mr. Robinson, I want to thank everyone who has done such a great task at making this last tribute of respect the kind of tribute that it should be. No one has done more than Ed Sullivan, and from the very first minute he has been sort of the assistant pastor of the Abyssinian Baptist Church. It is a great thing for the mayor of this great city to be present for this, the second largest job in the country, the mayor of New York, to come like this. To give his time, in another great tribute.

"We are all here today because we love Bill. Bill Robinson, better known as Bojangles, was born in Richmond, Virginia, on the twenty-fifth of May, eighteen hundred and seventy-eight, with the given name Luther Robinson. He was born the son of Maria Robinson and Maxwell Robinson. His parents died when he was but an infant, and he was reared by his grandmother who had been a slave. At the age of five he entered the public schools of Richmond but stayed only two years, running away from home to Washington, D.C., picking up nickels and dimes on the way by dancing.

"There wasn't a single outstanding nightclub or vaudeville house in the country, *including Miami,* that Bill Robinson didn't play at. North and South, he was the pet of police chiefs and country sheriffs.

"Bo had two sins, ice cream and gambling. . . ."

The nationwide radio audience heard the echo of ten thousand people laughing both inside and outside the church at the odd combination. But those who knew

Bojangles knew some story about those two vices. When the laughter subsided, Powell's rich, sonorous voice and his wry look bored into the minds and faces of the audience; Powell had a few points to make:

"Here before us this afternoon, my beloved friends of Harlem and those of you from outside our community, there rests the remains of a legend, for Bill was a legend. Born within the shadow of slavery and dying at the middle of the twentieth century, the most glorious century of mankind, Bill Robinson was a legend. He was a legend because he was ageless and raceless. Long after his bones have disintegrated and gone back to the kindred elements from whence they came, little kids from uptown and downtown and all around the states will be dancing up and down the stairs that Bill Robinson first discovered. He was a legend because, though he was an artist, he never missed an opportunity, whether seeing a little boy on the corner, or Shirley Temple in Hollywood, of teaching part of his artistry to someone on the way up. And that's greatness, too. Too often, people who are great like to keep what they have for themselves, but Bill was always ready to teach anyone, anywhere, how to dance. He was a legend because he was raceless. Bill wasn't a credit to his race, meaning the Negro race, Bill was a credit to the human race. He was not a great Negro dancer, he was the world's greatest dancer. Bill Robinson was Mr. Show Business himself. He stood out there at the end, as sort of a beacon light to all the little kids, the little hoofers, breaking their hearts out, Saturday's children, who loved the boards and the lights and the crowds, living in their little rooms and starving themselves just for the chance to work now and then. He was Mr. Show Business. He was Broadway.

"In some way the legend got around that Bill was an 'Uncle Tom.' Oh, no. You didn't know Bill if you had heard of that story. I was talking to some of the boys in Duke Ellington's band the other day and they were telling about a place they were playing in the Midwest and how they went around the corner on a cold day between shows to get some coffee and doughnuts, and the owner said, 'We can't serve you here.' Bill was on the bill with them, and they came back and told Bill the story. And Bill said, 'What!' Bill grabbed his pearl-handled gold gun [the crowd laughed again, for Bill and his gold gun were as legendary as their owner] and went around the corner. He said to Johnny Hodges, Lawrence Brown, Cootie [Williams], 'C'mon, fellas.' They went around the corner and packed into this place and sat down and Bill laid this pearl-handled gold gun on the counter and said, 'Coffee and doughnuts!' and they had coffee and doughnuts!

"There has been no one that I know of in show business who literally gave their heart, for Bill Robinson died, not from a broken heart, for he was happy, he died from a heart that had become weakened because he had danced so much. He had a remarkable physique and perfect health, but just because he loved show business he gave his heart, literally, to dancing. And who is to say, outside of God Himself, that making people happy isn't the finest thing in life. Surely not me, His minister. Maybe some of you can sit in the cynic's seat, but I can stand here as a man of God for twenty years in this pulpit and tell you that only He, to who we all must go, can decide. One thing I do know, no one ever raised as much money for human suffering as Bill Robinson. There was never a benefit—there was never a human being in need that Bill, *if he had the money,* didn't give to. The money that he raised for the house of Israel, for this benefit, for that, would total probably a hundred million dollars. The bonds that he sold during wartime. You know, there is something about the way he died that I love. He made four million dollars and he died without a cent. I like it. You know why? It showed that he not only had faith in God, but faith in his fellow man. He knew that whatsoever a man sowed he would reap. He knew that he couldn't dance for sixty years, he couldn't pack Madison Square Garden, he couldn't give away so much money, he couldn't raise money for the poor and suffering, without when the time came that they would remember. And so, they have remembered. And it's right. It's fitting that we should see that Bill's last bills were taken care of. Thank you, Ed Sullivan, for Bill. Thank you, all the committees that have raised money for Bill. You can *never* pay him back, but he knew that you would take care of him. He had faith in man, and faith in God.

"Bill Robinson fed them when they were hungry. He danced for them to get clothes when they were naked. There wasn't any charity that he'd ever turn down. And the Master said, 'The greatest rule in life is to love thy neighbor as thyself.' And He also said, 'Do unto others as you would have them do unto you.'

"The curtain has come down. The lights have dimmed. The last hand is finished. The theater is emptying. No more stairs to climb. No more boards to tap.

The last click is gone. . . . Somewhere, I know not where, but I know it is somewhere, Bill says, 'Copasetic!'"2

After the funeral, a cortege took Bill's body to Brooklyn, where he was to be buried in the actors' section of Evergreen Cemetery. Mayor Paul O'Dwyer and the other honorary pallbearers marched on either side of the hearse as the cortege made its way from the church to Lenox Avenue; they then fell out and stood with heads bared as the procession continued to 135th Street. There, it moved west to Seventh Avenue, then south to 110th Street, where the mounted police escort was replaced by a squad of motorcycle patrolmen. An elderly well-dressed black man walked directly behind the hearse, though he was not scheduled to be there. But the Harlem residents knew who he was—another soul whom Bill Robinson had helped.

The motorcade continued west to Central Park West and then south as people stood five and six deep behind the police lines. At Columbus Circle, the procession continued down Broadway to Fifty-seventh Street, turning there to Seventh Avenue and proceeding south to Duffy Square, where traffic had been diverted and a crowd, estimated at fifty thousand, waited. An American Legion color guard stood at attention before the statue of Father Duffy, and Noble Sissle's thirty-piece orchestra played "Give My Regards to Broadway." On the marquee of the Palace Theater across Seventh Avenue was draped a black-bordered banner that read SO LONG, BILL ROBINSON. HIS FEET BROUGHT JOY TO THE WORLD. From Times Square, the cortege moved south on Broadway to Fortieth Street and then east to

Second Avenue, down Second Avenue to Chrystie Street, and across the Manhattan Bridge to Brooklyn, where it followed Fulton Street to Eastern Parkway, to Bushwick Avenue, and finally to Conway Street and the cemetery. There, Bill's weary old dancing bones were laid to rest at last, seventy-one years after those miraculous feet came into the world and about sixty-three years after they first tapped across a professional stage, some 250 miles from his birthplace, Richmond, Virginia, and light-years away from the circumstances of his birth, as Reverend Powell had put it, "within the shadow of slavery."

Even in death, Bill Robinson continued to make history. The funeral, witnessed by many thousands of people, was the largest that New York had ever seen. But few in attendance that day could realize how the name Bojangles would be sullied in the years to come—especially by future black generations. As his legend spread, and as his fame as one of the greatest black American entertainers grew, so did his vulnerability to undefended accusations increase. He was called an Uncle Tom and criticized for not having done more to fight segregation. But his critics rarely had any understanding of the circumstances of his life or of his time.

Richmond, Virginia, Bill's birthplace, had been the seat of government of the ill-starred Confederacy. The city had fallen on April 3, 1865, and suffered under Union occupation during five years of Reconstruction until it was allowed to return to self-government under Virginia's new constitution. In 1869 the state General Assembly had empowered Governor Gilbert C. Walker to replace the Richmond City Council, which had held office under General Edward R. S. Canby, commander of Military District No. 1, and in the subsequent mayoral election in Richmond, a man named Ellyson had won. But the old mayor, George Chahoon, was anxious to retain the office and refused to recognize the validity of Ellyson's election. Submitted to a panel of judges, the decision as to who would be mayor of Richmond was to be rendered on April 27, 1880, and supporters of both sides packed the courtroom on the top floor of the State Capitol. As the judges filed in and the spectators rose, first the gallery, then the main floor of the room collapsed.[3] The "Capitol Disaster" was the last of a long line of disasters, in the view of the white residents of Richmond. The black residents were quite certain that there were more disasters in store for them, now that the Federal troops had pulled out. For a brief time they had enjoyed some political rights: twenty-one blacks had served in the lower house of the Virginia Legislature and one black Virginian, John M. Langston, had been elected to Congress. But now that they no longer enjoyed the protection of Federal troops, blacks faced the erosion of even the small amount of power they had enjoyed, not to mention their gains in education and employment opportunities.

In the year of the "Capitol Disaster," Maxwell Robinson, a machinist, and his wife, Maria, a "choir director," lived at 915 North Third Street with their two-year-old son, Luther.[4] A few years later, a second son, William, was born. By 1885, Maxwell and Maria were dead. There exists no documentation of the circumstances of their deaths, though it is thought that they died from a questionable accident, rather than of natural causes. A fire destroyed all Richmond's census and government records prior to 1885, and all official white documentation was lost. But even if the census records had survived, so many histories were lost also because the methods of information-gathering were slanted heavily against the black population. Certain black children who lived in white homes were simply recorded as servants' children with no other identification, for blacks were considered mere property. Orphans also went unrecorded, and after the death of his parents, young Robinson would have failed to make the census.

But Bojangles's history was always an exception. One man survived to tell the true stories of Bo's beginnings.

Lemmeul V. "Eggie" Eggleston was interviewed in 1973, a few days after dedicating the new Bill Robinson statue in Bojangles Park in Richmond. He was one of Robinson's two closest friends during Bill's last years in Richmond, and a partner in their many "mis-cheevious" adventures. "I'm not gonna tell ya anything bad about Bill Robinson. There's a whole lot of things Bill did that I never told anybody yet," Eggleston said while tapping his finger for emphasis. "I don't think it'd be advisable for me to tell them particular things because you couldn't rectify any mistakes you made back then." Eggie sat down thinking he would tell a few minutes' worth of Bojangles stories, but wound up talking through breakfast, lunch, and almost dinner. He said that Robinson's famous, or infamous, temper showed clearly even back then.

There was justification for it. Perhaps when young Bo was in school, he acted out anger at being abandoned by his parents' death. Part of his problem was his name. With a moniker like Luther, he was the brunt of more jokes than he cared to take, and so he decided to appropriate his younger brother's name. The story goes that Luther and William had a terrible fight, and the younger boy must have taken a bad beating, for henceforth not only did Luther carry the name William, or Bill, but the younger brother had a name his older brother had bestowed upon him—Percy, one that no doubt occasioned him as much discomfort as Luther had caused Bill. "Oh, I thought that was a joke," Bill's third wife, Elaine, said in 1974, "although I do remember someone once calling him Luther in a show. Maybe they had got it from some article about him. He got angry and yelled, 'Don't call me Luther!'"

After their parents died, the brothers were taken into the home of their grandmother, Bedilia Robinson, who had been raised as a slave in Richmond. Bedilia was the exception to the tradition of the nurturing black extended family that welcomed orphans and brought them up as their own. On the contrary, Bedilia Robinson didn't want the responsibility of raising her two small grandsons. However, according to Rae Samuels Forkins, wife of Bill's longtime manager, Marty Forkins, Bedilia Robinson gave them as much love as she could. In 1974, Rae Samuels recalled accompanying Bill once when he played Richmond, Virginia. A very old, very aristocratic woman showed up at the theater and asked to see "Snowball." This was none other than Bill Robinson, whose grandmother had taken him along when she went to work for the wife of a wealthy white banker. He would sit in the laundry basket while his grandmother took the clothes from the line. Bill never explained how he had acquired the nickname "Snowball." Perhaps it was suggested by his little brown face peering out from beneath a pile of freshly laundered sheets. Or perhaps the wealthy white woman was the person who introduced Bill to vanilla ice cream, for which he had a lifelong passion.

Bill's grandmother was old and infirm and incapable of caring for the two children. She did not want them and fought the responsibility of their custody. The case was brought before Judge John Crutchfield, the famous "Justice John" of Richmond's criminal court, whose fame rested greatly on his fairness and his concern for the wayward youth of the town. More than anyone else, he was the source of these youths' healthy respect for the law, a quality that distinguished not just Bill Robinson but other youths of Richmond, black and white. If Bill was present during the conversation between the judge and his grandmother, it must have been traumatic to hear the woman he loved the most list the reasons why she should not take care of her son's children. From then on, all family life was gone for young Bo. Judge Crutchfield took the boys into his own home until a suitable guardian could be found. Lemmeul Eggleston recalls that Bill was living with his grandmother and a man named Simon Robinson on the 800 block of St. Paul Street, when he and Bill hung around together. But Eggie was rarely inside the Robinson home. Bill's grandmother, a religious Baptist, would never let Bill dance or even utter that evil word in her company. And Eggie, to Bedilia Robinson, was just another street kid who aided and abetted young Bo in his most serious street crime—dancing. Eggie was smart enough to know he would not be a welcome guest.

Eggleston was about four years Bill's junior, but he was his closest friend. Young Bill may have chosen a younger friend because it was a way for him to control the relationship. He had a habit of insisting on being right and arguing his case until his opponent capitulated; Eggie was inclined to let him have his way. Eggie went to the Navy Hill school, but apparently he found time to join Bill in a variety of childhood escapades and entrepreneurial pursuits. In those days before child labor laws, there were a number of ways an energetic youngster could make money. "I knew Bill for some time, but we weren't social," Eggleston recalled in 1973, while seated at his dining-room table. "We shelled peas in the Jefferson Market [the main shopping area of Richmond at that time]. Then we started bootblacking because it was in contact with us daily. Most of the dancing was done around Seventh, Eighth, or Ninth and Broad. Broad Street—Twelfth and Broad. Neighborhood there from Seventh and Grace to Seventh and Marshall down to Eleventh and Twelfth and back up to Twelfth and Broad. By the Olds Hotel and back up to Seventh and Broad, which had a theater. But that's a long time ago.

"Five cents was the price of a shine," Eggleston continued, "and I've got the brush and the rag right in that box over there. That's the box Bill Robinson and I shined shoes with. Now, why I have that box: Bill got twenty cents from me and he didn't pay me that twenty cents and I swiped that box." Besides bootblacking, the two boys also danced outside the Ford

Theater. But even if they could earn the price of admission, they couldn't go in. The shows were for whites, and all the performers were whites, even though they darkened their faces with burnt cork and played "darkies."

The shows were minstrel shows, the first truly American contribution to the history of theater and a form that was then in its decline.[5] Born on Southern plantations among slave bands, the minstrel show was first brought to the towns by semiprofessional black bands under the direction of enterprising whites. By the early 1800s, some white performers had begun to imitate the blacks, making up their faces with burnt cork and performing jigs and other dances to popular songs about blacks. But it was a little-known performer named Thomas Rice who brought minstrelsy into its own around 1830. Taking the name, and the funny little dance, of an old slave named Jim Crow who happened to be singing and dancing in the stable behind the theater where Rice was performing, Daddy "Jim Crow" Rice became an immediate hit. (The term "Jim Crow" later came to represent institutionalized discrimination against black people.)

Minstrel groups sprang up across the South and soon took the entertainment north. The Virginia Minstrels, Buffalo's Christie Minstrels, and the Ethiopian Serenaders were just some of the all-white troupes who performed in blackface. By the mid-1850s, there were at least ten major minstrel houses in New York City, and a correspondingly large number of such houses in smaller cities.

As they became institutionalized, the shows took on

an established pattern. There were three acts. In the first, a line of performers was seated onstage in a semi-circle. An interlocutor, or straight man, in the middle of the group engaged in a series of humorous exchanges with the two end men, called "Mr. Tambo" and "Mr. Bones":

END MAN: Why did the chicken cross the road?
INTERLOCUTOR: I don't know. Why?
END MAN: To get to the other side!

The second act was called the "olio" and included songs and dances, banjo playing, animal acts, and anything else the performers could come up with. The third act, called the "after-piece," also featured variety entertainment, but usually involved theatrical or dramatic pieces and takeoffs on popular plays or operas.

From start to finish, the minstrel show depended on white perceptions of black culture, from the songs and dances, to the dialect, to the burnt cork on the performers' faces. The shows presented caricatures of blacks, but they were not without sympathy, and their humor was, in the main, not cruel. The early minstrels visited plantations to study black music, dancing, and humor, and thus maintained a certain freshness and a somewhat accurate portrayal in their performances.

All this changed after the Civil War. The structure of post–Civil War minstrel shows followed the same traditional formula, but the attitude was different. No longer did white minstrels seek out blacks for fresh material; therefore, the caricatures became wooden. White southerners had no sympathy for former slaves, and so the caricatures became cruel. Blaming the blacks for the war and its effect on southern life, the primarily southern-based minstrels created stereotypes that still exist in the minds of some whites today. So thoroughly ingrained did these stereotypes become in the view of the theatergoing public that when black performers entered minstrelsy after the war, they had to conform to the original formula, including performing in blackface. In effect, they had to play caricatures of caricatures of themselves—a practice that continues to this day in many film and video portrayals of blacks. Eggleston recalled, "The actors used to use burnt cork on their face. Now the colored, some of them, was colored and didn't need the burnt cork. I had to black my face when I was in the show and my lips around here. We had large collars. . . ." Eggleston paused. He was looking at a picture of himself in costume. His face changed and looked troubled. "I was criticized so much about that play 'cause I used 'Old Black Joe.' I was twenty years old when I played that. Bill Robinson never used burnt cork."

According to Lemmeul Eggleston, the big shows that came through town were sponsored by George H. Primrose and his various partners, and all were white shows. "Primrose and Dockstader. Primrose and West. That's where I started, imitating Primrose and West." Whenever the minstrels arrived in town, they'd go into full costume formation and parade along the town's main street, Broad Street in Richmond, and perform music, songs, and dance numbers to announce and advertise the show. Bill also credited George Primrose as his most important early influence, though he would also accord this honor to others.

According to Carl Wittke in *Tambo and Bones,* Primrose, whose real name was Delaney, began his stage career as a juvenile clog dancer in 1867 with McFarland's Minstrels in Detroit. After appearing with various minstrel companies and circuses, he formed a partnership with William H. West, and Primrose and West's Minstrels were on the road for thirty years. In the 1890s these shows included *The Forty Whites and Thirty Blacks,* though it was hardly an example of early integration on the stage. Really two separate shows, each had its own stage managers, and the performers traveled separately and stayed in different lodgings. Later, Primrose teamed up with Lew Dockstader, whose real name was George Alfred Clapp and who performed in blackface throughout his career. Primrose and Dockstader were among the last minstrels to tour the large cities.[6]

For two small bootblacks it was natural, when business was slow, to lay down their rags and try a few steps. "We actually started dancing for pennies in front of the Ford Theater," said Eggleston. "No colored people went in that theater; no colored dancers was in there. Now it's called the Globe Theater, over on Broad Street, Twelfth and Broad. We danced on any corner where people would throw us pennies." Eggie did the soft-shoe. Bill's specialty was the buck-and-wing, a minstrel term that referred to a combination of jig and "pigeon wing" or "chicken wing," a dance in which the neck was held still and the arms and legs flailed about like a bird's. They danced without benefit of music.

"Music wasn't even thought about," said Eggleston. "The *p*'s, *t*'s, that's how we got the music."

The *p*'s and *t*'s were part of the scatting chorus they used in their performance. Eggie used a comb and a piece of paper to make music when he wasn't singing a song that he and Bill wrote and composed:

> *Kid had a cow*
> *Cow had a calf*
> *Sold the cow for seven-and-a-half*
> *Then we went down the river*
> *But we couldn't get across*
> *Paid five dollars for an old gray horse*
> *Now the horse wouldn't pull*
> *So we sold it for a bull*
> *Bull wouldn't holler*
> *So we sold it for a dollar*
> *Dollar wouldn't pass*
> *So we kicked it in the grass*
> *There comes somebody . . .*

While reciting these lyrics, Eggie would make a funny lisping sound at the letters *p* and *t*. In fact, if you got too close, you would get sprayed with spittle. *That* was their music.

"Folks would throw us pennies," Eggleston recalled. "If I got more money than Bill, then he would just take it away from me, and I took it away from him. We weren't putting no hat around." Neither Bill nor Eggie entertained dreams of making a living by dancing. For them, dancing was just one of many ways to get pennies.

Another way was shelling or shucking peas. According to Eggleston, "The farmers of the country used to raise peas and then bring them into Richmond in the shells. We got two cents a quart for shelling them. 'Course, if a bag of peas were laying around and weren't doing nothing . . . that's where the situation started. Something happened we had control over but I don't want to say anything about that. But anyhow, the police got after us, chased us for a considerable length of time, and then they caught us. Took us to the police station, and Bill danced up those steps, danced all the way up those steps. When we got inside, one of the policemen said, 'Let me see some of those steps, you dancing man.' So Bill started dancing." While the police officers were watching Bill dance, Eggie saw his chance to make a quick getaway, and he took off. Bill took off after him. "So," said Eggleston, "they lost the bag of peas, they lost me, and then they lost Bill Robinson."

Some of the money they earned was spent on food. As Eggie said, "We were what you call 'habitual eaters.' There was a man used to make some stuff we called 'slung dung.' That consisted of everything the bakers had left over—pie crusts, doughnuts. You could get a whole lot for a cent. You always wanted a corner piece 'cause more crust was on it. There were two bakers in Richmond, Briggs and Broom, on Martha Street. Broom run us out, but we could still get it from Briggs."

When Eggleston was asked where some of the other money went, he smiled and quickly said, "A cancellation comes to that. I just can't tell. We were never what you call fancy dressers here in Richmond 'cause we were among old folks—always seemed like that. We cut down pants. We had to go by the old people. After the old people died, then we kids commenced to running wild. At those times we were known as 'mis-cheevious.'" And what happened when they didn't have money for something to eat? "There'd be an apple on a stand, a plum, a pear, anything, and Bill and I'd pass by there and that apple left the stand and followed us."

One time, Bill stole a rather large fish and tried to hide it under his coat. Unfortunately, the tail of the fish stuck out from beneath the coat's hem. Hauled up before Justice Crutchfield, Bill was advised by the learned judge, "Next time, either steal a smaller fish, or get a longer coat."

But it was one "mis-cheeviously misappropriated" item, a beaver hat, that led to Bill Robinson being given the nickname "Bojangles." A man named Lion J. Bou-jasson owned a hatmaking and hat-repair shop in the 800 block of Broad Street. The neighborhood young-sters, confronted with such an unfamiliar name, called the man "Bojangles." Lemmeul recalled, "One day a beaver disappeared. A beaver was a tall hat, you see. Now that beaver disappeared and we, between the two of us, we couldn't sell it. So, I saddled the thing on Bill Robinson." The episode became a joke on the street. "Who took Bojangles's hat?" someone asked. "Why, Bo-jangles took it," another would reply, parodying the hatmaker's name and pointing at Bill. The name stuck.

Others tried to claim credit for having given Robin-son his famous nickname, but Bill himself stated he had gotten it back in Richmond. There is a ring of authen-ticity to this story of children mispronouncing an unfamiliar name and jokingly parodying that name. Lemmeul Eggleston tapped his finger to insist his story was the truth, and in 1973, when he told it, there was no one left alive to dispute him.

According to Bill Robinson, it was also back in the early Richmond days that he coined the word "copasetic"—everything is better than all right, better than fine and dandy. Bill was shelling peas at the Jefferson Market, a *New York Daily Mirror* reporter asked him how he was, and the reply just popped into his head: "I'm copasetic." He used the word the rest of his life, but it was not popularized until he used it to open his vaudeville and radio performances—"Good evening. Everything is copasetic!"—and in the movies he made with Shirley Temple in the mid-1930s. After that, the word was included in *Funk and Wagnalls Standard Dictionary.*[7]

Over the next few years, Bill and Eggie continued to dance on street corners, much to the consternation of both their families. Whatever anger Bill ever expressed against his grandmother in later years concerned her strict Baptist faith and her disapproval of dancing. Eggie's family was more flexible, only prohibiting his dancing on Sundays. His mother used to preach, "Son, don't you dance on Sunday. Don't you dance on Sunday. It's a sin and a shame." Neither paid much attention to their families anyway, and in that they were not unlike many other boys in Richmond, black and white.

Over in South Richmond a white youth named Lemuel Gordon Toney played baseball in the streets when he should have been out earning money to help support his family, whose fortunes had not survived the

Civil War. (His brother, at least, was a local barber in the Jefferson Market, not far from Broom, the baker.) A stray ball and a broken window introduced him to Judge John Crutchfield, who urged him to continue playing. Toney related, and no doubt embellished, his favorite Crutchfield story in his autobiography, *What a Life, I'm Telling You.*

"He said, 'What is your name young man?' 'Lemeul Gordon Toney, they call me Dots for short.' 'I don't care how tall or short you are. Officer, what's the charge against this man?' The officer told him. The Judge said, '$25 or two months in jail.' The Judge repeated again, 'Come up with the $25.' 'Oh, Judge, you can't get blood out of a turnip.' 'O.K. then I will put turnip in jail for two months.'"[8]

Besides baseball, Dots Toney loved minstrelsy, and by the age of thirteen or fourteen he had taken to staging blackface shows for the local churches. Able to attend the Ford Theater, unlike Bill and Eggie, he may have seen the two black youngsters dancing when he went to those shows. His interest in dancing would naturally have led to an interest in other talented dancers, even two colored kids named Bill and Eggie who hung out on street corners. None of them considered dancing a potential career, but Dots, who was about seven years older than Bill, had concluded that it could be his ticket out of Richmond. He had worked up a blackface act, based on what he had seen at the Ford, but decided that he needed a gimmick. "Picks," short for "pickaninnies," were popular in white minstrel shows at the time. A pickaninny was any small black child who could sing, dance, tell jokes, and look cute up onstage. White performers used them when their act needed a big punch. Toney decided to include a couple of "picks" in his act. According to Eggleston, Toney talked to them about going on the road together, but there could be no serious discussion about leaving Richmond, since they didn't have any money.

One night not long afterward, Toney had a stroke of luck. He was working in a "Free and Easy" on Franklin Street in exchange for three meals a day, and biding his time until he could afford to leave Richmond. A big spender came into the club and, seeking to impress the hostesses, gave Toney a twenty-dollar bill, telling him to "bring in some real champagne." Toney went to find Bill and Eggie. "Come on, Bill," he remembered saying. "Let's get out of this town, there's nothing here for you and me." "What are you going to use for money?" Bill wanted to know. "See this twenty, we will go to Washington, D.C." "You're not going to pay your way, are you?" "Oh, no, we will beat our way on a freight train."

According to Lemmeul Eggleston, Toney asked both of them to go, and they set off for the train station with him. "So I started down to the depot with Bill, and my mind struck me to come back. And that is the reason, probably, I didn't go with Bill, on account of my mother and father. It would bring bad luck to dance on Sunday. I consider that I owe my longevity to the wishes of my mother. Well, I came on back and every time I went to New York for the Elks convention, Bill would tell people, 'He's a boy I tried to make something of but he wouldn't come with me.'"

Toney and Robinson grabbed the truss rods of a box-car and hoisted themselves to the top. The train was traveling at about thirty-five miles per hour when Toney slipped. Only Bill's quick reflexes saved him. As Toney wrote, "Bill caught hold of my leg and held me in this manner about five minutes until the brakeman came along. Together they managed to pull me up and save my life. We gave the brakeman a piece of change and he put us down in the box car and finally we landed in Washington."[9]

On their arrival in Washington, D.C., the two boys picked up odd jobs wherever they could, usually dancing in beer gardens around town. Neither took their dancing very seriously; in fact, both tried to get into other lines of work. Toney wanted to be a professional baseball player and spent as much time as he could over in Baltimore with the Orioles. Baseball, since it was still segregated, was not a place for Bill. Instead, he got a job rubbing down the "hots" (rubbing down a sweated horse after a race or workout) at nearby Bennings Racetrack and started dreaming about a career as a jockey.

Black jockeys predominated in the early days of horse racing. Isaac Murphy's record of three Kentucky Derby victories in 1885, 1886, and 1888 went unbroken for nearly a century, and several other blacks were nationally famous. Bill was slight of build, a prerequisite for jockeys then as now, and he enjoyed the racetrack milieu with its sporting-life characters and preoccupation with gambling. In fact, it may have been at the track that he developed his lifelong obsession with gambling in all its forms. After all, his day-to-day existence was a gamble. What were the odds against a twelve-year-old runaway? Where would he sleep or eat if he was broke? How would he survive if it was below zero outside, and inside he was burning with fever? One place he couldn't go was home. His grandmother was the only family he wanted to love, but couldn't. Bedilia Robinson, who had suffered the bondage of inhumanity as a slave and who sought salvation through her faith, would never allow anyone, not even her grandson, to tarnish her beliefs. He was not allowed to dance in her home. In fact, he was punished for even saying the word. He had to take the gamble and leave her. He had to gamble that he'd find some other way to earn her love, her respect, and his living. By age twelve and for the rest of his life, gambling would be an outlet for frustration—for not being able to earn his grandmother's respect, and for having to break down racial barriers that stood in the way of his accomplishing his goals.

But fate wasn't kind to Bojangles, and soon he was out of work at the track. Without a job, he was reduced to stealing the bread and milk that were customarily left on the doorsteps of houses by early-morning deliverymen. He would take the bread outright, but, following his own peculiar code of honor, he always drank the milk right there and left the empty bottle so the family would not lose their bottle deposit. He sold newspapers on the streets, then fell back on the only other thing he was good at—dancing. Again, Robinson formed a street partnership, this time, with a young white boy whose father also disapproved of his entertaining career. The white boy sang while Robinson danced to drum up newspaper sales. The white boy later became better known as Al Jolson.

Bill and Lemeul Toney, who later took the stage name of Eddie Leonard, kept in touch and occasionally worked together. According to Leonard's autobiography, they went to New York as soon as they had the money for train fare and new suits. The older youth got the first big break. He was hanging around with the Baltimore Orioles when he was discovered by the minstrel impresario George Primrose, an Orioles fan, who hired him on the spot after hearing him sing "Just Because She Made Them Goo Goo Eyes." Primrose put him in the Primrose and West shows and named him Eddie Leonard.

Bill's first break came when the impresarios Whallen and Martel hired him for their show *The South Before the War* around 1892.[10] Eddie Leonard had used his influence to get Bill a job as a pickaninny with the show, which was advertised this way:

> Don't fail to see Whallen and Martel's *THE SOUTH BEFORE THE WAR*. The greatest production of the century, not excepting Uncle Tom's Cabin.
>
> In ante bellum times—before the war—the colored people assembled from the various plantations for the annual festivities, and "Cake Walks," "Wing and Buck Dancing" and other characteristic sports were introduced.
>
> These are all faithfully reproduced in the great picturesque spectacular *The South Before the War*.
>
> A colored camp meeting, surely a great treat to attend. Those who have never witnessed it can see its real life depicted—the shouting, the singing, the exhorting of dominoes, the drawing of razors, the firing of pistols, the dancing of quadrilles to the accompaniment of a tin horn band, are all introduced in this show.
>
> What can be more enjoyable than listening to the sing-

ing, by genuine colored people, of the good old fashioned melodies which were sung on the plantations years ago. Such tunes as NANCY TEEL, HARD TIMES, YELLOW ROSE, ROSE LEE, and many others, accompanied by the old fashioned sheepskin banjo and the home made fiddle.

Hear whoops of terpsichorean ecstacs [*sic*], shrill whistles, catcalls, the rhythmic clapping of hands, and see the colored folk shuffle their enormous feet on sanded floors, do live jigs, sing, and do comical antics of niggerdom.

Bill's job in *The South Before the War* was as a "pick" for Mayme Remington, a former French burlesque dancer who became a top headliner in the late eighteen-nineties. She often traveled with as many as fifteen pickaninnies who did special dancing to various "Hawaiian," "Indian," and "African" numbers. Besides Bill Robinson, others of note who "picked" for Mayme Remington at one time or another were Coot Grant, Dewey Weinglass, Luckey Roberts, Archie Ware, Eddie Rector, Lou Keane, and Toots Davis.[11]

The show traveled up and down the eastern seaboard, and Bill stayed with it for more than a year, playing dice or cards backstage whenever there was a game. As a pickaninny, however, his days were numbered, for after a time he grew too large and was no longer cute enough for the job. After that, his career possibilities narrowed considerably. He tried, like many other former pickaninnies, to form his own act. Black performers could not get work as solo acts at the time; white show managers did not believe that blacks had enough brains to entertain whites as solo acts. The only time a black performer came close to performing solo was in tent shows, carnivals, or medicine shows.

For the five or six years that followed *The South Before the War*, Robinson said he "just messed around." One source states that he was in a production called *1492* around the turn of the century. Bill later admitted that it was during those years that he suffered his first knife and razor lacerations. Within his lifetime, he would be stabbed, slashed, and shot, but he never missed a performance on account of a wound. He had a quick temper and admitted that he fought freely when it was necessary. Bill was almost always armed with a gun, but he is not known to have inflicted any critical injuries. Lemmeul Eggleston remembered Bill's temper, saying, "He'd crack in a minute. In a second. Bill was friendly, but he had that enormous temper."

In 1898 he was back in Richmond, where he tried to enlist in a colored regiment to fight in the Spanish-American War. So eager was he to serve his country in some capacity that, failing to make the outfit as a regular soldier, he accompanied it as a drummer. In a dancehall in Brattleboro, North Carolina, he suffered his first bullet wound. "The second lieutenant shot me," Robinson explained. "I think he was cleaning his gun." He liked to show the scar on his knee where the bullet entered, and to point out that no similar scar existed to indicate its exit. The bullet was somewhere inside.

Over the years, Bill's memory of the origins of most of the other wounds on his body faded, like the scars. "Some," he said, "might have been done in Chicago, but some must have been done in New York."

2

Bojangles

Bill was in New York in 1900, according to Tom Fletcher, author of *One Hundred Years of Show Business*. Fletcher recalled meeting Bill in the early part of the year at the Douglass Club, 114 West Thirty-first Street, which was named perhaps for Frederick Douglass, the black abolitionist and "race leader." Its president was a three-hundred-pound black named Charles Moore. One of the many professional clubs where entertainers and sporting-world figures congregated after hours, it was staffed primarily by former entertainers, among them "Frog," the bartender, a former contortionist who had been billed professionally as "The Frog Man." What distinguished the Douglass Club from other late-night cabarets was that it was also, as Fletcher puts it, "the favorite 'slumming' place for the city's wealthy and famous." Alfred Gwynne Vanderbilt was the club's vice-president.

Other regulars were Diamond Jim Brady and Harry K. Thaw, who in 1906 shot and killed architect Stanford White in Madison Square Garden because Thaw was jealous of White's attention to his wife, showgirl Evelyn Nesbit. Many of the greats from the newspaper world were also regulars. No doubt because of its members' connections, the Douglass Club ignored with impunity New York City's one o'clock curfew for cabarets.

If the club was a slumming place for well-to-do whites in the city, it was also a veritable oasis of racial liberalism for the black entertainers who frequented it. While they enjoyed more privileges than ordinary blacks because of their ability to entertain, nevertheless they did not presume to expect equal status. Black entertainers had their "place," just as ordinary blacks did; and on occasion their place was more uncomfortable because it was less anonymous.

The racial lines were distinctly drawn in New York at the turn of the century. Of the 60,666 blacks in the city in 1900, the majority were concentrated in Manhattan, and most of them were squeezed into two neighborhoods: the Tenderloin, a folk designation for an area with no clear boundaries that generally covered the West Twenties, and San Juan Hill, Sixtieth to Sixty-fourth streets, Tenth to Eleventh avenues, its name a parody of the interracial battles in the district. A smattering of blacks lived in areas between these two neighborhoods, among them the top show people.[1] Bert Williams, George Walker, Ada Overton Walker, Will Marion Cook, J. Rosamond Johnson, and others lived on West Fifty-third Street. They earned money that was beyond the wildest imaginings of the average black New Yorker and enjoyed some popularity among white audiences at midtown clubs and theaters. But when racial tensions were high, they were as endangered as ordinary blacks, and sometimes in greater danger by virtue of their fame. In the summer of 1900 a fight between a white man and a black man on the corner of Eighth Avenue and Forty-first Street touched off a riot after the white man was killed. A vengeful white mob massed outside the clubs and theaters where well-known black entertainers were performing. "Get Cole and Johnson!" "Get Williams and Walker!" the mob shouted. Instead of trying to help the blacks who were being beaten by the mob, white policemen joined in the beating.

At the Douglass Club, black entertainers would arrive after completing gigs elsewhere and do their acts again. They received no salaries, but big tips from well-to-do patrons were more than enough to keep them coming back to perform. Besides, they enjoyed the opportunity to be with other entertainers in the relaxed atmosphere of the club. Tom Fletcher recalls that when he met Bill Robinson there, Bill had a partner named Theodore Miller. They were a dancing act, but what Fletcher remembered best was the singing routine with which they opened their performances at the Douglass Club. Bill would sing "Old Uncle Eph," a song from *The South Before the War* that was popular then, while Miller would sing an entirely different song. According to Fletcher, "[Bill] would manage to make his tune blend and harmonize with whatever other song his partner chose to sing, and this part of their act alone soon made him a big favorite, not only with the guests but also with the other performers. As a matter of fact, nobody paid much attention to Bill's dancing. . . ."

Bill was about twenty-one years old then, and had

already learned that he could please an audience with his personality alone. He also had a sizable ego and did not like the dismissive way his fellow performers regarded his dancing. He boasted to anyone who would listen that he had won many dancing contests when he was in *The South Before the War*. But he did not really get the denizens of the Douglass Club to pay attention until he announced that he was going to Brooklyn's Bijou Theater, where *In Old Kentucky* was playing and holding its weekly Friday night dance contest. Robinson was going over there to challenge Harry Swinton, a cast member of the show who was considered the best dancer of his day.

In Old Kentucky was the most outstanding of a new breed of traveling shows that emerged with the new century. American entertainment was in flux. The minstrel show, though past its prime, continued in popularity, and performers like Eddie Leonard and Al Jolson performed in blackface well into the 1920s. Vaudeville shows, which had developed from the olio section of the mid-1880s minstrel shows, spawned vaudeville chains, groups of houses controlled by a single manager. The largest of such chains, the United Booking Offices—later named the Keith Vaudeville Exchange, headed by Edward F. Albee—would eventually have four hundred theaters in the East and Midwest, while Martin Beck's sizable Orpheum Circuit would control houses from Chicago to Los Angeles.

Motion pictures were introduced as part of vaudeville shows in 1896 both as added attractions and as a way to clear the house between shows. Then there were the road shows, which combined elements of vaudeville and minstrelsy but which had an underlying theme that set them apart from either of the two forms. These were forerunners of the modern American musical. Some were called "Tom" shows because they presented some version of *Uncle Tom's Cabin*. Others were called "plant" shows because they were staged as plantation scenes. Still others were called "tab" shows, short for tabloid, and were abbreviated minstrel or vaudeville shows. In the early years of the century, the *Black Patti Troubadours* was among the best-known tab shows.[2] Written by composer Bob Cole and produced by Voelckel and Nolan, it followed the general minstrel pattern and starred Sissieretta "Black Patti" Jones, who was a popular singer of operatic music.

In Old Kentucky, which was organized around 1900, symbolized the in-flux state of American entertainment in that it was an "integrated" show—the actors were white while the musicians and dancers were black—though, like Primrose and West's *The Forty Whites and Thirty Blacks,* it would hardly be called integrated today. In 1902, James Hubert "Eubie" Blake, then nineteen years old, joined *In Old Kentucky* briefly after spending a year with Dr. Frazier's Medicine Show, in which he had played the melodeon, a small reed organ, and buck-danced on the tailgate of a horse-drawn wagon. He was hired to play in the pit band of *In Old Kentucky* while it was performing at Colonel Mapleson's Academy of Music on Fourteenth Street in New York. "We were there two weeks," Blake recalled years later. "A wagon pulled up to the theater, unloaded us, picked us up after the show, and took us to a dump on Bleecker Street where we slept. Same thing every day—I never even saw 14th Street."[3] But the teenaged Blake had sense enough not to complain or to challenge the public impression that he and other young black musicians and dancers were as happy as could be. As a newspaper column about the show in 1908 put it, "The lads are well·cared for on the road and are the happiest darkies in the world, at home and abroad. This is one of the features that has helped make *In Old Kentucky* a perennial."

Written by C. T. Dazey and produced by Jacob Litt, the melodrama's plot centered around a "sweet and homely love story that goes straight from the first curtain to the last." Having an underlying theme throughout was unusual. There was action galore in the four acts. The villain lit a bomb under his enemy. The heroine leaped a chasm. A $25,000 racehorse was trapped in a fiery stable. There was an elaborate racing scene with real horses. And there was an energetic pickaninny band. Earl "Tiny" Ray, who played the part of the jockey in one company, once said, "The great moment came when the Old Man told us: 'If Queen Bess loses, you play "Massa's in the Cold, Cold Ground." If she wins play as you've never played before.' Then, when Queen Bess won, the famous pickaninny band went to town."[4]

If all that weren't excitement enough, the show often included a "special feature," the Friday night buck-and-wing dance contest between members of the company and local buck-and-wing celebrities. Each contestant was given a number, and judges were placed under the stage, in the wings, and out in front. The accompaniment was the stop-time banjo, one plunk at the beginning of each bar. It was this contest that Bill Robinson had decided to enter.

At that time, the star dancer with *In Old Kentucky* was Harry Swinton, whom Eubie Blake, among others, greatly admired. "He came out in roustabout clothes with a paper cone full of sand and did more dancing just spreading that sand than other dancers could with their whole act," Blake remembered. And that was just the preliminary to his dance. But according to Tom Fletcher, even Harry Swinton backed off when it came to competing against the buck-and-wing dancers of Brooklyn. He avoided the competition by taking a low number.[5] Contestants performed in numerical order, and generally those who went on later were more energetic and more likely to win. Thus Fletcher and others at the Douglass Club wondered how Bill Robinson had the nerve to enter the Brooklyn dance contest. But one thing Bill had in abundance was nerve.

The night Bill entered the contest, Fletcher and a few others, including Eubie Blake and entertainers Bert Williams and George Walker, were in the audience. As expected, Swinton took a low number, leaving Bill free to compete against the local talent. He won hands down, though Fletcher and the others did not feel it was a fair contest between Bill and Swinton. Eubie Blake, years later, said, sniffing, "When you mention Swinton's name, Bill Robinson shut up." But Bill Robinson had the gold medal and the valuable publicity attendant to winning the contest. News traveled fast in the small world of show business, and now Bill Robinson was the man to beat at buck-and-wing dancing.

In his memoirs, Fletcher also documented one of the earliest times that Bill used the name Bojangles professionally: "It was in the summer of 1901, when my partner, Al Bailey, and I were with J. W. Gorman's Alabama Troubadours, playing the summer theater at Savin Rock, New Haven, Connecticut, that we saw an advertisement of a show playing Pleasure Beach in nearby Bridgeport. The ad read: 'Hear Smokey Moke and See Captain Bojangles.' We knew Smokey Moke. He was one of the top-flight entertainers of the society folks in and around New York City. But the Captain Bojangles was a new one to us. We had never heard of him before. One morning Al and I got up early and took the trolley that ran from New Haven to Bridgeport. There we found out that Captain Bojangles was Bill Robinson. Al and I had always called him Willie. The company Bill was with was called *The Valhallas* [*sic*]. There was actually no regular company, the show being made up of performers who were laying off from other shows."6

By the summer of 1901, Bill's partner, Theodore Miller, had quit the team for the more stable job of managing and acting as resident entertainer at the Davis and Johnson Club, 108 West Thirty-second Street in New York. Tom Fletcher and Al Bailey were also not working together at the time; they were holding out for more money before signing for a new tour. In the interim, Fletcher was filling in as stage manager for J. M. Moore's *New Orleans Minstrels* at Hubert's Museum on Fourteenth Street, not far from Tony Pastor's theater at Union Square. He told Bill that if he could find a partner he could have a few weeks at Hubert's. Fletcher recalled in his memoirs, "Bill showed up with a girl named Lula Brown, a marvelous dancer, and they worked together fine for a few weeks until one night she made a mistake. When she came off stage Bill said to her, 'Just three more mistakes and you'll get out of the act.' Just when she made them I don't know, but she must have made those mistakes because not long afterwards Bill left for Boston by himself and joined an act headed by Tricky Sam and Charles Randall. Bill became one of the drum majors in the act."[7]

Bill worked wherever and whenever he could, and with a variety of partners. At one point, he worked for Bert Williams and George Walker. Around 1902 he teamed up with a young singer and dancer named Johnny Juniper, who was playing with J. W. Gorman's *Alabama Troubadours* show. But this partnership was also short-lived, for Bill was called back to New York by George W. Cooper, a well-known black vaudevillian who with his partner, Bailey, was one of the very few black acts on the Keith Circuit. Bailey was getting drunk on the job and becoming unreliable, so Cooper decided to replace him, even though the team was in the middle of a week's booking at Keith's Union Square Theater in New York City. According to Tom Fletcher, Bill and Johnny Juniper were laying over in Boston when Bill received a wire from Cooper—could he come to New York right away? Bill took the first train out of Boston.

Working as Cooper's partner was a comedown for Bill in some ways. With Johnny Juniper he had been the head of the team. With Cooper he played second fiddle. Cooper was the straight man; Robinson had to play the fool to his foil. While Cooper dressed in a suit and tie, Robinson had to put on a comical getup—not a small consideration for Bill, a natty dresser. To make matters worse, he was not allowed to dance. And because the names Cooper and Bailey were well known, and they were booked for the next six months (an unusually long time) on the Keith Circuit, Robinson was not billed under his own name. For those six months at least, he had to be Bailey. But these disadvantages were far outweighed by the opportunity to join the circuit and have a mentor like Cooper. In fact, for Bill the opportunity to join any circuit was worth jumping at. The infamous T.O.B.A Circuit (whose initials stood for Theater Owners Booking Association, though performers said it meant Tough on Black Asses) wasn't even organized until the middle teens. Until then, most black performers could not count on regular bookings for even a few weeks out of a year. Not only did the Keith Circuit guarantee bookings, but it was one of the best circuits in white vaudeville.

Benjamin Franklin Keith of Hillsboro, New Hampshire, was a circus concessionaire before he opened a curio museum in Boston in 1883. Two years later he joined Edward F. Albee of Machias, Maine, in operating the Bijou Theater in Boston. The Bijou offered continuous variety shows from 10:00 A.M. until 11:00 P.M., and proved so profitable that Keith and Albee began buying up other theaters. Their profits increased when they introduced motion pictures into their programs. Recalled Albee in 1919, "Mr Keith [brought] the first machine to the United States. It was an old Vitascope, which displayed a small picture of about 8 × 8 feet. We exhibited it at Boston, then at Union Square. Then came the Cinematograph. We were their first exhibitors, putting it on at the Union Square Theater, then Boston. It made an instantaneous hit, for the picture was very much larger. I remember one of the first pictures presented was a troupe of cavalry men making a charge. They dashed down to the front and quick as lightning came to a halt. The people in the audience would rise up in their seats thinking [the cavalry] were coming from the curtain into the audience—it was so realistic. Then the surf breaking upon the shore made a wonderful impression upon the audience. I first advertised the Biograph in Boston by sending out a bicycle brigade of twelve men, the first carrying a bugle to herald their coming. All wore white suits, white hats and white shoes, and on the backs of their white coats was painted, 'Go to Keith's and see the Biograph.'"[8]

With their ever-increasing profits, Keith and Albee absorbed most of the smaller chains in the East. By 1914, when Keith died, the enterprise, which had been renamed the Keith-Albee Circuit, had grown to encompass nearly four hundred theaters, and the business continued under Albee and A. Paul Keith, B.F.'s son.

Though Albee, as general manager, was at least 50 percent responsible for the Keith Circuit's success, he always credited B. F. Keith with establishing the circuit's reputation for quality entertainment. Wrote Albee after Keith's death, "Mr. Keith has extended his influence for decency and cleanliness in vaudeville all over the world, and the men associated with him were inspired by his spirit, and have profited by his determination to give nothing but what was clean and wholesome. Years ago, when Mr. Keith first started, the performers very often took exception to cuts that Mr. Keith made in their acts and to his suggestions as to their dress, etc. They couldn't understand it, as they had been accepted in Fargo, Dakota [*sic*], and in variety houses. These houses were only attended by men and they made no objection to what they saw or heard, but when it was pointed out to the performers that things were different, that we were catering to ladies and children, and that the future of vaudeville and their own future depended upon the respectable conduct of both the theater and what it presented on the stage, they readily fell in with Mr. Keith's idea."9

The Keith Circuit was a class circuit. The bookings were more solid than on other circuits, where it was not at all unusual to face unexpected cancellations and to be stranded in some small town. Only about six black acts were booked. They included the famous teams of (Bert) Williams and (George) Walker, and (Flournoy) Miller and (Aubrey) Lyles. With Cooper, Bill Robinson could earn the huge sum of a hundred dollars a week, with a guarantee of twenty-six weeks or more. No wonder he said good-bye to Johnny Juniper.

As the bogus Bailey, Bill completed the contracts that Cooper had signed, got great press notices, and apparently pleased his new partner. Veteran vaudevillian Leigh Whipper described Cooper as "kind of an upstage fellow. He wasn't quite as friendly as he might have been." Bill was careful not to be *too* good, and by the end of 1902 Cooper had consented to change the billing of the act to Cooper and Robinson. On January 10, 1903, they officially became Cooper and Robinson—Comedians. Ironically, the future's greatest dancer in the world was still not earning his living as a dancer.

It was many years before Robinson was able to extricate himself from the role of buffoon. Cooper continued to wear a suit and tie. Robinson's stage getup consisted of a clown outfit and a tutu, worn over long pants, and a derby perched atop his head. This was fairly standard attire for the clown partner in such an act—Bert Williams wore a sheepskin tutu over black tights, a military jacket, and a stovepipe hat.

Cooper and Robinson's new act was titled "Going to War." It featured comedy routines in which Cooper played the straight man and Robinson a combination of Tambo and Bones. Among Bill's most popular routines were his impersonation of an automobile having a fit and his imitation of a mosquito or trombone with his lips. Their skits were heavy on ethnic humor—Negro, Jewish, Irish. Joe Laurie, Jr., in *Vaudeville: From the Honky-Tonks to the Palace,* reported that they once dressed up like "Hebes" (Hebrews) and did a heavy dialect. They were not alone in relying on the lowest ethnic humor to get laughs. Comedy routines burlesquing "micks" and "kikes" and "wops" were almost as common as "coon" routines in the early years of the century, signifying a lack of originality, if nothing else. Such practices were so offensive to ethnic communities in Boston and New York that both municipalities passed ordinances banning racial epithets onstage. According to Tom Fletcher, Cooper and Robinson's "Yoi Yoi Yoi Yoi Mary Ann" was introduced not long before these ordinances were passed: "Many people gave Cooper and Robinson credit for speeding up the passage of the ordinance through their introduction of this particular number. Bill's own shrewdness in meeting and overcoming the problems of racial and religious prejudice subsequently helped to strengthen the suspicion that the number was introduced for that purpose. Bill has never said." It is unlikely, however, that the team had any purpose other than to be popular.

As their popularity grew, so did their income. They played all the leading vaudeville houses, and, according to Fletcher, even went to London, where they were a tremendous hit with English audiences. Each year they put on a new act: In 1905–1906 it was called "Looking for Hannah," in 1907–1908 it was "A Friend of Mine," and the following year, "The Elephant Hunt." All the shows followed a fairly standard formula—jokes and skits and, increasingly, Bill's dancing. There were many stock situations for dance numbers in vaudeville:

> FIRST DANCER: What do you call that dance you just finished?
>
> SECOND DANCER: I call that beautiful number "Boston Baked Beans." What do you call your dance?
>
> FIRST DANCER: I call that "Tomato Catsup" because I put it all over your baked beans."[10]

Bill rarely had a chance to feature his dancing, however, for the act was a comedy act, and Cooper, who retained control over the material they used, was not foolish enough to relinquish it to his partner.

Cooper had his own cross to bear in the partnership, because Bill was constantly in trouble. According to Eddie Hunter, who later performed with Cooper, "He had a lot of trouble with Bill, keepin' him out of trouble and gettin' him out of scrapes. Bill was quick-tempered. They would be goin' somewhere to appear in a theater and George would learn that he had to bail Bill out of trouble or jail before they could go on. Yeah, Bill Robinson was a mess." The trouble usually involved gambling—pool, dice, or cards. Bill fancied himself a denizen in good standing of the sporting life and was not known to be generous in defeat. No doubt Cooper was delighted when Bill decided to get married; maybe having a wife would calm him down.

By 1907, Bill was in his late twenties, well established on the Keith Circuit, and making enough money to support a family, which he dearly wanted. He may also have sought some stability, for his respectable earnings in vaudeville always seemed to evaporate. If he wasn't giving his money away to some down-and-out acquaintance, he was spending it on his impeccable offstage wardrobe, or gambling it away. Perhaps a wife could help him save some money.

He met Lena Chase at her aunt's boardinghouse in Worcester, Massachusetts. Most black entertainers stayed at the boardinghouse when they were performing in the city. When they met, Lena was twenty-two years old and studying to be a schoolteacher, the highest profession to which a young black woman could aspire. After meeting and falling in love with Bill, she apparently changed course and moved to Boston, where, according to Leigh Whipper, she worked in "one of those big stores." Whipper described her as a very nice girl. She and Bill were married in the parsonage of St. Mark's-in-the-Bouwerie in New York City on November 14, 1907, and they took up residence in Bill's apartment in the West Fifties between Seventh and Eighth avenues until they could find a new place to live. In March 1908 they moved to 450 Sixth Avenue. One week later, and four months into their marriage, the honeymoon came to an abrupt end. On March 21, Bill was arrested for armed highway robbery.

AFFIDAVIT—ROBBERY

FIRST DIVISION, CITY MAGISTRATE'S COURT, 2 DISTRICT, CITY AND COUNTY OF NEW YORK, S.:   Hyman Sussman of No. 55 West 31 Street, aged over 21 years, occupation tailor, being duly sworn, deposes and says, that on the 21st day of March 1908, at the City of New York, in the County of New York, was feloniously taken, stolen and carried away from the person of deponent by force and violence, without his consent and against his will, the following property, viz.: good and lawful money of the United States of the value of two dollars the property of deponent and that this deponent has a probable cause to suspect, and does suspect that the said property was feloniously taken, stolen and carried away by force and violence aforesaid, by . . . William Robinson (now here) under——
——reason of the following facts and circumstances, viz: At about 8:30 P.M., the said date the defendant came into the deponent's place of business at the above address and threatened that he would kill deponent unless deponent gave him forthwith whatever money deponent had. Then defendant at the same time placed his hand in the pocket of the sack coat then and there more after the person of this defendant and whereas defendant had a revolver and when deponent struggled with defendant then defendant thrust his hand into the pocket of deponent's coat and took therefrom the said sum of two dollars, without deponent consent and against deponent's will and despite such resistance as deponent not [sic] about to offer and departed with said money.

Deponent therefore charges the defendant as above and after that he may be held to answer as the————.

Sworn to before me this 22 day of March 1908: Hyman Sussman

(Otto H. Dwyer)
City Magistrate[11]

(Robinson's Plea)

FIRST DIVISION, CITY MAGISTRATE'S COURT, 2 DISTRICT, CITY AND COUNTY OF NEW YORK, SS.: This defendant being duly examined before the undersigned, according to law, on the annexed charge; and being informed that it is his right to make a statement in relation to the charge against him; that the statement is designed to enable him if he see fit to answer the charge and explain the facts alleged against him; that he is at liberty to waive making a statement, and that his waiver cannot be used against him on the trail.

Question. What is your name?
Answer. Will Robinson (colored).
Question. How old are you.
Answer. 23 years.[12]
Question. Where were you born?
Answer. Richmond, Virginia.
Question. Where do you live, and how long have you resided there?
Answer. 450 6 Avenue. 1 week.
Question. What is your business or profession?

Answer.   Performer.

Question.   Give any explanation you may think proper of the circumstances appearing in the testimony against you, and state any facts which you think will tend to your exculpation.

Answer.   I am not guilty.

(signed) Wm Robinson

Taken before me this 22 day of March 1908, ss.:

Otto H. Dwyer
City Magistrate

Four days later, a grand jury indicted Bill on charges of robbery in the first degree, grand larceny in the first degree, assault in the second degree, and criminally receiving stolen property. Bail was set at one thousand dollars.

The Illinois Surety Company, 5 Nassau Street, put up the bond on April 1, and Bill, who had been staying in the downtown Manhattan prison affectionately called "the Tombs," was released. He may not have understood the conditions of his release on bail, just as he assuredly did not apprehend the seriousness of his situation. He immediately went back on the road with Cooper, and on August 22 the Illinois Surety Company, fearing that he had skipped bond, authorized the police to pick him up. Fortunately, the misunderstanding was cleared up, and Bill was set free again until his trial.

3

Bill Robinson
on Trial

Bill's case went to trial on September 28, 1908, before the "Hon. James T. Malone in the Court of General Sessions of the Peace in and for the County of New York, Part III." The handwritten transcripts state simply, "A Jury, is duly empanelled and sworn," and so we have no records as to the complexion of the panel of Bill's "peers," but undoubtedly they were all white, and of course all male, since women had not yet secured the franchise. The jury heard the indictment against Bill: robbery in the first degree, grand larceny in the first degree, assault in the first degree, and criminally receiving stolen property. Assistant District Attorneys O'Connor and Symonds and Bill's attorney, H. Coleman, Esq., were introduced. Then Hyman Sussman, plaintiff, was called to the witness stand.

Sussman identified himself as a merchant tailor who

lived and conducted his business at 55 West Thirty-first Street; the building at 1408 Broadway, where he had formerly operated his business and where the alleged crime had occurred back in March, had been "throwed down."

Sussman testified that it was between seven and eight o'clock on the evening of March 21, 1908, and he was about to close up, when Robinson appeared. "He just come around and closed the door behind his back and he says to me, 'I kill you if you wouldn't give me all your money.' I went on my knees. He put his hand in my pocket and ripped the whole coat up and grabbed out the money.

"I said, 'You wouldn't get much by killing me.' He said, 'I am a gambler and I lost my job and I will kill you.' I said, 'You wouldn't get much, I support my mother, take everything I got.' He put his hands in my pocket. Ripped his hand through and grabbed out what I got. I lost $13, but there was found in the street pieces."

Assistant District Attorney Keyran J. O'Connor then asked Sussman to identify the coat in question, which O'Connor produced, and which Sussman identified. O'Connor then asked, "Did he do anything to you after he had taken the money from you?" Sussman answered, "He held me up this way, he said if you make any holler I will kill you."

"What did he have in his hand?" asked O'Connor. "Gun," was Sussman's reply.

O'Connor asked if anyone else was in Sussman's shop at the time, and Sussman said that a gentleman had been there changing a pair of trousers (removing them so that Sussman could press them). His name, Sussman thought, was J. Phillips.

O'Connor then asked what happened after Bill had pulled the gun and taken the money. "Well, he tried to run, he tried to run from the door, they caught him at the barber shop, about 15 feet away from my store," Sussman replied. "He tried to run, he throwed a woman around and everybody but they hold him so tight he was arrested right then and there."

On cross-examination, Bill's attorney, H. Coleman, Esq., concentrated on the question of the gun. Had the defendant actually displayed a gun or had he simply suggested its presence by keeping his hand in his coat pocket? Sussman made this confusing reply: "When he asked of me he held the revolver in front of my face, yes sir, that is true, he held it here [indicating someone holding a revolver in a pocket]." The trial transcript does not indicate if Coleman sought clarification. He then asked why Sussman had not mentioned a revolver when he first reported the incident to the police. Said Sussman, "I was so excited, that they didn't let me talk so much. I forgot all the circumstances."

Next, Coleman asked Sussman, "Did you ever seen Robinson before this time?" Sussman answered, "I seen him coming around with another fellow. Robinson did not go down to my place to have a coat made, no sir. Robinson never had a coat made by me at any time. I am sure about that. I never took his measure, he didn't ask me."

Coleman asked, "Do you want the Jury to understand that without any cause or provocation this man walked into this place and deliberately pointed a revolver at you and asked you to give up your money to him?" At first Sussman did not understand the question. After the judge rephrased it, he answered, "Yes."

Attorney Coleman asked for more information about the "other fellow" with whom Sussman had seen Robinson in his store. Sussman said the man's name was Jackson and that he came from South Carolina. Coleman then asked, "Do you know Jackson by the name of Charlie Hall?" Sussman answered, "Charlie Hall has clothes made in my place."

Coleman pressed. "Isn't it a fact that the defendant went down to your office and left his measure for an overcoat and paid thereon $5?" "No sir," said Sussman. "Never did pay me anything, and I never took his measure."

"Isn't it a fact that when he called there afterwards and you had not the coat made or done anything about it that he demanded the payment of his $5 back again?"

"No sir. I am sure about that."

"Well, you recollect now trying to please him, told him you would make things all right and that you handed him two $1 bills."

"No sir, I didn't because I didn't know the man."

"And that he told you he wanted the other $3 which he had paid with the $2?"

"Never."

"And isn't it a fact that it was only after he got the $2 that you called for your wife and your wife came down, then you began to holler?"

"No sir, my wife was not there at all."

Attorney Coleman had no more questions at that time. On redirect, Assistant District Attorney Symonds offered Sussman's coat in evidence as People's Exhibit I.

Jacob Phillips was then called to testify for the People. He corroborated Sussman's story, saying that on the night in question he (Phillips) was behind a screen, taking off his suit, when Robinson came running into the shop, locked the door behind him, and demanded all of Sussman's money. Phillips said he rushed, undressed, to the door, turned the key, and ran out into the street and yelled, "Help!" The defendant rushed outside; a police officer came along. "There were hundreds of people around. I saw a little colored boy there. I didn't see him do nothing, the defendant with the little colored boy, but I saw the little fellow rush inside and rush out again."

In cross-examining Phillips, Attorney Coleman wanted to know the exact location of the screen behind which Phillips had been standing and in which direction the shop door opened. He also asked Phillips when he had last spoken to Sussman. Phillips answered, "When I received this paper [subpoena] to come here. That was Saturday. That was not the first time that I ever had a conversation with him before about this case at the time the defendant was locked up. I have been in Jefferson Market Court when the case was up. They called me in front of the judge and I said the same as I am saying now." There is no indication in the transcript that Coleman questioned Phillips further about the "little colored boy."

The next witness for the People was Peter Roland, police officer. On direct examination by District Attorney O'Connor, he testified: "On the night of 21st of March 1908 I saw the defendant in front of 6th Avenue and 31st Street and I heard some person hollering 'Police.' I ran in the direction of where the voice was coming from; it was in front of 54 West 31st Street. There I saw the defendant—the complainant having hold of him, Mr. Phillips, and the complainant's wife. He [Sussman] said this man came into his store to assault and rob him."

Asked if he had found anything in the possession of the defendant, Roland replied, "I did; $2. He had it in his hand—two single dollar bills, and one was torn."

Roland then stated that at that time he asked Sussman what had happened. He also said, "The defendant made no statement to me."

O'Connor, after offering the two one-dollar bills in evidence, asked, "You say the defendant did not say anything at all to you?" Roland answered, "No, he made no statement to me." The People rested their case.

Robinson's attorney, Coleman, called Bill and asked him where he lived. "I live at 450 6th Avenue," Bill replied. He was then withdrawn.

Coleman called Officer Roland to the stand. "At the time you arrested the defendant did he have a revolver on him?" No," answered Roland. "He had no revolver."

Coleman then called Bill back to the stand. Bill opened his testimony by saying, "I am 23 years old," and for the purist that did not bode well for the rest of his testimony. He was more like thirty, but he obviously did not look it. He had probably started shaving years off his age way back when he had worked as a "pick," and he wasn't about to come clean now. Moreover, since he did not take the trial seriously in the first place, he saw no reason to jeopardize his future career by being truthful about his age.

He continued. "I live at 450 6th Avenue when I was

locked up. I have been living in New York City off and on about 14 years. I am a performer, working nearly all the time. I guess I worked about 13 years out of the 14.

"The first time I was in the complainant's place was about 8 years ago, when he started making my clothes. He has been making clothes for me off and on. He made about three suits for me, I guess, and I paid him."

Coleman asked if Robinson had left an order with Sussman prior to "the trouble." Bill replied, "I left $5 deposit on an overcoat, the coat was $50. He measured me, he tried the coat on. I couldn't say about what time that was. It was about 3 months before we had this trouble. I had been down to his place several times between the time I left my measure for the overcoat and the trouble. I went there for my $5 or my overcoat.

"This Hyman, he has been making my clothes for about 8 years. This man used to keep a place in 31st Street near 7th Avenue, between 6th and 7th Avenue. He made me a suit there. He used to keep another place in 31st Street near 6th Avenue where colored people used to go in through his shop to get into this gambling house. He made me a suit there. He kept the place in 31st Street where we had the trouble. He made me a suit there. He made me an overcoat and he was keeping upstairs on 26th Street and 7th Avenue and he took the measure for the coat. I picked out the goods. I said, 'I will come up next week to get you to measure the coat.' When I come back he had moved on 6th Avenue between 28th and 29th Street, he had taken my measure and this gentleman was his witness. . . . [Phillips] has been with him ever since I have been in New York. I don't know whether he worked there but he is in the tailor shop all the time. He made me an overcoat, I tried it on and didn't like it. He [Sussman] said you make me cut up my goods and now you don't want the coat. I said, 'It ain't made right.' He told several fellows I stuck him. The fellows said, 'Why don't you take the coat? It is a good coat.' I goes around, tries it on and I don't like it. The fellow say, 'That coat is fine'; so I go back to get it. He had moved from 6th Avenue back to his old place where we had the trouble, and he had the overcoat hanging in the window. I said, 'I guess I will go and get it.' I goes around after it, $45. Mr. Hyman says, 'It ain't finished, I have got to fix the lining inside.' I said, 'I'm going out of town.' He said, 'All right, I will have it ready when you get back.'

"I goes to Scranton, Pennsylvania, and while in Scranton [he] claims the overcoat is stolen, he claims some fellow said he see me in his tailor shop on a Saturday night, and I left New York Saturday for Scranton. When I came back from Scranton I went to New Haven, and this Charlie Hall meets me and he says, 'There is a warrant out for you.' I said, 'What for?'"

At this point, Bill's attorney and the judge reminded him essentially to confine himself to the case in question, and his attorney asked him to relate what happened on the night he went to Sussman's tailor shop.

"That night I was going away from town. I went in, I said, 'Can I have my $5, please?' He said, 'No, not unless you pay me for the coat.' I said, 'I know nothing about the coat.'

"This man was sitting in a chair, his witness, in a chair. Mr. Hyman, he stood up. I said, 'I want my $5.' He said, 'I am not going to give it to you.' He said,

'You stole the coat.' I said, 'Why don't you have me
locked up if I did.' He says, 'I won't give it to you.' I
said, 'I think you are a pretty cheap man,' and Hyman
says, 'If you say that to me I will punch you in the nose.'
I said, 'It ain't necessary to do that,' and Mr. Hyman
closed the door up, Mr. Hyman closed the door and I
was standing like this and Mr. Hyman hollered, he said,
'Don't shoot me, don't shoot me, I will pay you.' I said,
'I didn't come in here to fight or shoot. All I want is my
money.'

"Mr. Hyman handed me $2, he gave it to me, I put it
in my pocket and when I put it in my pocket this
Hyman and this other gentleman grabbed me and both
began to holler. His wife came downstairs and she said,
'What is the matter?' Mr. Hyman says, 'Nothing, get
$3, and I will pay him,' and in the meantime this other
gentleman opened the door.

"The barber next door, Mr. Hyman, his wife, were all
holding me and when the two barbers came up he said,
'This man is going to kill me.' The officer shoved me in
the store and said, 'What is the mattter?' Hyman said,
'He has a gun there.' The officer pulled out my hand
and pulled out $2."

Attorney Coleman asked, "What about the gun?"

Bill answered, "I didn't have any gun, and the officer
locked me up on what Hyman said. I have been a customer with this man for 10 or 12 years, and the same
night he claimed I took his $2 I had my salary coming.

"I at no time while in there made any threat against
him, and I did not at any time threaten to shoot him, I
couldn't shoot him."

Attorney Coleman having concluded his questioning

of his client, the judge asked Bill, "What kind of performer are you?" "Vaudeville performer," Bill answered. "How long have you been performing on the public stage?" asked the judge. Said Bill, "I guess since I was big enough to go on the stage." "About 13 or 14 years?" "Yes sir."

On cross-examination, Assistant District Attorney O'Connor wanted to know how one of the dollar bills had been torn in half if the two bills had been given to him by Sussman. Bill answered that he did not know, that it was torn in half when he had received it. O'Connor then asked if Sussman's coat was torn. Bill answered that it wasn't.

O'Connor continued. "Now you say everybody is robbing you, don't you?"

"How?" Bill asked.

O'Connor reviewed Bill's testimony relative to Sussman's and Phillips's. Then he asked, "Didn't you bring a man named Jackson in there?" "No sir." "Do you know Jackson's name, or Jones?" Bill answered that question with a question of his own: "Jackson's name or Jones?"

Although the written transcript does not record it, Bill's attorney objected to this line of questioning, and the court sustained his objection. For some reason the prosecution was trying to link Bill with a man named Jones or Jackson.

The judge wanted to know Bill's reaction to Officer Roland's testimony that Bill had said nothing when he was arrested. Asked the judge, "Did you make any reply?" Answered Bill, "I certainly did sir." "You certainly did?" "Yes sir." "What did you say to him?"

"The police officer asked us what was the matter. I said, 'Nothing, I just come to get the money this man owed me,' and Mr. Hyman he did the talking then he says, 'That is my money he has just taken,' and naturally the officer kept the money, and they locked me up."

But Bill had to be pressed to say that the officer had not told the truth.

Defense Attorney Coleman had only two more questions. He asked Bill again if he had made a statement (to the officer). Bill said he had. Coleman asked if there was anything else Bill wanted to say. Bill answered, "No sir, that is all."

The defense rested.

Remarks by counsel to the jury were not recorded, nor was it recorded how long the jury took to render its decision. It is unlikely that they took very long. Upon its return, two days after the trial had begun, the jury rendered a verdict of guilty of robbery in the second degree.

Bill was sentenced that day, September 30, 1908. At the sentencing, Defense Attorney Coleman moved for a new trial on the ground that the verdict was against the weight of evidence. He also tried to introduce a new witness. But the judge interrupted. "No, I don't care about hearing any witness. If you have anything that has been committed to paper, I will read it. The Court does not grant a new trial or partial trial after the Jury has passed upon it."

Coleman tried again. "Will you let me say a word to you privately?" "No." "If you cannot suspend sentence, will you kindly send him to Elmira?" If the judge responded, there is no record of it.

The judge then turned to Bill and informed him that "everything was done that could be done for him," and that a "discriminating and intelligent jury" had found him guilty of robbery in the second degree. "The crime itself is one of the most atrocious in the catalogue of crimes. Crimes of violence are always atrocious. There have been many robberies and many burglaries committed, but your crime, the circumstances under which it happened, shows the total disregard of societal duties or regard for it. Your position as an actor and the opportunities that you have had led in the direction of such [a] monstrous crime as robbery. The Judgement of the Court in your case is that you be imprisoned at hard labor in the State's Prison for not less than 11 years nor more than 15 years."

As he was hustled back to the Tombs to await transfer to Sing Sing prison, Bill was in shock. He had not taken his arrest or his trial seriously. In his view there was no question that Sussman and Phillips had lied, and since this fact was clear to him he had expected it to be equally clear to the judge and jury. It had not occurred to him that he needed to buttress his story, to provide witnesses who would testify in his behalf. If that need had occurred to his attorney, Bill had not given the man any help. He himself had been the only witness in his defense, and while the trial transcript does not reveal the tone of his testimony, according to the *New York Morning Telegraph* of October 18, 1908, it had been flippant: "Robinson did not realize the seriousness of his situation, thinking he had done nothing wrong at all, and by his joking manner caused both judge and jury to think him fresh enough to warrant their banishing him from the metropolis."

Bill's attorney had not pursued his defense aggressively. There were two serious implications made by prosecution and prosecution witnesses that Coleman should not have allowed to go unchallenged, or that he should have challenged more strongly:

1. The attempt to connect Bill Robinson with a man named Jones. While it is not stated in the transcript, apparently it was common knowledge that Jones had recently been convicted of highway robbery. His implied association with Bill cast doubt on Bill's character.

2. The implication on the part of prosecution witness Phillips that "a little colored boy" had run into the tailor shop for some purpose; this would have provided a possible explanation for the absence of a gun in Bill's possession when he was arrested.

There were also a number of points that Coleman should have made, but did not:

1. If, as Bill testified, he had known Hyman Sussman for years, why were no witnesses called to verify Bill's statement?

2. If, as Bill testified, Phillips had worked for Sussman for years, why were no witnesses called to verify this statement?

On both points, if the defense could have proved that Sussman and Phillips were lying, then the rest of their testimony would have been seen as suspect.

3. Both Sussman and Phillips testified that Bill had a gun. Officer Roland testified that Bill did not have a gun. Why

didn't Coleman pursue this discrepancy in testimony among prosecution witnesses?

Now George W. Cooper stepped in. Before the trial, Cooper and Robinson had been doubling at the Alhambra Theater and at Hammerstein's Victoria Theater daily for a week. The team had contracted for future bookings elsewhere, and now Cooper was forced to cancel them. Having lost his partner, Cooper had also lost his livelihood. When Cooper informed the managers of Robinson's conviction, they were shocked. They agreed with Cooper that Robinson had been railroaded, that Sussman and Phillips had perjured themselves, that Robinson's attorney had not mounted an adequate defense, and that Bill himself had not given his attorney any help. Cooper went to Karlin and Busch, attorneys, who agreed to look into the case and to ascertain whether there was enough evidence to request a new trial. In a month they had all the evidence they needed.

Among the documents they collected were affidavits attesting to Robinson's good character from fourteen people, including theater owners and managers and fellow performers. Edward F. Albee, manager of B. F. Keith Theatrical Enterprises, stated that he had known Bill for a number of years, that Bill was a man of considerable ability as an entertainer and theatrical performer, and whose services were worth about two hundred dollars per week. He stated further that he knew many other people who knew Bill, that he had discussed with them Bill's reputation and character, and that he knew "the reputation of the said William Robinson for honesty, veracity and integrity to be very good." In conclusion, Albee stated in his affidavit that had he been requested to appear at the trial to testify to Robinson's good character and reputation, "he would have unhesitatingly appeared and testified to him accordingly."

Bert Williams and George Walker submitted identical affidavits. They stated that they had known Robinson for about eight years, "in a business way." Williams stated that Robinson "was at one time employed by me in one of my theatrical enterprises."

Similar affidavits were signed by William Hammerstein, manager of the Victoria Theater in New York City, F. F. Proctor, Jr., assistant general manager of the Keith and Proctor theaters in New York City and elsewhere, Martin Beck, general manager of the Orpheum Vaudeville Circuit, Philip E. Nash, one of the managers of the United Booking Offices of America, Percy G. Williams, owner of the Colonial and Alhambra theaters in New York City, David D. Tobias, secretary of the Gotham-Attucks Music Publishing Company, and Samuel McKee, vaudeville editor of the *New York Morning Telegraph*.

More to the point, three men, including Charles Hall and Martin Wright, two employees of the Waldorf Club, a social club on Sixth Avenue that Bill frequented, submitted affidavits stating that Hyman Sussman had known Bill Robinson for years. Charles Hall's affidavit stated, "That he was present and accompanied the said defendant to the then place of business of the said Hyman Sussman, on or about the 7th day of March 1908 . . . when the said defendant ordered an overcoat to be made by the said Hyman Sussman and paid him a deposit of $5.00 in cash thereon. That no receipt was asked or given therefor. That deponent is personally acquainted with the said Hyman Sussman for a period of about 6 years and that the said Hyman Sussman has made clothing for the said defendant on numerous occasions. That deponent has had business transactions with the said Hyman Sussman and has had clothing made by the same Hyman Sussman and on various occasions has met the said defendant in the place of business of the said Hyman Sussman."

Armed with these affidavits, Karlin and Busch approached the members of the jury that had found Robinson guilty. Eleven of the twelve men endorsed the application for a new trial, saying that had the affidavits been presented to them during the trial they would not have convicted Bill. On October 28, 1908, Karlin and Busch presented the affidavits and the jurors' signed statements to the Court of General Sessions of the Peace and moved for a new trial.

Referring to the list of affidavits attesting to Bill's character, the motion stated, "Deponent at the time of the trial did not know that the persons abovementioned would have testified as stated and did not give their names to his counsel and believes that if he had given the names of the persons mentioned to his counsel and their appearance in Court had been secured it would have had a tendency to result in a verdict of Acquittal."

The motion stated further that Karlin and Busch, through interviews with the trial jurors, "have learned that several of them were influenced in some degree in reaching their verdict by being led to believe by the questions put to the defendant on his cross-examination by Keyran J. O'Connor, Esq., Assistant District Attorney, that he was in some way connected with one Edward Jones, who previously and at the same term of Part III [of the Court of General Sessions of the Peace] had been convicted of Robbery in the first degree and had been sentenced to a term of not less than nineteen years and not more than twenty years in the State's Prison. That although objections entered by counsel to such questions were sustained, it is manifest that they operated to the prejudice of the deponent, and deponent is further informed that two of the trial jurors in his case also sat in the case of the said Edward Jones."

Judge Malone took a month to rule on the motion for a new trial. In the interim, Karlin and Busch secured an affidavit from Bill's partner, George Cooper, dated November 18. Why such a statement from Cooper was so long in coming is not known. He had more specific information about Robinson's relationship with Sussman than most of the others who had submitted affidavits: ". . . to my personal knowledge, the complainant, Hyman Sussman, has known the defendant, William Robinson, for 4 years and has made clothes for Robinson on at least two occasions. Robinson has twice borrowed money from me to pay for clothes bought of Sussman.

"Furthermore, I know Robinson was 'on the road' playing with me at the time his overcoat was originally stolen. He has been my partner in the theatrical business nearly 7 years, during which time I have known him to be so neat and hardworking. During the past year he has only been in N.J. or Brooklyn 8½ weeks working; had been working steadily 'on the road' from September 1907 until 2 weeks before arrest."

Cooper's late-appearing affidavit may have swayed Judge Malone at last, for nine days later he granted the motion for a new trial, and Bill was released on bail pending that trial.

As reported in the press, the December trial had the atmosphere of a tribute to Bill Robinson. His supporters came out in force, including most of the membership and staff of the Waldorf Club. The men who had submitted affidavits on his behalf testified; the most important testimony came from two employees of the Waldorf Club, Charles Hall, waiter, and Martin Wright, barber.

Charles Hall told of the difficulty he'd had getting back a fifteen dollar deposit when he decided not to buy some clothes he had ordered from Sussman. He testified that at first he hadn't pressed for the immediate return of the deposit:

ASSISTANT DISTRICT ATTORNEY GARVAN: Did I understand you to say you did not need the money?

HALL: I did not need it at that time. I had known Hyman for a long time and did not want to crowd him. Later, when I wanted it I got it in twos and threes. The last five came in two from him and three from his wife. If I had not got that two and three on that particular day I might today be in the same position as Robinson.

By the time Martin Wright, the barber, was called to testify, things looked so bad for Sussman and his one "witness," Jacob Phillips, that Wright was understandably confused by one of the first questions he was asked.

GARVAN: Do you know this defendant?

WRIGHT: Wait a minute before I answer. Which is the defendant? [1]

On conclusion of testimony, Garvan did not want the case to go to the jury, but rather that the court render a verdict. Judge Malone put the case to the jury, which took exactly fifteen seconds to acquit Robinson. Not long after the trial, Sussman and Phillips were indicted for perjury.

Asked what he intended to do now, Bill said, "My wife saw me four times at the theater last Sunday while I was out on bail, but she was in no mood for it. I'm going to take her to a show tonight and let somebody else make her laugh, and me, too." [2] But the whole affair had been upsetting for Lena; it was hardly the way for a marriage to start out. Moreover, Bill was soon back on the road with Cooper, and Lena was left alone again. In retrospect, Bill's marriage to Lena never really had a chance.

One of Cooper and Robinson's first engagements, in early January 1909, was in Albany, New York. On the Empire State Express train north, Bill asked the conductor if it was possible to slow the train down as it passed Sing Sing prison. The conductor said that it wouldn't be possible; did Robinson want to get off? "Not at all," Bill replied. "I only wanted to see what promised to be my country home looks like from the outside." [3]

The following week, the team played the Alhambra in New York City. One day it snowed, and seeing the snow piled up around the door as the performers arrived for rehearsal, Bill grabbed a shovel and began clearing a path. Cooper arrived and asked if he'd turned from actor to laborer. "Since my recent absence from the stage," said Robinson, "I have come to like certain kinds of labor styles. Every time I get a shovelful of snow I think of how much better this is than making little ones out of big ones [referring to rock piles], which they threatened to have me doing for many a year."[4]

Later that month, Cooper and Robinson did a stint at Hammerstein's Victoria, and one night they hosted a "peculiar theater party." The honored guests were sixteen guards at the Tombs with whom Bill had become friends during his time there. "He was never so funny as he was last night," reported the *New York Morning Telegraph*. "He says he felt that way, seeing that he won't be in Sing Sing for the next eleven years."

Although he was able to joke about it, Bill's near imprisonment for a crime he did not commit had affected him deeply. He never again mentioned his arrest or trial, at least not publicly; and in later years he concocted stories to cover the time he was on trial and in the Tombs.

4

Shuffling
Along

For the next six years, Cooper and Robinson played steadily on the Keith and Orpheum circuits, crisscrossing the northern half of the continent. Rae Samuels Forkins, "The Blue Streak of Vaudeville," who would later become one of Bill's closest friends and associates, believed that the Orpheum Circuit was the best in vaudeville, for its theaters were first class and it was highly organized:

"I started in Duluth, but you didn't have to," she explained in a 1974 interview. "You could start with the Palace Theater in New York or the Palace Theater in Chicago. From Chicago you would go to St. Paul. From there you would go to Winnipeg, Canada. From Winnipeg you would go to Calgary; it was cold, very cold there. From Calgary you would go to Edmonton, almost up to Alaska, and you'd freeze your ears off.

From there down to Vancouver. From Vancouver down a little further—it would get warmer there—to Seattle, then to Portland. From Portland to San Francisco—two weeks there—then you would go down to the Valley to Oakland, San Jose, and Fresno. Sometimes you would also play Sacramento, a little north. Then down again to Los Angeles, where you'd play two weeks more. From Los Angeles you'd come down to Salt Lake City, from Salt Lake City to Ogden, Ogden to Lincoln, Nebraska, to Omaha. Then to Sioux City, Iowa. Then to Des Moines, then to Kansas City. You didn't always play the entire circuit. You were 'picked up' for a number of cities. If you played the full circuit it was called 'playing the wheel.' I used to play it twice a year. When you got your ticket, it would be about three feet long. The time it took to do the loop depended upon the time it took for some of the jumps."

At the time, the vaudeville wheel was America's modern equivalent of a syndicated radio or TV network. For a performer, it was the only means of mass exposure. It meant putting together five to fifteen minutes of new material twice a year, then playing that routine up to eight times a day, six days a week—and getting well paid to do so.

By 1912, Cooper and Robinson had established themselves on the circuit and had gained considerable favor for something they weren't responsible for—their race. The fact that they were "real Ethiopians" was the stuff of headlines in the *Denver Tribune* of May 14, 1912:

> Two "colored gentlemen" bearing the names of George W. Cooper and William Robinson are the best thing at the Orpheum this week. The men, who are honest to goodness

Ethiopians, not burnt cork 'make-believers,' have that provoking flavor of real down South 'darky' about them which with homemade maple syrup is fast becoming a thing of the past. Cheap imitations have spoiled both.

Both Cooper and Robinson are the genuine article and their chuckling guffaws, pigeon wing steps and cachinnating songs are a real vaudeville entertainment.

More important than newspaper headlines to vaudeville performers were the formal reports from theater managers to the home office. H. B. Branton, Des Moines, Iowa, wrote: "I herewith beg to submit report for the following acts playing during the week of Feb. 25, 1912 at Orpheum Theater." The show had eight acts and an overture. Five acts, made up of jugglers, singers, dancers, and athletes, got fair or good reviews from Mr. Branton. Three acts—the Kinodrama entitled *A Doubly Desired Orphan,* Rae Samuels, and Cooper and Robinson—got very good notices. Rae Samuels's report read: "19 minutes, oil in 1. Singing character and popular songs, assisted by a pianist. Stopped the show in the afternoon and went big with the audience at night." Of Cooper and Robinson, Branton wrote, "17 minutes, street in 1. 2 colored men, one straight and other comedy. Singing, talking and dancing. Very good with audience."[1]

By this time Robinson was equally as important to the act as Cooper. He was no longer second fiddle, except in billing, and he no longer had to wear his clown-tutu outfit. He also had clout in the world of vaudeville, at least in the eyes of those who had yet to make it, among them Ada Beatrice Queen Victoria Louise Virginia Smith, later known as Bricktop, saloonkeeper par excellence in Paris, Mexico City, and Rome.

In 1914, Bricktop was a member of the Panama Trio, resident performers at the Panama Club in Chicago. The group also included Cora Green and a young woman named Florence Mills who had grown tired of working as a single on the Negro T.O.B.A. Circuit. Bricktop claimed that it was she who persuaded the managers of the Panama to keep Florence on, for Mills was a soprano, and very shy, a quality that worked to her disadvantage at the raucous Panama. As Bricktop recalled some sixty-five years later, "I don't think it would be remiss for me to take a little pat on the back for giving a few pointers to the girl who would go on to become one of the greatest Negro stars.

"Florence, Cora, and I started doing some numbers and billed ourselves as the Panama Trio. We were singing harmony and dancing together long before the Boswell Sisters became big stars. When the three of us were out on the floor, we really kept the audience applauding and wanting more. One night Bill Robinson complimented us, and then we knew we were something special.

". . . At the time, he was part of a top vaudeville duo on the Keith Circuit—Cooper and Robinson. He told us we were great and that he was going to send someone in to hear us. A few nights went by, but there was no sign of anyone saying that Bill had sent him.

"One night a man and woman came in just before closing time. The place was almost deserted. Florence, Cora, and I were anxious to get out of the place, so we went out on the floor, *walked* through two or three songs, and then got off. I was standing by the door when the couple left. I remarked that their faces looked familiar. He looked like the head of the Keith circuit and she looked like Eva Tanguay, 'The Girl Who Made Vaudeville Famous,' the highest-paid single performer in vaudeville. I was to find out the next day that the lookalikes had been the real thing.

"Bojangles could be a very explosive fellow, and when he came to see us the next day, he really took aim at us and fired! There was no fighting back, because everything he said was true. We'd been unprofessional. How did we expect to get anywhere? That was the last time in my life that I didn't go out on the floor and do my best. . . ."[2] As for Robinson's later feelings about those women, he forgave them. In fact, he, too, claimed credit for having taught Florence Mills a few dance steps, though if he taught her in his usual fashion, he demonstrated a few that she could manage to learn, then a few that she would hardly be able to follow. He enjoyed reminding his students he was the master.

Bill Robinson was a staunch professional. He would go into a rage if other performers made noise backstage when he and Cooper were on. As Tom Fletcher recalled, when Bill was the leader of a partnership, he allowed three mistakes, then the partner was out. He practiced steps that he had been doing for years and constantly worked on his timing—often at 4:00 A.M. He put the same effort into a performance for a scanty audience in Duluth as he did into a performance at the Palace in Chicago. But the counterpoint to his utter professionalism onstage was his complete lack of responsibility off it.

His marriage to Lena had no effect at all on his gambling habit. He was on the road so much—she didn't travel with him—that she had little opportunity to encourage more stability in his life or help him save money. They never found the time, or the means, to build their marriage. They saw each other only when he appeared in New York, and even then only after he came home after a night out with the boys. Bill spent many waking hours offstage either playing cards, or playing pool, or borrowing money to pay his gambling debts, or fighting fellow gamblers who he felt had cheated him. "He was a good pool player," according to U. S. "Slow Kid" Thompson, vaudeville and circus performer, "but he thought he was a better pool player than he was. The boys used to take his money and he'd raise hell and fight with them."

Sometime in 1914, Cooper and Robinson were appearing at the Olympic Theater in Des Moines and Bill, as was his habit, was spending a good part of the time offstage in a pool hall at Thirty-first and State streets. One day he got into a brawl, and in the course of extricating himself from the fray, swinging the heavy end of a pool cue, he hit a man on the head. The man happened to be a police officer. A short time later that same officer waited backstage as Bill did his last performance with the team of Cooper and Robinson. When the act was over, Bill was arrested and shortly afterward the partnership of Cooper and Robinson dissolved, though it is unlikely that the arrest was the only cause.

Many years later, Rae Samuels told the story of Bill's

arrest, almost apologetic about revealing anything nega-
tive about the man whose reputation she and her husband had helped to protect for so long: "I was playing
in Des Moines, I'll give it to you, I didn't bother telling
this to anybody else. . . . I'm going back to the Coast
after my first season and I'm coming back to go into the
[Ziegfeld] Follies, so now I'm a seasoned performer. I
was all dressed up and I was really something. I see a
colored boy sitting in the wings with half a pie in his
hands eating it, and a policeman standing behind him.
'Oh boy,' I said to myself, 'I wonder what he's done.' I
found out that he was Bill Robinson of Cooper and
Robinson. He was a great pool player, you know, and
he'd had a fight. The policeman was going to take him
to jail, but he waited and let him do his act. So, they
took him to jail, but they turned him loose and sent him
back. Marty [Forkins, Rae's husband] wasn't managing
him yet. It happened plenty of times. The police never
did anything to him. My God, he used to be down at
the police department all the time. He'd go down to
night court, and if anyone had been arrested that had
never been arrested before, he'd find out who they were
and what they did and he'd get them out. He could talk
[the police] out of anything, and he put up [bail]
money, too."

Thus, if Rae Samuels's memory is correct, Bill's arrest
was hardly worth breaking up Cooper and Robinson.
The team was at its peak. Cooper had managed to excuse Robinson's earlier brushes with the law; why not
this one? Given the "two colored" rule that blacks in
vaudeville could only perform in pairs, never as singles,
Cooper would have to find a new partner if he let

Robinson go, and for all Robinson's peccadillos, he was a superb performer.

It is more likely that time and vaudeville legend have telescoped many incidents into one and that if it was Cooper who ended the partnership it was not the poolroom incident alone that caused him to decide he could no longer work with Robinson. It was probably a history of such incidents, and of Robinson's offstage unreliability in general. Even in his statement to the court back in 1908, Cooper had offered the information that Bill had borrowed money from him twice to pay for clothes ordered from Hyman Sussman, and given Bill's gambling penchant it is likely that he borrowed money from his partner for other purposes as well.

U. S. Thompson felt that the major reason for their breakup was money, and Bill's habit of drawing both his and Cooper's pay in order to gamble. "In St. Louis he'd be a big hit and go out to the box office after a matinee and draw two hundred dollars. And if he'd lose that he'd go to the box office and draw some more money. . . . All up West was gamblers, all kinds of games, and [they] knew they could beat Bill. They used to follow him all around. Pool players would go and follow him, and these stud players and cooncan players. He wanted to be the champion of everything, see. That's why him and Cooper split. Cooper told me Bill would go out front and draw up all the money: 'The night payday come, I wouldn't have none for myself. He done lost the salary.'"

Eddie Hunter, who later worked with Cooper, supports the idea that working with Bill Robinson could be frustrating: "George used to tell me about Bill. He

[Robinson] was a stubborn man to get along with. George always had to watch him and keep him out of trouble. He was always a troublemaker. Always gettin' in trouble. George would be gettin' him out of scraps."

But Hunter also suggested that the real reason Cooper and Robinson broke up was Cooper's decision to marry a white woman. Hunter described the woman as "a very pleasant woman. White. She was white, yeah. Nice, refined." He offered the information that "Cooper always got along with people. They respected him, and they respected his wife." He did not offer any information about how Bill Robinson felt about the marriage, nor explain why he felt that Cooper's marriage to a white woman was the real reason for the breakup.

According to Rae Samuels, "[Bill] couldn't entertain the thought of a colored man being married to a white woman." It is possible that it was Robinson's idea to dissolve the partnership. More likely, however, it was not Robinson but outside forces. The respectful people to whom Eddie Hunter referred were not white theater owners or vaudeville bookers. Once these kinds of people learned that Cooper was married to a white woman, they would not have booked him. The marriage forced Cooper out of white vaudeville.

The story was put out in the newspapers that George Cooper had died of cancer—and indeed, if prejudice and discrimination are considered a form of cancer, the papers told part of the truth. Cooper's career did essentially die with his marriage. He played small black theaters for nearly fifteen years, until he had a chance to appear on Broadway.

Bill Robinson was more fortunate than his longtime

partner. In fact, the breakup of the team gave Robinson the opportunity to become a vaudeville star on his own, though he might not have been successful as a single without the help of Marty Forkins, Rae Samuels's husband.

Rae had been watching Bill, and liking what she saw. "Bo had that personality. It was God-given, and he knew what to do with an audience. He could take the toughest audience in the world and take them in his hand and put them in his pocket—I don't care where you put him [in the show lineup]." When Cooper and Robinson broke up, Rae Samuels urged Marty Forkins to manage Bill.

Forkins was a streetwise Irishman from Chicago whose first job was waiting on tables in the bar his father owned. He attended Notre Dame University and Law School, but he never practiced law. He started managing boxers and soon moved into the entertainment business. He cut his teeth in theatrical management by working for C. S. Humphrey and the Western Vaudeville Managers Association. By the time he met Bill Robinson, he was already established as one of the top independent theatrical managers in the Midwest, counting among his clients Fred and Dorothy Stone and Will Rogers. At the urging of his wife, he agreed to meet Bill Robinson in his office in Chicago, not long after Robinson's partnership with Cooper had ended.

Robinson had performed without burnt cork in modern white vaudeville shows for years, but he had always been restricted by the "two colored" rule. Until now, he had been willing to accept that rule. But now that Cooper was gone and he was facing Marty Forkins for the first time, Bo had a proposal to make. He was tired of discrimination. Although he couldn't learn material without someone reading it to him, he knew he was smart enough to hold an audience on his own. He wanted to try a solo act. Forkins must have been surprised when Robinson told him of his dream. For his part, Bill was aware of how risky it would be for himself and for Forkins, and he must have been equally surprised when Forkins accepted the idea of managing the first black solo act in vaudeville, provided that he could sell the concept to a booking agent. The deal was confirmed with a handshake, and thus began a thirty-five-year association that was then, and remains today, extremely rare in show business. Robinson and Forkins never had a signed contract, and their relationship was marked by mutual respect and trust, though Robinson always called his manager Mr. Marty or Boss, and Forkins always called his client Bill or Bo.

One of the keys to Forkins's success as a manager was his awareness of the importance of public relations; he never made a move without assessing its PR implications. One of his first concerns as Bill Robinson's manager was how to present Bill. He thought it best not to remind either vaudeville managers or the vaudeville-going public that Bill had once been part of the team of Cooper and Robinson. There would be too many questions about what had happened to the team. Also, by promoting Bill as formerly of a team he would be reminding vaudeville managers and bookers of the "two colored" rule, which was the last thing he wanted to do if he hoped to promote Bill as a solo act. The presentation of Bill Robinson as a solo act required a different tactic, and a different history. Forkins decided to present Bill as a solo "discovery" and to start him off with the proverbial clean slate.

Forkins came up with the story that he and Bill had met in a restaurant where Bill was working as a waiter. Bill had spilled hot oyster stew in Forkins's lap, and while apologizing had explained that he was not a waiter but a dancer. This had interested Forkins enough to start their professional relationship. Lame as it was, Forkins, Rae Samuels, and Bill all stuck to the story, and within a few years it had become a part of Bojangles legend, although to some people it always seemed to invite more questions than it answered.

Having come up with the story of how they had met, Forkins got to work on creating a short history for Bill Robinson as a solo act. He knew that Gertrude Hoffman, star and producer of Chicago's successful Marigold Gardens Theater, was looking for a new dance instructor. For the job, Forkins strongly suggested Bill, who Gertrude Hoffman already knew was one of the best dancers in the business. She understood that Forkins was angling for more exposure for his client than a mere dance instructorship would give him, and she didn't faint at Forkins's suggestion that Bill perform, too. She accepted Forkins's terms and hired Bill on the spot.

As dance instructor, Bill worked with the Marigold Gardens chorus girls, two of whom—Ruth Etting and Joan Crawford—would later become film stars. As sometime solo performer, he was well received, and caused no race riots. Gertrude Hoffman deserves considerable credit for sharing his vision and having the courage to give him the opportunity to realize it. Many years later, she too gained national fame as Mrs. Odetts, Gale Storm's eccentric next-door neighbor in television's *My Little Margie*.

Bill spent about a year at the Marigold Gardens. His popularity there allowed Marty Forkins to get him bookings at small theaters elsewhere in Chicago at first, then in an ever-expanding Midwest area. Within two or three years, he had become the first major black single dancer on the Keith Circuit. He was impressed. "Before that," he once explained, "I never pictured myself as a star."[3]

Sadly, by the time he became a star, he was unable to share his happiness with his wife, Lena. Their almost nonexistent marriage was doomed from the day it began, not only because of Bill's arrest and imprisonment in New York in the Hyman Sussman case, but also because of his constant absences, his gambling and fighting, and his inability to save money, none of which had worn well with Lena. They had been unable to have a child, and that, too, had weighed heavily on their relationship. Around 1916 they separated, though it was several years before they actually divorced.

In the following year, 1917, the United States entered World War I, a turn of events that proved disastrous for large commercial theaters and the actors and actresses who performed in them. But in some ways the war was a boon to variety artists, whose lifeblood was performing. The U.S. War Department encouraged entertainers to give shows for the troops at various army and navy posts. The armed services paid for their travel and lodging. For Bill, it was a fine opportunity to gain more exposure as a solo artist, and he was happy to perform for the troops.

He never publicly complained about having to perform first for white troops, then for blacks, or about the comparative venues in which the men of both races were entertained. Nor did he complain about being denied lodging and accommodations that white entertainers accepted as their due. Bill Robinson was a patriot and as respectful of the military as he was of the police. He kept for the rest of his life a letter of commendation that he received from the War Department:

WAR DEPARTMENT
Commission on Training Camp Activities
Washington

September 25, 1918

Mr. Bill Robinson

My Dear Mr. Robinson:

The War Department, through the Commission on Training Camp Activities, desires to express its thanks for your very kind assistance in entertaining the men in the camps through the volunteer service which you have just rendered.

We are sure that from your experience in the camps you fully realize the pleasure which your act has given to the men and also the extreme need for contributions such as yours.

Of course you realize the Government is furnishing these entertainments in the Liberty Theatres at a substantial expense in the operating of the theatres and their expenses and it is only through co-operation such as yours that it is able to meet the situation.

> Again thanking you, we remain,
> Very truly yours,
> J. Howard Reger[4]

That same year, 1918, Bill introduced the stair dance into his act. It was at the Palace Theater in New York, showplace of the Keith circuit and the undisputed crown jewel of vaudeville theaters (one at which few black performers appeared, and certainly not as singles). During World War I Bert Williams, the team of Greenlee and Drayton, and Bill Robinson were the only black dancers to appear there. The stage was flanked by four steps on each side, which was convenient for performers who wished to descend into the audience or for an individual or a group that wished to go up onto the stage. The story goes that during one matinee Bill saw some friends in the audience and on impulse danced down the steps to greet them. The audience applauded his deft moves, and he decided to work them into his routine.[5] Thus was his famous stair dance born, though Bill and Lemmeul Eggleston date its origin to many years earlier. Since many theaters did not have steps leading to the stage, Bill was unable to do the dance regularly until he had his own portable staircase built, probably about six years later. Still, in 1918 his dance caused enough of a stir to raise the hackles of another staircase dancer named King Rastus Brown. According to Stearns and Stearns in *Jazz Dance,* around 1918, King Rastus "was loudly and insistently grieved by a young upstart named Bill 'Bojangles' Robinson, who stole his Stair Dance. He challenged Robinson to a cutting contest on any stage, anywhere, anytime." But Bill never took up the challenge. Al Williams, when interviewed by Stearns and Stearns, claimed, "Robinson never seemed to be around when King Rastus was in the back room of the

Hoofers Club. Bill Robinson came to shoot pool in the front room."[6]

Neither man could claim to have originated the idea. Vaudeville legends abound with "firsts" in this area. Some credit Al Leach (and His Rosebuds). Then there were the Whitney Brothers, who did a musical stair dance at Hyde and Behman's Theater in 1899. A team called Mack and Williams did a single, a double, and a triple stair dance in 1915. Paul Morton and his wife, Naomi Glass, also did one as part of their act. What distinguished Bill Robinson's stair dance was showmanship. His stair dance, when perfected, involved a different rhythm for each step—each one reverberating with a different pitch—and the fact that he had a special set of portable steps enhanced his claim to originating the dance. By the spring of 1921 it was a standard part of his act, as evidenced by a telegram he received on April 4 from F. W. Vincent, one of the managers of the booking department of the Orpheum Circuit. There was a dispute between Bill and another dance act. Vincent asked that Bill eliminate the stairs "this week" as a "personal favor."[7]

Apparently, the dispute involved the use of a staircase dance by The Four Mortons, who may have been Paul Morton and his wife, Naomi Glass, plus their children. Rae Samuels recalled a time when "we were playing in Minneapolis and an act called 'The Four Mortons'—a father, a mother, son and daughter who were dancers— deliberately tried to take his stair act away from him. They showed up with a set of stairs, and they were scheduled to go on before Bill. So then when Bill saw those stairs he came flying into my dressing room and said, 'Miss Rae, you're not going to let them do this to me.'" Bo also contacted the management of the Keith chain. But while F. W. Vincent advised Bill to back down, Rae Samuels took his side and persuaded the theater manager to forbid the Mortons to use their stair routine.

After that, Bill tried to secure a patent on his stair routine, and though the U.S. Patent Office in Washington, D.C., declined to accept his application, Bill rarely had to go to great lengths to protect his "professional territory" again. Soon, he was so well identified with the stair routine that no one would dream of impinging on his territory. Dancer Fred Stone once used it and sent Bill a check for fifteen hundred dollars and a note that said, "In part payment for the stair dance I stole from you." Bill cashed the check.

Bill's routine probably would not have suffered unduly from the brief elimination of the stair dance. He had plenty of other steps he could use, none of which he had invented, but all of which he invested with his own particular style. To quote Stearns and Stearns: "Sandwiched between a Buck or Time Step, Robinson might use a little skating step to stop-time; or a Scoot step, a cross-over tap which looked like a jig; hands on hips, tapping as he went, while one foot kicked up and over the other; or a double tap, one hand on hip, one arm extended, with eyes blinking, head shaking, and derby cocked; or a tap to the melody of a tune such as 'Parade of the Wooden Soldiers'; or a broken-legged or old man's dance, one leg short and wobbling with the beat; or an exit step, tapping with a Chaplinesque waddle . . ." All the while he told jokes and stories and did imitations—a mosquito's hum, a trombone—his comedic timing as perfect as his tapping. And as if his dancing and comedy were not enough, he was physically very appealing. To compensate for a slight build, particularly lack of height (he was about five feet seven), he was in the habit of hunching up his shoulders, which had the effect of making him appear not so much taller as more vulnerable. His face was open, good-natured, his smile infectious. "In a sense," dancer Charles "Honi" Coles once remarked, "Bo's face was about forty percent of his appeal."

But there was also the obvious delight Bill seemed to take in dancing, and the sheer professionalism of his performances, a professionalism that would not brook shoddy musical accompaniment. According to Rae Samuels, "He loved good musicians. The bad ones he disliked personally, and he didn't want any part of them at all. I remember I played one time with him in Minneapolis and there was a great pianist, one of those fellows that just played the kind of music that Bo loved to dance to. He was a big hit there. He said [to the other members of the band], 'You fellows must be tired of doing these shows. Why don't you just sit back and rest.' Then he looked down at the man at the piano and said, 'Howard, I want to do a little soft-shoe. Why don't you carry me, will you? Just give me a little of that "Alice Blue Gown." You just carry on.' Why, he would have danced for hours."

Bo's talent, ability to project his personality across the footlights, and sheer love of dancing proved an irresistible combination. By 1921 he was stopping shows almost everywhere he appeared. The dancing that had earned only scorn from his grandmother now generated ovations and respect for the image of black people onstage. It was a shame that he could not share that success with her.

Bill appeared everywhere. Based on his scrapbook, here is an incomplete itinerary for August–December 1921:

August 8—Manhattan—Keith's Palace Theater
August 18—Mt. Vernon, N.Y.—Proctor's Theater
August 26—Manhattan—Royal Theater (Keith)
September 13—Boston—Keith Theater
September 20—Providence—E. F. Albee Theater
September 27—Manhattan—Royal Theater (Keith)
October 1—Manhattan—Riverside Theater (Keith)
October 11—Brooklyn—Bushwick Theater
October 18—Pittsburgh—Davis Theater (Keith)
October 25—Youngstown—Hippodrome
November 1—Dayton—Strand (Keith)
November 8—St. Louis—Orpheum
November 14—Chicago—Palace
November 22—South Bend—Orpheum
November 29—Rockford—Palace
December 2—Madison—Orpheum
December 8—Chicago—Lincoln

Even though he was provided train tickets by the vaudeville circuits, he had to find his own lodging in each town, and that made being on the road harder than for a white performer. Rae Samuels, for example, could recite the following litany of lodgings for herself:

Minneapolis—Radison Hotel
St. Paul—St. Paul Hotel
Winnipeg—The Vancouver Hotel
San Francisco—The St. Francis Hotel
Los Angeles—The Alexandria Hotel
Salt Lake City—The Salt Lake Hotel
Denver—Metropolitan Hotel
Kansas City—The Baltimore Hotel

Bill had to be more creative. His litany of lodgings would have been more like:

Minneapolis—Mrs. X's boardinghouse
St. Paul—Mr. and Mrs. Y's home
Salt Lake—Mr. Z's spare room

Eddie Hunter worked in vaudeville back then. A comedian who from time to time worked with George Cooper, among others, Hunter had performed in blackface until he realized that he could make people laugh without it. He remembered that life on the road had its rough spots: "You ran into prejudice. Certain kinds of people didn't want you in a hotel, didn't want you in this or that. I'd get into a town and the stationmaster would know who's coming in on those late trains. They'd wait to receive you, and then they'd close up and take you to a rooming house where they knew you could stay. One time we pulled into a town in the wee hours of the morning. Everything white with snow. Cold! Pull up to a place, a rooming house, man rings the bell. 'Got a couple of people down here who want a room. One colored. One white.' The man hollers down,

'I'll take the white. Won't take the colored.' The white fellow spoke up, 'You can't take him, you can't take me.' Oh, I don't know. The things you go through in life. I told him, 'Don't do that because of me. No sense in you suffering.' He said, 'No, I meant that. If he can't take you, he can't take me.'"

According to Hunter, however, "Eating was no problem. I'd go to a restaurant and go into the back part, the kitchen. I'd say, 'I'm playing over here at the such-and-such theater and I'd like to eat here.' I could come in through the back. Like that. You'd work out things. Or maybe I'd arrange to have my food sent over to the stage door. There's always a way."

Unlike Hunter, Bill did not rely on helpful station-masters to find lodgings. "He knew each week where he was going to stay," Rae Samuels said in 1974. "There was one place, though, where Bill didn't know where he would stay. It was in Louisville, Kentucky; we were there for the Derby. He said, 'Oh, Mr. Marty, where I'm living is terrible.'" Forkins suggested that he move to the place where he and Rae were staying, but Bill realized he would not be welcome to stay overnight by the hotel management. He did, however, agree to take meals with the Forkinses. Rae Samuels recalled, "I want to tell you, when that waiter brought up that food, and he saw that black man sitting there, he knew who he was, and pretty soon there were a whole bunch of black heads poking through the door, and whispering, 'That's him. That's Bojangles!'"

As a rule, however, Bill made his plans beforehand and made no changes once he arrived in a city. While the white performers in the troupe went to their hotels and rested, Bill went straight to the local police station, presented his revolver, and asked for a permit. That accomplished, he went to the railroad station and bought a ticket out of town. Having covered himself against possible unpleasant incidents, and ensured a quick getaway if necessary, he went to his lodgings and began to prepare for the show.

While some of these precautions were necessary because of Bill's gambling and fighting habits, they were also advisable because he was black. Ever on the alert for trouble with whites, he could never be sure when a racial incident might occur. Onstage, he was in the habit of quipping that he was "having the best time I've had since I was colored." Offstage, he was continually reminded of his second-class position in society by being denied service by whites and suffering the numerous indignities particular to the life of a black man on the road. He realized he could do nothing as an individual, but if black vaudeville performers had some sort of professional organization, they might at least attempt to influence conditions on the road.

White vaudeville entertainers had such an organization, the National Vaudeville Artists' Association. It provided health and burial insurance and the use of a new million-dollar-plus Manhattan clubhouse—with private sleeping facilities, swimming pool, billiard rooms, indoor pool, and card rooms—among other benefits. Black vaudeville artists could not join this association, and yet, as a group, they needed health and burial insurance more than did the whites, as a group. The famous black composer Scott Joplin's having to be buried in a potter's field (a city-run burial site for beggars with unmarked graves) was partial evidence of that fact. Bill knew only too well what it was like for a black performer to become ill or die, for he had helped many fellow performers and their families pay hospital or funeral bills. By early 1921 Bill had decided to inquire about the possibility either of joining the N.V.A. or of forming a "colored branch" of the association. His letter of March 28, 1921, addressed to F. W. Vincent of the Keith circuit, has not survived. Based on the reply, which did survive, his letter may have been prompted by a request to buy tickets to an N.V.A. benefit. Vincent apparently did not feel competent to answer Bill on such a delicate matter and referred the letter to the boss, Edward F. Albee. Albee, one of the men who had signed an affidavit to release Bill from jail back in 1908, responded to Bill's letter.

On April 2, 1921, he wrote that he was thinking about a colored branch of the National Vaudeville Artists' Association. He had heard of no objections and saw no reason why Bill and all vaudeville artists shouldn't be members.

As a friend, he suggested that the few colored performers "would rather be among themselves in some part of the city best suited to their own convenience." He asked for Bill's advice on the touchy subject. Then Albee reminded Bill that if colored performers cared to join under these circumstances, they would receive all benefits, including the Insurance Fund, "with one exception—the clubhouse."[8]

Apparently, Bill did offer Mr. Albee some advice on forming a colored branch of the National Vaudeville Artists'. He wrote to the N.V.A. and received a response from Henry Chesterfield, secretary of the N.V.A., dated August 22. Mr. Chesterfield was careful about his phrasing. He seemed to quote the bylaws of the organization regarding the necessary qualifications for colored and other artists. They had to be actively engaged in vaudeville at the time of application—a safe hedge, since there were so few colored vaudeville artists at that time.

They also had to be nominated and seconded by a "brother artist." The letter also implied that Bill had suggested holding a benefit to raise the money for a new colored branch of the N.V.A. Mr. Chesterfield replied that the N.V.A. would arrange it, and "will not tolerate outsiders to handle the benefit without the sanction of this organization."9

Robinson did not follow up on Chesterfield's grudging invitation. His travel schedule made it difficult to organize even his own life, much less a group of black vaudevillians who were few and far-flung and had equally busy travel schedules. For the time being, he was forced to conclude that his idea was one whose time had not yet come, and that he would have to be content with being a vaudeville headliner who could not use the N.V.A. clubhouse or benefit from membership in the organization. He had reason to believe that the situation might change, however, once the era of the "new Negro" began with the opening of the first all-black show on Broadway in 1921.

Shuffle Along was the brainchild of two black acts, Sissle and Blake, and Miller and Lyles. Noble Sissle and Eubie Blake had teamed up in 1915 as "The Dixie Duo," and were among the first blacks to perform without burnt cork and in elegant clothes. Blake played the piano and Sissle sang, though they included the comedy bits that were a must in vaudeville. Flournoy Miller and Aubrey Lyles were a blackface comedy-dancing act that had started out in college theatricals at Fisk University in Nashville, Tennessee. Like Sissle and Blake, and like Bill Robinson, Miller and Lyles enjoyed the distinction of traveling on the white vaudeville circuit, and like the others they suffered the same indignities on the road. Bill Robinson knew these men and may even have tried to enlist their support in forming a black branch of the N.V.A., but it was more than likely that he rarely saw them. The policy followed by the white vaudeville circuits, like B. F. Keith's, was to book only one black act per show, and thus the performers' paths crossed only briefly at any given time. Though Sissle and Blake and Miller and Lyles had been active on the white circuits for several years, it was not until 1920, on the occasion of an NAACP (National Association for the Advancement of Colored People) benefit in Philadelphia, that the two teams had the opportunity to discuss the problems blacks had on the stage and on the road and to germinate the idea of an all-black musical comedy.

Built around their respective acts, and with a thin plot line, *Shuffle Along* remained little more than an idea until the Cort family, which owned several theaters in New York, offered the two teams the use of the run-down 63rd Street Theater and some old costumes and sets. The foursome built the rest of the show around these items, which explains why, in a musical about an election for mayor in all-black Jimtown, Mississippi, there was a scene in which the actors, dressed in Oriental costumes, did a number titled "Oriental Blues." The young singers and dancers recruited for the show rehearsed for free, so delighted were they to have the opportunity to appear in any kind of stage production.

Bee Freeman got her first big break when she was chosen for the cast: "I came to New York with an infant in my arms. The fellow that was playing the lead, Roger Matthews, was from my home, Boston. About two days after I got into New York City I was walking down the street and I ran into him. I told him I left my husband, I have the baby and need a job. He said, 'Here. Take this address and be there at about two o'clock.' This was about noon.

"So I went to this place. It was a rehearsal hall. Right around the corner from the Lafayette Theater. They were rehearsing when I arrived and they were supposed to leave on tour the following week. They were still tightening up the show and doing bits and pieces here and there. So Roger took me and introduced me to the leads—Miller, Lyles, Sissle and Blake. They wanted to know what I could do and I said, 'Nothing!' So Lawrence Deeds, who was the director, said, 'Well, you can walk across a stage, can't you? Just keep time to the music and walk across the stage.' I did and he told me to come back and do it again. Then I noticed Eubie and Noble starting to look at me and talk. They kept talking and then Noble leaned over the piano. Then Eubie started playing something and Noble told me to walk across the stage to their music. I walked across the stage and came back. Then Eubie called out, 'That's it! If you've never been vamped by a brown skin, you've never been vamped at all!' That song was written right there and then. And that was not quite a week before the show was supposed to open in Philadelphia."

It was customary to take a show on an out-of-town tour before opening on Broadway, and *Shuffle Along* went on such a tour—on a shoestring. Even so, by the time it opened in New York at the 63rd Street Theater, it was eighteen thousand dollars in debt and had attracted no financial backers or advance reviews. On opening night, major critics did not even attend. *Shuffle Along* was a sleeper whose primary publicity was of the word-of-mouth variety. But word got around, and once the major critics saw and reviewed the show, there was no looking back. George Jean Nathan, the most powerful critic in New York, saw it five times. The critics and audiences raved about the energy of the young singers and dancers, which was so contagious that, as Alan Dale of the *New York American* put it, ". . . gradually any tired feeling that you might have been nursing vanished in the sun of their good humor. . . ." Elsewhere in his review, Dale described the production as full of "pep," and it was this pep that attracted the audiences. So warm was the feeling the show conveyed that audiences did not even take umbrage at the presentation of tender, uncomic love between a black man and woman.

Until *Shuffle Along,* it had been unacceptable to show true love between blacks on the white stage; only a caricature of love was possible. Blacks could only do comedy, which is why Sissle and Blake and Miller and Lyles had chosen the musical comedy idiom. But they had decided to try a little experiment. In addition to the still-popular songs "I'm Just Wild About Harry" and "In Honeysuckle Time," Sissle and Blake wrote one called

"Love Will Find a Way" for Lottie Gee and Roger Matthews. Blake played the piano onstage during the number, and his three partners were so leery of its reception that they actually positioned themselves near the exit to facilitate a quick getaway should the audience start throwing things. To their amazement, the song was not only well received but encored.

Florence Mills achieved major stardom in *Shuffle Along,* though it wasn't easy. After the show had played on Broadway several months, its star, Gertrude Saunders, decided to quit and go into burlesque, which paid more money. Ada Smith, Florence Mills's former partner in the Panama Trio in Chicago, was in New York by this time, working at Barron's in Harlem. (Barron Wilkins, owner of the club, had given Ada the name Bricktop because of her flaming red hair.) According to Bricktop, it was she who suggested Florence Mills to replace Gertrude Saunders: "She was with an act on the Keith circuit called the Tennessee Ten, headed by Kid Thompson." She and Thompson needed an out. Bricktop told Noble Sissle that he should give Florence a chance, but he was not sure she was the right type. "She auditioned and auditioned. I don't know how many times they had her try out."[10]

Bee Freeman recalled, "The first time I saw Florence Mills she was walking onstage. People had already been talking about her. What would she look like and things like that. When she walked onstage she was wearing a black, rusty-looking dress. It seemed like she had no glamour at all. She looked like one of those little girls you would see working in a store. And we had been on Broadway long enough to think that we were very elegant. We all had magnificent wardrobes and we were really riding high and handsome. So she sang a few bars at rehearsal and we thought, 'Who is she?' and being just as obnoxious as we could be. 'How dare they inflict this thing on us.' But that first night she went onstage before the audience, she got on that stage and there was nobody who could get on. Nobody. She was just incredible. And the sweetest, most charming lady. She was so wonderful. And we were all so ashamed of ourselves. None of us had that talent. We had all the things that mean nothing, but she had that talent. She had all of that. She was a beautiful lady."

Bricktop also thought highly of Florence and her talent. "The night she took the floor from Gertrude Saunders, she had seventeen encores. *Seventeen encores!* She never looked back. After that, Florence Mills was a *star*."

Black performers began to feel a sense of real possibility as a result of the success of *Shuffle Along,* which ran a full year on Broadway and continued in various revivals across the country well into the 1940s. According to U. S. Thompson, "There was a big demand for colored talent after *Shuffle Along*. See, *Shuffle Along* kind of opened the doors for colored talent and performers. At that particular time, everywhere you turned there was colored performers and colored revues and nightclubs and theaters and things."

Some black entertainers were uneasy about all the attention they were suddenly getting from whites, particularly the invitations to mix with whites socially. Not only were they suspicious of the motives behind such invitations, but also they feared a white backlash. Bee

Freeman lost her job in *Shuffle Along* over such socializing. "One night I got a note from a man who said he wanted to drop me off wherever I wanted to go. He was somebody that I had met before, though I can't remember how we were introduced. So I sent word to him that we were all going uptown to a restaurant on One Hundred and Thirty-fifth, Tabs. We all got into his car, went up there, had a meal, and he left us there. Then the girls went their way and I went mine.

"The next day was Saturday, matinee day. While I was dressing, word came around that we were all to be onstage five minutes before curtain was to go up because management wanted to speak to the cast. Miller came onstage, all of them were there, but he was the one who said that it was his painful duty for him to have to discharge one of the most promising members of the show because they could not afford for their women to be going out with white men. Of course, the fact that after that he had all kinds of white women didn't matter. And that's what happened to my career. Just like that. And of course, if I had known then what I know now, my dear, I would have had so much publicity and all that it would have been running out of my ears. I had a case. And you see, the man, I think he owned the theater where we were playing, well, he was on his way to Miami when this happened. When he came back and heard, he gave them the devil and wanted to get me back. Sissle and Miller were the ones who were tough because Eubie and Lyles said it was ridiculous and would not condone it in any way. But Sissle and Miller stuck together and they said that if they brought me back to the show, that they would withdraw the show from the theater. I don't think they would have done that, but that's what they threatened. I couldn't say anything. I said nothing in my defense because it was such a shock. Then I found out that this man's wife had seen him give the note to the usher to bring backstage to me. I said nothing in my defense, you see, because to be fired for something like that was inconceivable to me. I just couldn't imagine that happening. And the funny thing is we were in this type of show in a white theater and everyone in the audience was white. I mean you could throw rice in the theater and not see it. And still they had that attitude. And that thing followed me because two or three times I was up for things and they would put thumbs-down on it because of what had happened. It was a very, very tight group at that time."

No doubt Bill Robinson heard the story by way of the show business grapevine, and wasn't surprised. He'd seen a lot of progress since the start of his career, not the least of which was his own success in getting past the old "two colored" rule in vaudeville. He was pleased with the success of *Shuffle Along,* although it had had no direct effect on him, and with the increased number of "colored revues" that *Shuffle Along* was spawning. But he was much too wise to expect any major changes in social relationships between the races. And, so far, he hadn't seen much improvement in traveling or lodging conditions for Negro performers on the road.

5

Below the Headlines

By the time *Shuffle Along* opened and closed on Broadway, black life in New York had undergone a fundamental change: For the first time, the city's burgeoning black population was becoming centralized. Harlem, which was fast becoming the "Black Capital of America," was originally planned as a "suburb" for wealthy whites. Development there had begun in the wake of construction on Manhattan's three elevated railway lines, which by 1881 had been extended to 129th Street. Plans were on the books for an additional extension northward, and since the influx of European immigrants had caused the city's population to pass the one-million mark by 1880, developers realized that more established white residents had to have somewhere to flee to. So they laid out a new residential community in an old Dutch farming community called Haarlem, shortened to Harlem over the years. They established broad, tree-lined avenues and neat side streets, and built luxury town houses and apartment buildings, assuming that by the time the buildings were constructed that the "Els" above 129th Street would also have been completed. Unfortunately, they overestimated the eagerness of wealthy whites to move north, as well as the size of the impending profits. By the early 1900s, the Els were ready to transport Harlem's new inhabitants, and the buildings were ready to receive them. But the expected northward migration of whites did not occur. One reason was that in the fury of building and overspeculation, both land and building costs had become inflated way out of proportion. By 1904–1905 the bottom had fallen out of the Harlem real-estate market.

In desperation, many realtors began to sell, and rent, to the city's growing black population, which tripled between 1890 and 1910. The old black neighborhoods in the Tenderloin and San Juan Hill districts were too small to accommodate them. At first, only the most well-to-do blacks moved to Harlem, among them Reverend Adam Clayton Powell, Sr., pastor of the Abyssinian Baptist Church, and his family. But by 1910–1911, ordinary blacks and black establishments had joined the northward trend, which sped rapidly after the victory of black heavyweight boxer Jack Johnson over Jim "Great White Hope" Jeffries. After the fight, mobs of furious whites destroyed sections of downtown black neighborhoods. Rather than reopen for business or resettle in their former areas, black families and firms simply relocated to Harlem. By 1920 even the venerable Abyssinian Baptist Church had begun preparations to move from West Fortieth Street between Seventh and Eighth avenues to 138th Street between Seventh and Lenox.[1]

Bill Robinson joined the northward migration to Harlem in the mid-teens, along with many other black show business people—Scott Joplin and his wife, Lottie, moved from the West Fifties to 133 West 138th Street in 1915. By then, one could enjoy the sporting life in Harlem, for there were many bars with live entertainment and gambling halls. Des Williams, a bartender, placed Bo in Harlem back in 1913. Williams said that one night Bo cleaned out every gambler in the house and that Bojangles was so happy he danced down 135th Street.

At first, Bill treated Harlem like any other new town. His first order of business was to make friends with the local police, in particular with Edward P. Mulrooney, captain of the 132nd Precinct. He often saw Mulrooney early Sunday mornings when he was going home after a Saturday-night card or crap game. He would say, "Howdy, Mr. Captain!" and do a little dance. Years later, when Bill was richer and more famous, he was one of the biggest contributors to the police welfare fund, but he never lost his awed respect for Mulrooney. Mayor Jimmy Walker once remarked, "You know, Bill doesn't really recognize the mayor of the city of New York. He thinks I'm sort of assistant to Mulrooney."[2]

Though he lived in Harlem, Bill was seldom there to watch and enjoy the emerging "Black Capital of America" or to play the "New Negro." He was too often on the road. Chicago seems to have been his headquarters because of its location in the middle of the country and the fact that it was Marty Forkins's home base. Later,

Bill also frequented Chicago because it was where Fannie Clay lived.

Fannie was a Tennessee girl, twenty years Bill's junior and equally distant from him in life experience. People in her morally correct social milieu believed that theater people were a short step above trash. They had an even lower opinion of vaudevillians, who were essentially rootless and were often out of work. When Fannie and Bill met, she was a student at the Illinois School of Pharmacy and dreamed of owning her own pharmacy someday.

Exactly when Bill met Fannie isn't known, but he was still married to Lena at the time. While Bill and Lena had separated around 1916, they were not divorced until 1922. Within days, Bill married Fannie. It wouldn't have looked good for Bill's fans to read that he was divorced one week and married the next, so this part of the Bill Robinson legend is muddied, too, full of contradictory statements by both Bill and Fannie. In interviews with reporters, neither gave the time or place of their wedding the same way twice.

One time Fannie said they were married at a friend's home in St. Paul. In an interview for the *Journal and Guide* in 1935, Fannie said, "Bill and I met about fifteen years ago. We have been married about fourteen years." In a third interview, Fannie said they were married in Minneapolis in 1924. But after reading the first of a series of Robinson scrapbooks, we suspect that they met sometime in late 1920 or early 1921, and were married by 1922. In a story about Bill developing ptomaine poisoning, the *Minneapolis Messenger,* January 21, 1922, reported:

Billy (Bojangles) Robinson, who appeared last week at the Orpheum theatre, was taken suddenly ill last Saturday (14) with ptomaine poisoning. He was able to appear with the aid of a physician. Mr. Robinson was feeling better on his arrival in Duluth last Sunday and during his act he averted a panic when the box office was held up by bandits. He is accompanied by his wife.

Beginning in September 1921 the first Bojangles scrapbook (eleven by fourteen inches, bound in red, with BILL ROBINSON embossed in gold on the cover) is fairly complete. During an interview with Michel Mok of *The New York Post* (December 12, 1936), Bill was using the scrapbooks to tell the reporter the history of his life. He gave one of his familiar deep-throated chuckles and said, "I sure do get a kick out of these here [scrap] books. I'm glad you came in so I had an excuse to go over them. I've had a swell time. I haven't had as much fun since I've been colored."

Given Bill's carefree manner, we suspect that Fannie had stepped in to organize and collect the articles about him that appeared as he traveled the vaudeville circuits. Bill and Fannie would have known each other several months by September 1921 and came to rely on each other in spite of their respective misgivings. Years later, after Bill died, Fannie described how her everlasting love for him began, in a small autobiography that appeared in the February 1953 edition of *Ebony* magazine. It was not an auspicious beginning. Fannie had her eyes on a career as a pharmacist. She did not have her sights on the men who frequented Walgreen's drugstore and ice cream parlor, especially not those men who were coming in from the poolroom or the many gambling dens in the area. Fannie had to be sharp to become a student at the Illinois School of Pharmacy. Her time was limited since she attended classes during the day and worked the evening hours. Studying and writing papers would often not begin until one A.M. Fannie was a down-to-earth woman with high values. She was not the type to fall for a well-dressed, happy-go-lucky gambling dancer and dandy—but she did.

At first, Bill had no idea he would fall for Fannie. If Walgreen's drugstore had been located at any other corner except 35th and State, their paths would probably have never crossed. But that ice cream parlor afforded him two of his most important things: ice cream, and someone to loan him money when he went broke. His usual easy touch was the store's supervisor. Then one day the supervisor was away and Bill needed a stake for a game. Out of desperation, he approached Fannie for a loan. He was his most charming self. Bill even promised her a gift when he returned her loan. Before she knew what hit her, Fannie was falling for his line, and for him. It took nearly a month for him to repay Fannie and hand her the gift, but he did.

Having decided that he was back in Fannie's good graces, Bill began to flirt with her as he had before the loan. Why would a woman be so interested in this kind of man? She knew he had a gambling problem and she knew this meant trouble to anyone who was a part of it. But just in case Fannie didn't know the pain that chronic gamblers can inflict, Bill gave her an education and taught her a bitter lesson. He stole her favorite jeweled pin. Bill pawned it to stake himself to a game.

There was no mistake in Fannie's mind that he was guilty. There was no excuse for what he had done. Chronic gamblers, and those affected by their behavior, often suffer from the desperate motivations behind Bill's action. Fannie must have realized the painful consequences of any continued relationship with Bill. How could he ever think of redeeming himself in her eyes? Days later, Bill purchased the pin from the pawnshop, returned it, admitted his guilt and apologized to Fannie. She freely expressed her anger and berated him for what he had done. She tongue-lashed him as though he were a child, with such fancy and educated words that he didn't know what hit him. Clearly, Fannie showed him she was no fool to be taken for granted. She had the perfect opportunity and excuse to get rid of him. They had no ties. They never even went out on a date. But she didn't get rid of him. She promised to help him and, at that moment, she probably fell in love with him forever.

Instead of writing Bill off as unstable and untrustworthy, Fannie became intrigued. Why would a man who showed no compunction at all about "borrowing" the prized possession of a girl in whom he was clearly interested be so anxious to redeem himself? Fannie realized that Bill was a compulsive gambler and unable to keep from resorting to whatever means were necessary to maintain his gambling habit. He was making one hundred to two hundred dollars a week, without taxes, and was unable to save a cent, even though Fannie often offered to save his money for him.

Like a doctor, nurse, or pharmacist, Fannie took him under her protective wing. She wanted to help him because he was hurting, not because he was a successful vaudeville entertainer. Up to that point she had never seen him perform. Show business was not on her mind. Fannie's first goal was to prescribe a cure for Bill's problem. She strongly suggested he open a bank account and save his money, not gamble it away.

Bill nearly died from hysterics when Fannie first suggested the idea. Though he was nearly forty, he had never had his own savings account. He never needed one. Unless he happened to be lucky that week, his salary was almost always gone before his next payday. But to please her, he agreed to allow her to open an account in his name and promised he would send part of his salary to her each week while he was out on his forthcoming Canadian tour. For the moment, Fannie was appeased and thought her patient was taking a turn toward partial recovery.

Bill was impressed by Fannie's sincerity and caring. Except for Forkins, Cooper, and Rae Samuels, no one else had ever taken this kind of interest in him without wanting something in return. Fannie's concern about his financial affairs made an impression. In fact, a few days later, just before he was about to leave for his Canadian tour, he took her up on her offer of financial help—not to save, but to borrow.

Once again, Bill was in trouble—big trouble—gambling trouble. The night before, he was having a bad run with Lady Luck. It was late in the game and he was out of funds. He was rolling the dice for a $150 marker on the floor against someone else's wad of cash. He rolled and lost. To make his marker good, Bill pawned his steamer trunks containing his clothes, shoes, and all the things he needed for his Canadian tour. He stooped so low as to practically live out of the pawnshop for a few days. After all, a vaudeville star could not be seen wearing the same thing twice onstage. He had his reputation to protect. When he went to Fannie, she had her future and her next term's tuition to protect.

At first he cried to Fannie that he needed to borrow the money to fix his trunks. But she was wise to him now and didn't fall for his line. Courageously, she pumped Bill until she got the truth out of him. That was a big step. Bill was not used to having to account to anyone for his actions. Fannie was glad he respected her enough to tell her the truth, even if it was the awful truth. Her patient was showing promise.

Most would have thought that Fannie was smart enough to prevent her better judgment from being convoluted by her emotions and risk everything. If he absconded with the money, she would not be able to afford her tuition. She would have to drop out of school temporarily, or permanently. At the time, Fannie still thought her education and career meant more to her than Bill Robinson. Against all sense and reason, she put it all on the line for Bill and loaned him the money.

Bill was amazed and couldn't thank her enough. He promised to send some money back to her every week while he was away. Fannie could only hope he would keep his promise. Happily, he did. Each week, she wrote letters to him and he wired various amounts back to her. How did he get the money? Perhaps he had given up gambling. Or, more than likely, he was getting lucky. Whichever it was, he continued sending money back until it became a habit. By the time he returned from his tour, he had sent back enough to pay back the debt, plus an additional amount in excess of one thousand dollars. On the morning he saw Fannie in Chicago again for the first time, he said the money was for her. It was his way of saying thanks for her kindness and generosity. She told him that she could never accept the money and that she had put it into his account. Fannie handed him the bankbook to prove it. Though he couldn't read his name on the book, he sure knew how to read the one-thousand-dollar figure. Never before did he have so much at one time without getting it by shuffling cards, rolling dice, or hustling at pool. Fannie saw the gleam in his eyes. Both knew that gleam meant one thing: by that night his money would probably be bet on cards, dice, or a pool cue.

Bill remained in Chicago for a short time and started seeing Fannie outside the drugstore. Then, as usual, he was on the road.

Fannie continued to write to Bill whenever he was on the road and he kept calling. U. S. Thompson, Florence Mills's husband, who was in Chicago at the time and knew Bill Robinson "before he knew Fannie," said that Bill never wrote to Fannie because he could neither read nor write. "Me and another boy named Kelly, we used to read his letters from Fannie for him, and to write his letters to Fannie for him. He used to send her a telegram and then call her up to see if she got the telegram. He was always pretty liberal with his women. He wasn't tight."

By then Fannie had come to know Bill well enough to realize that he did not spend all his money on gambling. He was generous to a fault and capable of giving away money to a friend or acquaintance he judged more needy than he. She also harbored no illusions about the ability of any woman to change him. He was Bill Robinson, original. He was soon back on the road again, and for several months they maintained contact only through her letters and his calls. In her *Ebony* article, Fannie wrote how Bill's complaints turned to a marriage proposal. It was definitely not a get-down-on-one-knee-and-say-"I-love-you" kind of proposal. Bill was not that kind of guy. He complained that all of his follow-up phone calls cost too much money. He told her to give up everything she wanted—being a pharmacist and one day owning her own drugstore. He told her to join him in Minneapolis, and she did.

In many ways Fannie was the opposite of Bill. Oddsmakers from Harlem to the West Coast would have backed any bet *against* their marriage. But Fannie was a young woman with a great deal of self-respect. She knew that in her own small way she had begun a fight to advance herself, and her race. Not many Americans were seeking higher education during the early twenties. Few were female and even fewer were black.

In one extremely important way, however, Bill and Fannie were very much alike. In pharmacy school and onstage, they each were the proverbial "raisin in the pound cake." Both knew it and both accepted the responsibilities of the position. They were blacks, constantly exposed in a white world, seeking greater achievements than most blacks of the day even dared to dream about.

Fannie quickly realized that through Bill, through the power of his tapping feet, they could do something that would make a difference—no matter how large or small it might be. Because in America's roaring twenties and during the age of the Harlem Renaissance, each little advance meant a great deal to future black generations. Fannie and Bo were out there fighting for small footholds into American equality. They were blacks willing to challenge white beliefs, and they were in the minority—both in the white world and their own. It was love, for each other and for their fellow blacks, that bound "Big Bo" and "Little Bo."

Bill and Fannie were not alone in struggling against discrimination. A few other blacks were also making progress in their own way. When interviewed, Eddie Hunter, one of George W. Cooper's partners after Cooper split with Bill, told what blacks had to do. "Fight your way through. Don't take it laying down. Stand up to them. Don't back down. What the hell ya gonna back down for? I got just as much right to live and live the way I want to live. It's my life. Not yours. You don't back down on those things. You fight 'em."

One of Eddie Hunter's greatest success stories came on the day he realized he didn't have to perform in blackface. Many black performers had become dependent upon burnt cork, thinking they couldn't perform without it. Hunter said, "Yeah. I used to put the black on my face. Then came the time I wouldn't do it. I stopped it, for I found out I didn't need it. I didn't need that stuff to make people laugh. I needed just a certain move. Expressions. Movements. Actions. I could make them laugh on that. When I found those things didn't mean nothing to me, I didn't need 'em. I found it out because in certain towns, on Sunday, you could perform without it. No makeup. You had to walk in like you were just off the street, then go on out there and do your business. And when I found out that I could make people laugh without all that stuff, I stopped using it. I wouldn't perform that way no more. I said, 'What do I need all this stuff for if I could make them laugh and scream without it.' And I liked it that way. You didn't have to put on no costume or nothin'. You could be yourself. When I found out I could do that, that was it. No more messin' around with this or that. And that's the way I performed and I was happy with it. Humph. Those days are gone."

While Bill Robinson had not experienced the problem of making the transition from blackface, and while he had successfully overcome the old "two colored" rule, life on the vaudeville circuits was no piece of cake for him. Thanks to Fannie's efforts, we have Bill's scrapbooks filled with reviews that graphically illustrate what Bill and Fannie were up against. Reading them takes one back to a time when white Americans could still hang signs outside their boardinghouses and hotels that read "No Negroes, Jews or dogs allowed," a time when racism was rampant, when "Strange fruit hanging from a tree" was not a reference to apples or oranges. Back then, Bill "Bojangles" Robinson was an oddity to white vaudeville reviewers. They didn't know how to write about successful black performers except for a handful like Williams, Mills, and Sissle and Blake. Or, to paraphrase a president, "Back when this country didn't even know it had a race problem."

The *Pittsburgh Sun,* October 18, 1921, said, "Bill

Robinson, not as black as the ace of spades, but a gentleman of color, nevertheless." The *Dayton* (Ohio) *Daily News* wrote on November 1, 1921, "Bill Robinson belongs to a race that has never received the best of it in this country." The *Rockford* (Illinois) *Republic,* November 29, 1921, stated: "Bill Robinson does as many monkey shines as any colored entertainer."

The *Davenport* (Iowa) *Democrat* referred to Bill as "a gentleman of color." The *Daily Times* called him "a real black dancing fool," and went on to say, "This colored boy stands them on their heads."

The *Calgary Daily Herald,* on February 3, 1922, said: "Bill Robinson has a perfect right to call himself the dark cloud of joy. Colored persons appear to come of a naturally jovial race, and for wit, humor and merriment, Bill might be a direct descendant of Uncle Remus. His stories were new and bright and his little imitations of a mosquito and a Ford car, done with his lips, were very novel. He is also a dancer of a finished type. Bill danced all over the stage, with every sort of known movement of the feet, danced down the steps and into the aisle, and down again, and up the steps and danced all the while. He is a dapper person and has a cheerful face."

The *Seattle Daily Times,* February 13, 1922: "Bill Robinson, a darky who doesn't need any burnt cork to provide a background for his flashing teeth and rolling eyes."

The *Morning Oregonian* said on February 20, 1922: "To tell about the most popular act on the Orpheum bill this week, one needs the pen of a Roy Octavus Cohen, whose accounts of the 'cullud quality folk' of Bummin'ham, Alabama, have become classics. One of Roy

Octavus' heroes is far and away the most entertaining act on the bill. He is Bill Robinson, a dapper, alert young negro man, a dancing hound whose feet are absolutely crazy and who smilingly observes that he 'has no sense at all.' Right in the middle of some of his most amazing novelties he was interrupted with applause, just as a lecturer is stopped every once in a while by hurrahs. Only Bill didn't stop. He went right on. 'As long as you like it I can furnish it,' Bill smiled."

On rare occasions some reviewers saw past Bill's color and concentrated on his dancing talent. The *South Bend* (Indiana) *Tribune,* November 22, 1921, wrote, "Then there is Bill Robinson, who has more music in his feet than most have in their heads. As an exponent of syncopated stepping Bill is a rare jewel."

The *Rockford Register-Gazette,* November 29, 1921, stated: "Bill Robinson, formerly of the team of Cooper & Robinson, made a decided hit. Mr. Robinson dances with an exceptional artistry which puts him in the front rank of 'hoofers.'"

In Winnipeg, Canada, George Brown, the "champion walker," joined the tour. In a number titled "Pedestrianism," he and Miss Marion Ardell, who had set a few hiking records herself in her native state of California, kept up with individual endless-stair machines, then invited volunteers from the audience to try to do the same. None of the volunteers could duplicate the feat. In Vancouver, George Brown gave an exhibition of his skill by walking a winding two-and-a-half-plus-mile route from City Hall to the theater in just fifteen minutes. Bill Robinson and Jess Libonati, a xylophone player also on the tour, accompanied him. In San Francisco, once again Brown staged a public walk, this time from City Hall to the ferry and back to the theater. Again, Libonati and Robinson accompanied him. The *San Francisco Call and Post* carried a photomontage of the event, and Bill kept the clipping for his scrapbook. Brown did not continue with the tour after it left California, but Bill had picked up some valuable tips on public relations and would use them to his own advantage later on.

Bojangles also exercised his dice-throwing arm, as he did everywhere he went. Only in San Francisco, however, was his game ever interrupted by an earthquake. Playing "African golf," as the game was often called, against Alexander Carr, star of *A Rainy Day,* he had made several passes with no luck. The pot totaled $150, and both Bill and Carr were feeling the strain. Bill's turn came again, and he rolled the dice. One showed a six. The other stood on edge and wavered a moment. Just as it was about to show another six, the table trembled in response to a minor earthquake, and the die fell to show a five. Carr argued that a six would have come up but for the earthquake; but Bill had his eleven, thanks to Mother Nature. He gathered up the proceeds and left quickly. However, this happy experience did not change his mind about earthquakes. According to Fannie, he was terrified of them.

On March 6, Bill played the Orpheum in Sacramento. Two days later, Bert Williams was buried in New York. Fannie clipped an article about the funeral and pasted it into the scrapbook. It was the first time in the state of New York that a black man had been buried according to the Masonic ritual. Both Williams and his partner,

George Walker, who had died some years earlier, had testified to Bill's good character during his 1908 trial. After Walker's death, Williams, as a single, had gone on to become the first black star of the Ziegfeld Follies.

W. C. Fields called Williams "the funniest man I ever saw; the saddest man I ever knew." Bert Williams was sitting on top of the entertainment world and being treated like trash. Though he often performed in ridiculous-looking costumes (his most famous, a chicken suit), he was able to write his own material. The songs—"Nobody," "When It's All Goin' Out and Nothin's Comin' In," and "I'd Rather Have Nothin' All the Time Than Somethin' for a Little While"—were his legacy to racial equality.

Segregated offstage, riding freight elevators when the white cast members rode the passenger elevators, unable to stay in the same hotels or eat in the same restaurants as the other performers, Bert Williams remained with the Follies for ten frustrating years because he realized he was a trailblazer. As he said, "We've got our foot in the door, we mustn't let it close again." In his song "Nobody," Williams—like Robinson—fought back. They were racial activists when the term hadn't been coined yet. Robinson used his feet to break into vaudeville. And when his feet weren't enough, he used his brains and other means.

Back in the twenties, most would have thought that Robinson and Williams had it all. But anyone who knew Bill Robinson soon realized that he, like others, was only starting to ask for more than the white world thought he, or any other black, deserved—recognition and equality for his race. What made people like Bojangles, Bert Williams, and Florence Mills most interesting was that sometimes they succeeded in their attempts.

In her 1953 *Ebony* article, Fannie described one time when Bill got even with a racist while they were traveling on a train between vaudeville cities on or below the Mason-Dixon Line. Two things made the story most interesting: one, that Bill fought back; and two, that he did it without getting himself arrested or killed.

The offender was a fellow performer who was known for his beliefs in old Southern ways. He had a way of teasing Bill and trying to get his goat. For a while, Bill understood who the statement was coming from and tried to let it go without a physical or violent incident, but the other performer wouldn't let up. The skirmish broke out in the car where the men usually passed the time smoking their cigars and shooting the breeze without the presence of the women. Fannie had no idea an incident had even taken place. After all, there were no gunshots, no men running through the cars, and no shouts of panic. She had no idea that anything had happened until she was about to join Bill and saw a smile on his face that she had come to understand as trouble. Capital *T* kind of trouble. The kind that could get a black man killed in the South during the twenties. In brief, the other performer was attacking Bill and challenging him to discuss why Negroes have such a wide variety of skin tones, and why Fannie was so much lighter than Bill. Bill's explanation was point of fact, even though he knew it did not pertain to Fannie's personal family background. He explained that in past times many children were the result of rich white fathers and poor slave mothers, or fancy Southern belles and big black Negroes. What got the other entertainer so upset was Bill's innuendo that the other performer or members of his family, being of Southern background, might be one of those children.

Not long after Bert Williams's death, people began to suggest that Bill was somehow his successor. On March 14, when Bill was playing the Orpheum in Los Angeles, The *Los Angeles Daily Times* made this allusion. Later, an article in the *Omaha* stated:

> More than one admirer of Bill has said that the mantle of the late Bert Williams has fallen on his shoulders. But there is one marked difference between the style of Bill and his illustrious predecessor. Bert's humor was of the lugubrious nature and he won his laughs by sorrowful song stories about his misfortunes. But Bill has the jolliest face of the jolliest man of the jolliest race in the world and gets 10 times as much fun and pleasure as the audience out of efforts to entertain.
>
> Bill Robinson is a legitimate dancer of the old school, with grace and music in every move and perfect rhythm in his buck and wing evolutions which have won him the title of the greatest hard shoe dancer in the world.[3]

The *Los Angeles Daily Times,* July 25, 1922, said:

> Everybody must know Bill Robinson by this time, so it is enough to say that, despite the fact that he is now doing five shows a day—three at the Hillstreet and two at the Orpheum—Bill steps with unabated pep. For the rest, it is the reviewer's unqualified opinion that there are few better dancers anywhere, and that Bill has a good chance of end-

ing up as another Bert Williams—it all depends on who gets hold of him next.[4]

That summer, when Bill was playing the Orpheum in Chicago, Fannie was able to put in the scrapbook the first advertisement in which Bill was given top billing:

ORPHEUM CIRCUIT—GRAND OPERA HOUSE
9 Big Acts and Pictures
BIG FUN SHOW
Come Have a Laugh with
Bill Robinson
"THE BLACK DAFFYDIL"
A Cloudy Spasm of Song, Dance and Fun
Also
Harry B. Watson
"RUBEVILLE"
With a Cast of Ten
Also
Sylvia Snow, Dan Sigworth and Michael Kurzene
"TIDBITS OF 1922"
A Timely Mixture of Melody and Dance[5]

But top billing was something that eluded Bill on the West Coast. Next he joined the show at the San Francisco Orpheum. It included Harry Carroll's "Varieties of 1922"; Milder Harris (Chaplin) in a playlet called "Movie Mad," costarring S. Miller Kent and Lavina Shannon; Leo Carriloo, master of character stories; Flo Lewis, who did impressions of female stars; aerial stuntmen Martin and Moore; and cakewalkers Chong and Rose Moey. Bill's act was one of three not accorded headline billing. He was not as well known on the West Coast, a situation he was determined to change. When the show moved on to the Los Angeles Orpheum, Bill went with it. In addition to two performances a day there, he did three at the Hill Street Theater, in a show that also featured Yost and Clady, who did a clay-modeling act; storyteller Wellington Cross; Ann Butler and Hal Parker, who performed a "wise-cracking" routine; the Singer Midgets; and a Selznick photoplay, starring Eugene O'Brien, titled *John Smith*. Thanks to Bill's exhausting efforts, by the third week of July he was a headliner in L.A. as well. Or at least Marty Forkins had decided he was. Forkins paid for the following ad in *Variety* of July 21, 1922:

BILL ROBINSON

THE DARK CLOUD OF JOY

Playing Six Weeks at the Orpheum Theatre in
San Francisco This Season And Incidentally
The Only Act to Repeat At The Golden Gate
BOOKED SOLID KEITH-ORPHEUM THEATRES[6]

Shortly after Forkins's ad appeared, Bill spoke to a reporter for the *Los Angeles Evening Express* (July 22, 1922):

"They say I'm a dancin' hound and a wise coon, and all that," beamed Bill Robinson, colored dancing hit, who appears on next week's bill at the Hill Street Theater, "but I'm just one of my race that has been fortunate. I say I've been fortunate meaning it in every sense of the word, too."[7]

The headline act was John Steel, a tenor and successful recording artist who permitted audiences to select his program, with the result that it varied from popular concert songs to dance songs, to "Questa o Quella" from *Rigoletto,* to the vaudeville hit "Mother Machree," to the Hebrew liturgical song "Eli, Eli." Steel's accompanist, Jerry Janrigan, proved as able as Steel in skipping around the musical spectrum.

Steel, after working with Robinson for the first time, was so impressed with Bill that he wrote to Irving Berlin in New York about him. In a covering memo dated August 6, 1922, Steel wrote he hoped it would achieve "the desired effect"—to get Robinson into the Music Box. Steel also sent good wishes to Bill's wife.[8]

John Steel's memo indicated more than good wishes. It is one of the few written documents that links Fannie with Bill prior to 1924—the year that most sources say they were married.

In his letter introducing Robinson to Berlin, John Steel said there was a "young colored boy" on the Orpheum "making a sensational hit." He also wrote that Robinson was the best dancer he had seen and that he would be sensational in the Music Box. Obviously, John Steel had not worked with or seen Bill at the Palace because he also wrote that Bill "would be a 'find' for the East." He closed his letter saying he was confident Mr. Berlin would have some "hit" songs for him, then sent best wishes to Sam Harris.[9]

Bill did not go to the Music Box in New York, then

or ever. He was virtually unknown in New York, except on vaudeville stages, and there didn't seem to be much chance that he would break into the legitimate theater. Eventually, however, he and Irving Berlin got to know each other; and Berlin was one of the pallbearers at Bill's funeral.

By the third week of August, Bill was headed east to Baltimore and the Maryland Theater. He joined a bill that featured Oscar Adler's jazz orchestra, singer Eva Shirley, eccentric dancer Al Roth, a playlet called "Highbrow," dancers Nelson Snow, Charles Columbus, and Harriet Hector, Spanish opera star Don Jose Moriche, and others. Bill was not a headliner, not in Baltimore, Maryland. In fact, this appearance was one of his rare ones below the Mason-Dixon Line. The previous season, Eugene O'Neill's *The Emperor Jones,* which had opened in 1919 in New York starring veteran actor Charles Gilpin and enjoyed a long and successful run, had done little business in Baltimore principally because many objected to seeing a Negro acting in a serious drama before a white audience. Theoretically, the happy darkies of vaudeville should not have evoked resentment. But according to *Variety,* Bill Robinson did:

HISSERS OF COLORED ACT TOLD TO LEAVE THEATRE. WOMEN IN MARYLAND, BALTIMORE, AUDIENCE DISAPPROVE OF BILL ROBINSON.

Baltimore, August 23

At the Monday afternoon performance at the Maryland here a colored dancer, Bill Robinson, was billed for the deuce spot. He appeared, and after the applause from his first number hisses were heard throughout the house. Everyone turned and necks were craned, but the performer went on, unperturbed, and did another dance. Again he drew big applause, but after the applause had died down the hisses again came directly from midway in the orchestra.

Again the performer kept on. After the next applause the hisses accompanied and were located.

Three women, apparently refined and certainly well dressed, of middle age, were requested to leave the theatre. The audience, immediately after, encouraged the Negro and gave him as much applause as most headliners get.

This evoked a speech from Robinson. He said that in 30 years in the show business such a thing had never happened to him before, and that he had been taught that, should it ever happen, to ignore it. He did, and won the house by the neat way he turned the tide.[10]

On November 13 in San Francisco, Bill appeared at the Orpheum earlier than expected. Though he was in town, he was not due to join the show for a couple of days. Then he learned that Jack George, a blackface comedian who was the opening act on the current bill, had been taken ill and hospitalized, and that the management was looking for a replacement. Bill went to the manager and offered to take George's place, but he didn't want George's salary. In fact, his one condition was that George be paid his full salary and that he be paid nothing. "Imagine that," exclaimed George in an *Oakland Tribune* interview, "a headliner opening the bill, just to give a fellow like me a chance."

"I was born in the South," Jack George explained to a

reporter the following week, "and I must confess to my shame that I had all the lack of respect for the Negro as a unit that the Southerners have. I say, 'had,' for Bill Robinson has unconsciously taught me a lesson, because he didn't know me except as a trouper."

Bill refused all kudos for his part in bettering American race relations: "Aw, gwan. What's the matter with that fellow anyway? That's nuthin' at all."[11]

The next week, nine members of the Orpheum show challenged local newspaper sportswriters to a baseball game. The N.V.A. baseball team consisted of Billy Galson, Val Stanton, Ernie Stanton, Ed Ruby, and Bill Robinson, the only black. The writers' team included Tom Laird, George Davis, Abe Kemp, Howard Smith, Scoop Gleson, and a man named Eppinger. The game was held at Recreation Park, and the eventual score was 13 to 6 in the N.V.A. team's favor. During the game, George Davis boasted of his running ability, and the N.V.A.'s third baseman, Bill Robinson, remembering George Brown's walking exhibition, challenged him to a race. Bill offered to run backward. In the race from left field to the first-base line, Bill won by a heel in the first documented public exhibition of his backward-running ability. There would be more demonstrations as the Orpheum Actors' Ball Club made their way along the West Coast.

Bill was an exceptionally talented ballplayer. In the early years of the century he played second base on a team of black vaudevillians who, unable to get into a white baseball organization called the "White Rats," dubbed themselves the "Black Rats." They played both white and black teams. Later on, Bill was able to get on teams that were predominantly white, not only because he was among the few blacks on the tour, but also because he was so good.

In a June 1950 *Negro Digest* interview with Era Bell Thompson, Fannie talked about how Bill loved and lived for baseball and how she learned to love it, too. She knew how to argue a call with an official or a fan and she knew how to appreciate a good hit or catch. She was completely absorbed by the sport and Bill respected her appreciation of the game. So much so, that once while Bill was suffering from an extended case of laryngitis, he even allowed her to do his deeds and speak for him. He placed her on his knee the same way his friend Edgar Bergen would place one of his wooden pals on his knee, and let Fannie go to town. She yelled at the ump, the fans, and probably even shouted out Bill's bets.

In Sacramento, after an exhibition game against a group of locals calling themselves the "All-Ins" (which handed the Orpheum team their first loss), Bill held another race exhibition. He challenged three local runners and was given a ten-yard handicap because he would run backward. It was no contest. Bill beat the three forward-running challengers. His close attention to the off-stage stunts of George Brown, the "champion walker," was paying off. The publicity Bill was receiving from running was spreading his name beyond the small theater sections of local newspapers.

In December, at the Orpheum in Fresno, Bill held an exhibition of another kind, this time onstage. It was probably the first occasion on which he officially per-

formed on his future trademark—his own, specially
made dancing stairs. For the December appearance, Bill
brought a set of collapsible stairs onstage. His act was
described by the *Fresno Morning Republican:*

> There are six steps, and each of those steps plays a part
> in the act. You have heard of the clever conversationalist
> who kept going a whole evening saying nothing but the
> words from one to ten, backward and forward, with longer
> and shorter series, permutations and combinations, so that
> the interplay of repartee and jest, quip, rejoinder and sur
> rejoinder were all thrilled. This is what Bill does dancing
> up and down those steps. A turn up, or two steps down
> will make the audience howl, as he taps resonant pine with
> his toes. It is an accomplishment in the art of making
> nerves tingle.[12]

By the end of the year, Bill Robinson's infectious
smile, yellow cane, pearl-colored derby, and wooden-
soled, split-clog tap dancing were well known among
West Coast vaudeville aficionados. More than one critic
predicted that he would soon be creating a sensation as
the star of some musical revue on Broadway. No doubt
others besides John Steel had recommended him highly
to colleagues back East. But the city that jazz musicians
had started calling "The Big Apple" by this time was a
hard nut to crack, particularly for a black, and for a star
who would have to take at least a two-thousand-dollar
cut in salary. But the reviewers kept writing that Bill
should head up one of those "colored revues" that had
been spots of joy on Broadway.

In the first week of January 1923 in Salt Lake City,

Bill was reminded of his tentative position, even in vaudeville. A week before the opening, he was informed that he would be placed dead last on the bill. Bill sought E. F. Albee's advice on the matter. Albee telegrammed back, "Be a sport." He did not order Bill to do it, but suggested that he "open if necessary." Albee said that Bill would be successful no matter what his position in the program, and by opening he would "teach a lesson to others."[13]

The Orpheum Circuit managers may have assessed, correctly, the racial atmosphere of the Mormon stronghold. Bill followed Albee's advice and performed in a spot in the program generally reserved for unknowns. Ever the professional, as a black he was also ever publicly mindful of his "place."

One of Bill Robinson's favorite dances was the "Old man routine."
(Photo courtesy James J. Kriegsmann)

A close look at Bill's left shoe illustrates the split-clog. *(Photo courtesy James J. Kriegsmann)*

This pose became famous when first illustrated by Hirschfeld. *(Photo courtesy James J. Kriegsmann)*

ABOVE: The look and smile that captured world audiences *(Photo courtesy James J. Kriegsmann)*

OPPOSITE: The image of Bill Robinson's vaudeville and Broadway legacy—top hat, tails, dancing cane, and stairs *(Photo courtesy James J. Kriegsmann)*

LEFT: The close-up he fought for and got in Hollywood *(Photo courtesy James J. Kriegsmann)*
BELOW: Only a dancer would sleep on split-clogs. *(N. R. Mitgang Collection)*

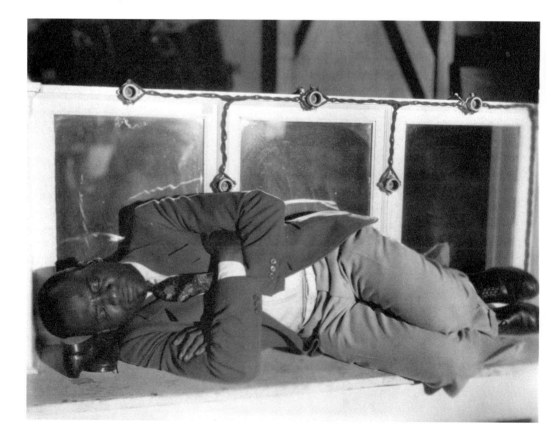

ABOVE: This studio publicity photo offers a rare look a Bill Robinson without a smile. *(20th Century-Fox Film Corp.)*
LEFT: Bill owned a $17,500 Duesenberg and employed a chauffeur when this photo was taken. It was unlikely he would have needed a hitch. But on Broadway and in Harlem, you could bet he would get one. *(Photo courtesy James J. Kriegsmann)*

The Little Colonel. Hattie McDaniel, Shirley Temple, and Bill
Robinson *(20th Century-Fox Film Corp.)*

ABOVE: *Scandals.* Bill Robinson, Alice Raye, and James Dunn *(20th Century-Fox Film Corp.)*
RIGHT: Bill and his young bride, Elaine *(Photo courtesy James J. Kriegsmann)*

ABOVE: Bill and the cast members of *Memphis Bound (N. R.
Mitgang Collection)*
BELOW: Rae Samuels and Marty Forkins *(N. R. Mitgang Collection)*

Championship bookends—Bill Robinson and Joe Louis (*N. R. Mitgang Collection*)

Just Around the Corner. Bert Lahr, Joan Davis, Shirley Temple, and Bill Robinson *(20th Century-Fox Film Corp.)*

Rebecca of Sunnybrook Farm. Bill Robinson, Shirley Temple, and
William *(My Three Sons)* Demarest *(20th Century-Fox Film Corp.)*

(Photo courtesy James J. Kriegsmann)

6

Tides and Times Keep Changing

Fifty-six years separated the end of the Civil War and the opening of *Shuffle Along* on Broadway in 1921. While white Americans were about to roar through Prohibition, emancipated black Americans still couldn't vote in many cities. But black Americans had begun a renaissance, one that was allowing their voices to be heard in the greatest political pulpit in the nation—the American stage. In a time when talking pictures were years away and network radio and television were still figments of scientists' imaginations, there was nowhere else that black voices could be heard so loud by so many in such a short time. Among those voices being heard the most was Bill Robinson's; onstage and off, it was beginning to reach the ears of the president, governors, mayors, people of influence, and ordinary citizens.

Bo was on his way, and Marty and Fannie were making sure that nothing stood in the way of his reaching the top, even if it meant redefining how high a black was "allowed" to go in show business. Attitudes, social patterns, and images were changing. But, as always, change was not readily accepted.

Sometimes, Bo had to forge his own revolution toward social justice. There was the time he entered a small-town all-night diner at 4:00 A.M. and ordered a breakfast of bacon, eggs, toast, and coffee. When the attendant refused him service, saying, "We don't serve your kind," Robinson tried placing his order a second time. Again the attendant refused. This time Bo reached inside his jacket, removed his gold-plated, pearl-handled gun, and reordered with a smile. He was served, taken into custody by a rookie deputy, then released by the town sheriff, who had become a friend over the years. Bill's police connections were beginning to pay off. If the offender had been any other black man, he probably would have been tossed in jail for an extended period or lost forever on a chain gang. But the offender was Bill "Bojangles" Robinson, which meant the white attendant had to learn a lesson in social decency.

Other changes were silent and hardly noticeable, but very important to the future image of black entertainers. One change had to do with what a black man was allowed to wear onstage. Until the twenties, because most blacks were forced to play buffoon characters, what clothes they wore made little difference. However, for Bill, with his ever-increasing stature on and off stage, the difference had become an obsession. Having previously played a demeaning role, now he was performing first-class song-and-dance material in the best clothes money could buy. He thought nothing could make him revert to a degrading style of dress. In fact, Bo had a fetish about clothes, though, curiously, he preferred buying them off the rack to having them specially made—perhaps because of his experience with Hyman Sussman.

According to many sources, no one could take care of Bo's clothes except Bo. Suits were dressed at attention, cleaned and ready for action. Each was spaced inches apart in the tradition of the marines. Shoes were polished and all his gear was stowed away under the protection of specially designed dustcloths. A spec of dust or lint wouldn't dare approach his things. He could find anything he needed, anytime, with or without the lights being on. He was obsessed with neatness. He was a "Neatnik" to the nth degree and was told he had the cleanest dressing room in vaudeville.

He was a perfect size 38. Whenever he was in Chicago he went to a tailor named Hill, picked out ten or twelve suits, and all the tailor had to do was shorten the trousers. When Fannie started traveling with Bill, the task fell to her to have his suits pressed after each wearing. He seemed to find relaxation in attending to the other ministrations to his wardrobe. His suits were always hung a certain number of inches apart in his closet, his hats placed upside down on the shelf. After his death, Fannie recalled that "his favorite indoor sport was brushing his clothes with a whisk broom. He even brushed his clean white socks which he traditionally wore on the stage. The nap mustn't be fuzzy."

In later years, after he had become a major star, Bill had a dresser, but he insisted on caring for his wardrobe himself. "He had a valet and a dresser," according to Rae Samuels, "but he wouldn't let them touch his things. He'd pack his own trunks and make sure everything was in its place. And he wore those longies to dance in. He'd wash them out himself. He wouldn't let them touch anything. He was the cleanest human being you'd ever want to meet."

He was even more concerned about his shoes, his most important professional tool, specially made for him in Chicago by the Aiston Shoe Company. They were split-clogs, ordinary shoes with a wooden half sole, about three eighths of an inch thick, and a wooden heel slightly higher than the leather heel on a street shoe. The wooden half sole was attached to the leather sole from the toe to a point behind the ball of the foot and thereafter was left looser to permit flexibility. Earlier in his career Bill had worn lightweight bicycle shoes, and that accounted, he believed, for the bunion on his right foot that acted up on occasion.

The Aiston Shoe Company had a good customer in Bill Robinson, for he wore out twenty to thirty pairs a year. When the sole of only one of a pair split, it was necessary to discard both shoes, for the slightest difference between the resoled shoe and the old one would be noticeable in his taps, so delicate was his touch. He had a good company in Aiston, which would make up new pairs of shoes on a moment's notice and send them to him wherever he happened to be.[1]

For many other things, Bill depended on Fannie. He was her career. She was his personal stage manager, director, accountant, co-publicist, and legal adviser in Marty Forkins's absence. She also scouted new musical arrangements and wrote many of his comedy routines. Little Bo was Big Bo's perfect definition of a theatrical wife. Fannie treated and ran the show-business parts of his life as a well-managed business. But Big Bo was also Fannie's lover, her best friend, and often, since they were without children, the little boy they never had. His sheet music, an important and very expensive part of his ability to perform, was a constant source of childish consternation. He would forget to pick it up after a rehearsal. Fannie had a hard time distinguishing his sheet music from the rest of the company's, so she copied the style of his scrapbook (red with large gold-embossed letters reading "Bill Robinson") and had special binders made to hold each arrangement. Finding and protecting his music became possible and made that part of her job a little easier.

Still unable to read, the only way Bill could learn his lines was to have Fannie read them to him. Fannie played all the roles of the other performers, or repeated song lyrics until Bo committed them to memory, which didn't take long. Rae Samuels said, "He could learn a good new song by listening to it twice." Eventually, Bill came to call the process the kitchen routine.

Ed Sullivan, an up-and-coming sportswriter from Port Chester, N.Y., got to know Bill well during the twenties. He reminisced in an interview:

> Bill was self-educated and could hold his own with anyone with any conversation. A lot of those early vaudeville performers had little or no education. They started out as kids like the Foys [Eddie Foy and the Seven Little Foys] and when they started out they picked up on education.

That goes not only for Bill but for a lot of white performers. They had a practical education that was beyond compare.

Lillian Alpert Wolf, Marty Forkins's assistant, remembered:

Bill didn't have to read. His mind was his eyes and ears
and they could understand more than those who professed
to be well educated. He knew and understood everything
and everybody and he remembered everything. You
couldn't beat him. He was interested in everything that
was going on in the world. He was worldly.[2]

According to U. S. Thompson, Fannie also taught
Bill to read and to write his name.

There is ample evidence in the Robinson papers that
Fannie paid careful attention to politically correct corre-
spondences—Christmas cards and congratulatory telegrams to vaudeville circuit managers and others who
were important to Bill's career. She also streamlined his
efforts to maintain good relations with law-enforcement
officers across the country. Although he had long before
developed the habit of making the local police station
the first stop upon arrival in town, Fannie went him one
better by preceding their arrival with a note to the chief
of police containing felicitations to him and his wife and
a pair of tickets to the show. She was a better PR representative than Marty Forkins, who was no slouch himself when it came to keeping Bill in good with the
police; according to Rae Samuels, Marty would add a

couple of suits to a police chief's wardrobe from time to time.

Through the end of February 1923, Bill played the Orpheum Circuit. At the beginning of March he also joined the Keith Circuit. After playing Toledo and Pittsburgh in late April, he opened at the Palace in New York. What made the Palace engagement particularly special was that Eddie Leonard, the same Eddie who had helped Bo run away from Richmond, was on the bill too. Bill was second on the program, Rae Samuels, "The Blue Streak of Vaudeville," was ninth and next to last. Within four days, Ruby Norton, a singer, had been moved from seventh to sixth place, and Rae from ninth to eighth. Bill was still in the number two spot. But on May 11, 1923, *Zit's Weekly Newspaper* pronounced them all the clear showstoppers:

> Brown-eyed Rae Samuels and blond-haired Ruby Norton, together with "Chocolate Drop" Bill Robinson, set all the pace and made the running on Monday night of this track. And, oh, what a pace it was. The track was afire and simply sizzled as they burned it up. This Bill Robinson is a dancing fool—nothing else but. Both literally and figuratively he was a "dark horse" at this track, *for nobody seemed to know much about him when he came out.* I want to tell the world, however, that everybody knew about him when he went off. [Emphasis added.][3]

Marty Forkins decided that Bill's reception at the Palace, despite his poor placement in the lineup, would be a good opportunity to exploit Bill's reputation for not complaining. He and Joe Page Smith, with whom he had formed a partnership at that time, took out the following bold-faced ad in the *New York Clipper:*

BILL ROBINSON

THE DARK CLOUD OF JOY

while playing the Palace said, "A lot of people kick about the Palace number two spot but I found the two spot like others found number five. Maybe I'm lucky."

Direction SMITH AND FORKINS[4]

The Keith management wasted no time in offering Bill a two-year contract, to commence after the next season, for he had already committed himself to the Orpheum Circuit for the current one. It would be his fourth consecutive Orpheum season, a record for a single dancer, black or white. By this time, Bill was well on his way to achieving another record, though it was never noted in the record books—twelve years of performing in vaudeville (1914–1927) without a single season's layoff. For ten years in a row, he danced *more* than fifty-two weeks a year, if you count the times he danced on two stages on the same night. One day in 1925 he called Marty Forkins from Minneapolis and said he would like one week off to attend the World Series. From then on, he decided that he could at least take off World Series week each year.

Years later, Bill's loyalty to his favorite team, the Yankees, paid off. The *Chicago Defender* (October 8, 1932) ran the following small story:

RICHER BY $12,000

And everybody thought he was only a dancer. Bill (Bo-jangles) Robinson, world famous tap dancer, picked the New York Yankees to win the world series from the Chicago Cubs in four straight games. When someone offered to take him up, giving 6 to 1, Robinson backed his own judgement with $2,000. Robinson, a favorite among the Yankee players, was special guest on the train which took the world champions home.[5]

As hard as he worked, no wonder he was a stickler for professionalism; and with the exception of the incident in Baltimore, where he knew he had to be on his best behavior, he was not likely to tolerate rudeness from audiences. U. S. Thompson recalled, "One time in East St. Louis, I think almost immediately after they had the riot there, there was a fellow sitting in the front seat and he kept making a lot of noise, like a Bronx cheer. Bill stopped the orchestra. 'Now wait a minute,' he said. 'There's a fellow sitting down there that don't like me. Now what is your story?' The fellow did the same thing again. So Bill jumped down off the stage and took him out. When Bill got back onstage, the people started applauding and Bill did his act."

For the balance of the year, Bill played the Keith Circuit in the Northeast, from Newark to Buffalo, Pittsburgh to Portland. In Providence, Rhode Island, in late November, he was on a program with Jack Benny, who, according to the *Providence Evening Tribune,* "tells some stories and tells them well and fiddles some in a way that makes the fiddle a sort of fellow comedian." Bill also did a number of benefit performances, among them one at the Lafayette Theater in Harlem and one for Catholic Charities. In August he participated in a program in honor of General Gouraud of France presented by the 369th Infantry. At the time, Lieutenant Noble Sissle was leader of the 369th Infantry band. Eubie Blake also appeared on the program, doing a "*Shuffle Along* Repertoire" with Sissle. Bill was listed in the program as "Bill Robinson ('Bojangles')." He also played several theaters on the Orpheum Circuit.

The beginning of the year saw him in Albany on a bill with the Gish sisters, then heading west on the Keith tour, which was joined in Cleveland by Sophie Tucker and Lou Holtz, both of whom were unscheduled "surprises" on the B. F. Keith Palace program. In Detroit in early February, he shared a bill with Rae Samuels again. He was always pleased when she and he were on the same bill, and was in the habit of sending telegrams to Marty Forkins announcing, "Mr. Marty, you know something? I gooled them. Then Miss Rae comes on right after me and gooled them better than I did." In vaudeville parlance, "gooling" meant being a hit. For her part, Rae enjoyed appearing on the same bill with Bill. "He was a great act to follow, but only if you had something. He would always leave them right in your lap, laughing." Show business legend holds that while in New York, Bill made a man laugh who had not done so in twenty-two years and who had made a standing offer of one hundred dollars to any man who could make him laugh.

The only thing Rae Samuels did not like about appearing on the same program with Bill was being hit up for money. "Fannie used to fight with him to save his money all the time and when he'd get broke in a crap game he wouldn't go to her. He'd come to me and say, 'Let me have five hundred dollars, Miss Rae, and I'll give it to you Saturday night.' Well, until I got onto him I'd let him have it. Then Marty would have to fight to get it back for me. Sure, he'd borrow from anybody."

Little Bo never did get used to her husband's gambling compulsion and to the havoc it played with her attempts to save money. Bill would find her secret money caches, pawn the expensive pieces of jewelry he had given her, obtain advances from the box office so that at the end of the week there was no salary left to be collected. She would have to face angry creditors and landlords, eke out money for food and shelter, stand up to her husband when he demanded money she knew they needed to live on. Yet, she was willing to put up with it all in order to have her Bo.

In 1925, Bill was in Chicago. There was nothing new about that. But two weeks later, he was performing with "genre entertainer" Nora Bayes. For that show, Bill introduced a song that became a favorite: "Your Lips Tell Me No, No; But There's Yes, Yes in Your Eyes." Like for the love song in *Shuffle Along,* the public's warm reception of this one indicated a slight thawing in American race relations. A few years earlier a black male entertainer would not have presumed to sing such a song to an audience of white ladies. Among the Robinson papers are two letters written in January 1925 by "Three 'Bill Robinson Fans': Miss V.B., Miss B.C., and Miss A.C." The first letter asks him to sing the song during the Saturday matinee at the Palace Theater in Milwaukee. The second letter thanks him for honoring the request.

In late February, Bill joined the Orpheum Circuit in St. Louis and spent the next two months in the Midwest. Forkins and his partner, Smith, ran another bold-faced advertisement in the March 19, 1924, *Variety:*

Isn't it great to have the public and all performers like you? Well, I'll tell you what will make everybody like you. When I started doing a single I wore a 7¼ hat. I have improved 100% and I still wear a 7¼. That's why everybody likes

BILL ROBINSON
my body and soul belong to
SMITH & FORKINS[6]

The end of April found Bill in Seattle, on a program with Sophie Tucker and the comedy team of George N. Burns and Grace Allen. He shared equal billing with Burns and Allen, though they were clearly not as well known as he. A reviewer for the *Portland Telegram* wrote, "George N. Burns and Grace Allen in a demonstration of how to treat 'em rough. If women could only be handled as George handles Grace, life would be a lot simpler."

In August he shared a bill with Fanny Brice at the San Francisco Orpheum, then moved over to the Golden Gate Theater for a week, where he was billed beneath Joe Fejer and his orchestra. In September he was billed under Brice again in Denver. Bill simply could not get headlines in white vaudeville, so he began to devote more of his energies to an activity that could garner him headlines: "freak sprinting." In the same towns, and in the same newspapers whose entertainment sections gave the other vaudeville stars top billing, he got top billing on the sports pages.

In Seattle he staged an exhibition of freak sprinting at a college track meet and did a hundred yards backward in fifteen seconds. In Los Angeles, at the end of May, the Olympic trials in track and field were held at the Coliseum. Identified as "Curley Robinson," he covered the same distance in 14.2 seconds. In San Francisco he competed against the best local runners and, with a twenty-five-yard handicap, won the race. In Denver he ran seventy-five yards backward, and bested the time of that city's racers running forward.

Denver was particularly entranced by this display, and gave him more coverage than he'd expected. *Denver Express* reporter Joe Myers wanted to know how he got started running backward. Cornered in his dressing room between shows, Bill didn't have time to think up a plausible answer. So he gave an implausible one:

Here's how Bill tells it: He was in London with the American Olympic team in 1908. Since a kid he had been a runner, competing for North Dorchester High and South Boston A.C. in Boston. He had been practicing running backwards just for fun for years.

While working with a squad of quarter-milers before the games, Bill gave an exhibition. They tried a competitive heat and Bill beat them. Then they hooked him up with a few sprinters at a handicap of 25 yards. Bill won again. He has done it hundreds of times since and never lost one of the freak races.

He claims Howard Drew and Charlie Paddock—joint holders of the 100-yard record with others—among his victims. Drew had his try in Bill's home town of Spring-field, Mass., where the actor was cutting quite a swath in darktown circles. Bill beat him with room to spare.[7]

Considering that during the major part of 1908 Bill was either on trial or in jail on the charge of having assaulted the tailor Hyman Sussman in New York, this was an audacious story. Marty Forkins's account of spilled oyster soup, which he created to cover the real circumstances of his and Bill's first meeting, pales by comparison. Fannie counseled Bill to be careful about not repeating this particular tall tale. In Minneapolis at a similar exhibition several months later, Bill told a reporter for the *Minneapolis Daily Star* that he had participated in the Olympic Games in 1901 and had qualified to do so again in 1908, but had been unable to go because of vaudeville contracts. He added, however, that he was the only black man who had ever run for the South Boston Athletic Club. One claim Bill made about his backward-running ability was true: According to the *Guinness Book of World Records,* he held the record for running backward (13.5 seconds) until Paul Wilson managed to do it in 13.3 seconds in Hastings, New Zealand, on April 10, 1977.

Bill staged most of his running exhibitions while with the Orpheum Circuit in the West and Midwest. The local Orpheum Theater usually helped publicize the event and provided the trophy. Beginning in 1925, however, theaters on the Keith-Albee Circuit sponsored similar exhibitions in the East. Bill was favored by the Keith management—to the extent that a black star could be favored. When the new E. F. Albee Theater opened in Brooklyn in January 1925, Bill Robinson was the one black act selected to appear on the premier bill.

The new theater was an imposing edifice. The Grand Hall sported marble columns, grand staircases, three seventeenth-century Jeanne d'Arc Aubusson tapestries that had hung on the choir pillars of Notre Dame Cathedral in Paris, and the largest rug in the world—forty feet by seventy feet, a ton in weight, woven by twenty-five women in Czechoslovakia. Backstage there were twenty dressing rooms, a tailor shop and a kitchen, a billiard room and a reading room, and even a tiled room with a bathtub for the stars of the animal acts.

Brooklyn Borough President Joseph A. Guider, a state senator, and an appellate judge presided over the dedication ceremonies, during which Guider read a congratulatory telegram from President Calvin Coolidge. Then the show began. E. F. Albee himself had selected the performers and considered them the best of every type of act available. As the reporter for *Zit's Weekly Newspaper* put it, "Bill [who had come from Milwaukee] was selected as Mr. Albee's choice of the colored performers, for this great showman knows that no vaudeville bill is complete without a member of the colored race."[8]

Marty Forkins saw his chance to capitalize on the event by running yet another bold-faced ad:

After 27 years of service for the Keith interests

BILL ROBINSON

THE DARK CLOUD OF JOY

was selected to appear on the initial program of the new E. F. Albee Theatre, Brooklyn, this week (Jan. 19). Many thanks to Mr. E. F. Albee and his associates for their kind appreciation for giving a colored boy this great distinction.
Direction Marty Forkins[9]

Bill, who came on just before the intermission, lived up to the honor accorded him by being "the first big hit at the new house" and *perhaps* by introducing on that stage the word that was to become his trademark. *Variety,* on January 21, 1925, reported that "Bill went very 'copasetty' and finished to wow returns from about 3,000 pairs of smacking dukes." The fact that the *Variety* reporter did not hear the word correctly indicates that Bill had not used it much before, at least not on New York stages.

It was after Bill's performance at the new E. F. Albee Theater that the Keith Theater in Providence, Rhode Island, sponsored his first exhibition run in the East. A month later, Bill shared a program with Harry Houdini on the Keith Circuit on the East Coast. Houdini extricated himself from trunks and straitjackets, and Bill danced. At the end of June, the B. F. Keith-Albee Vaudeville Exchange contracted with Bill for yet another season.

In late October 1925, Bill appeared at the New York Hippodrome with Florence Mills. It was eleven years since he had tried to help her and the other members of the Panama Trio in Chicago. In the intervening years she, too, had become a star. The two acts were so well received that one pair of agents in Brooklyn decided that they should star in a Broadway show. Rogers and Roberts saw Bill and Florence at the Hippodrome and wrote to Bo, saying they had "THE vehicle" for them. In 1925 they felt that a "Great Colored show is due" and "it wouldn't be a bad idea for us to get together . . . to hear the score."[10]

Bill did not formally team up with Florence Mills,

though they did occasionally enjoy working together. U. S. Thompson recalled, "When Florence was playing the Palace Theater, Bill was playing the Riverside and he made them put him on early so he could go down and make another appearance with Florence at the Palace. I had to frame up something they could do together."

The letter by Alex Rogers was not the first time Bill was mentioned as a logical choice to star in a Broadway revue. The occasional vaudeville reviewer had suggested this possibility, and some of the white intelligentsia in New York were ready for it. Carl Van Vechten was among them. *Shuffle Along* on Broadway had spawned an excited interest in all things black. Van Vechten, a music critic and photographer, became a self-styled conduit between the Harlem artistic community and downtown white society. He wrote articles, hosted parties, and took pictures. In an undated letter (probably written sometime after 1928, when Bill and Fannie had moved to an address mentioned in the letter), Bill Robinson responded to a note from Van Vechten regarding some photographs he had taken of Bill: "Yes, I would very much like to have those pictures. Copasetically, Bill."[11]

Led by Van Vechten and others, white downtowners had discovered the "New Negro" up in Harlem. Spurred by Prohibition and the interest in the "New Negro," white gangsters had opened whites-only nightclubs in Harlem that catered to a prurient interest in "exotic" blacks and at the same time served as outlets for bootleg liquor. The shows at such establishments as Connie's Inn and the Cotton Club were obviously imitative of Broadway revues, but none of them ever made the transition from Harlem to Broadway. Harlem was still off the beaten track for serious reviewers, and even if the serious reviewers had bothered to see the shows at the Harlem clubs in their professional capacity, they would have found them lacking. At first, most of the black entertainers and waiters were not Harlemites at all; rather, they were imported from Chicago, where the mob bosses were headquartered. They were also uniformly light-skinned. There was yet no place for a dark-skinned performer like Bill Robinson, no matter how great his talent.

But there was interest in Bill from other quarters. He had some contact with producer Lew Leslie at this time. Leslie was producing all-black revues at his downtown Plantation Club and had set his sights on bigger things. In association with British promoter C. B. Cochran, he had taken the second all-black revue to Europe in 1923. *Dover to Dixie* had starred Florence Mills. U. S. Thompson recalled in 1975 that taking a black revue to Europe in those days was no small accomplishment:

It was after the war. The labor people in England was against the importation of foreign acts. After the show came in and stayed twelve weeks, they wouldn't renew the labor permit. So, we had to close.

There was a man—he and Cochran was enemies—and he wanted to beat Cochran to the novelty of bringing in a colored show. So he brought over a revue called "Plantation Days" and played the Hippodrome in London. That show wasn't such a success. Anyhow, when Mr. Cochran brought Florence over in the *Dover to Dixie* thing, the the-

ater-going public was against the importation of this sort
of thing, because they figured that this man—Lord somebody—had already brought it in, it wasn't no sensation or
anything like that. Anyhow, that night we opened in *Dover
to Dixie*, there were a lot of people to hoot 'em . . . razz
them, give them the Bronx cheer and all that, see. When
the curtain went up the audience didn't get a chance to
hoot—it was action, action, action all the way down,
stopped the show. Leslie said, "Don't take a whole lot of
bows. Just take a bow or two and go ahead." And they
never did get a chance to hoot.

Hannon Swanson was a writer for the *London Express*.
He hated Negroes. He had been to New York and Florida
and knew all about the Jim Crow stuff. Before the show
came in, he wrote all this [bad] stuff. He had never seen
the show, but he just figured . . . But when the curtain
went down, the people stood up. Mr. [Will] Vodery, the
leader of the band, used to do all of Ziegfeld's arranging,
and the music was good and the talent was good and [the
show] wasn't too long, and it was a riot! London had
never seen . . . Hannon Swanson, who hated Negroes, had
never expected to see nothing like that before. But when
the twelve weeks was up, the musicians was out of work in
London. Actors and musicians was walking around in the
streets, playing the bass around the streets and passin' the
hat and things. They wouldn't extend our labor permit.
That's what we were up against.

Three years later, Leslie was game to try again. His
production *Blackbirds*, an all-black revue starring Florence Mills, opened at the Alhambra Theater in Harlem
in 1926 and ran for several weeks before going to Europe. It was judged better than *Dover to Dixie*. But nei-

ther Leslie nor any other producer was willing to try to take Bill Robinson to Broadway. Perhaps they were waiting for his "tryout" in Europe.

By the mid-1920s, the European economic situation had improved and Europe was captivated by American jazz. Introduced by black American servicemen during World War I, and brought over after the war by the all-black revues of Lew Leslie and others, jazz music and jazz dancing were all the rage in Paris, and to a lesser extent in London and the Scandinavian capitals. Ada Smith of the Panama Club in Chicago in 1914, now known as Bricktop, had been invited to Paris to be competition for Florence Jones, the one black American entertainer in Montmartre. Singing in a tiny club called Le Grand Duc, Jones had been "discovered" by Cole Porter and his set in the spring of 1925 (everyone who was anyone in the United States went to Paris that spring). Josephine Baker arrived in Paris that fall, and the rest is history. By early 1926 Parisians and other Europeans were clamoring for *le jazz hot,* and black American entertainers were only too willing to oblige.

The Bill Robinson papers unfortunately do not include correspondence on how his and Fannie's trip to Europe in the summer of 1926 came about. We can deduce, however, that they arranged a booking in England and then took it from there. They sailed for London on the S.S. *Leviathan* on July 3, 1926. The Bill Robinson scrapbook contains bon-voyage telegrams from Eubie Blake, among others. Bill and Fannie had apparently been dreaming of sailing on the *Leviathan* for some time, for Bill had appeared on the same bill with the S.S. *Leviathan* Orchestra at the Keith Theater in Philadelphia back in June 1923 and had clipped for his scrapbook an article about the "trial voyage" of the ship.

In London Bill opened at the Holborn Empire Theatre. He received good-luck telegrams from Lew Leslie and Rose Zits, undoubtedly connected with *Zit's Weekly Newspaper*. Fannie sent a postcard back home (July 14, 1926) to Mr. and Mrs. Carl Van Vechten, writing that they were well and that Bill's opening "was a *riot*. See you in late August."[12]

In Paris Bill apparently got in touch with his old friend Bricktop, who had become the darling of the Cole Porter set by virtue of her ability to teach the Charleston. No doubt she was eager to show Bill that she had learned professionalism from him and had gone on to make good. The Bill Robinson papers include a program from a charity benefit in Venice in late August 1926, organized by Mrs. Cole Porter, among others. Bricktop had very carefully identified the various luminaries on the program by writing "Count," "Duchess," "Contessa," and so on in front of their names. The bottom of the program states: "Direttrice Miss BRICK-TOP" and it is enclosed in handwritten parentheses. Also in her handwriting, following her name, are the words "Ha Ha," a written chortle over how far she had come since the days when Bill Robinson had tried to help the Panama Trio in Chicago.

While in Paris, Bill and Fannie met up with Florence Mills and her husband, U. S. Thompson. "We were performing in Paris at the Ambassador [in Lew Leslie's *Blackbirds*]," said Thompson in 1975. "Bill only played a couple of weeks in London and then he came on to

Paris to visit, you know, he and his wife, and we had quite a few days together in Paris. We went to museums and things like that."

Following their sojourn in Paris, the Robinsons returned to London, where Bill played the Holborn Empire again. Then, on August 10, they sailed on the S.S. *Leviathan* for home.

7

Bo on
Broadway

After his return from Europe, Bill went back to the vaudeville circuits, but interest continued in his starring in a Broadway musical. In early December 1926, while he was playing at the Hill Street Theater in Los Angeles, he received a telegram from Louis Schurr, who was casting a new musical, *Show Boat,* produced by Florenz Ziegfeld. Schurr was confident in Bill's talent and in casting him for a role in the new show, writing, "Kindly advise immediately how soon you will be available and what is your salary."[1]

Schurr was a theatrical agent who would later represent Lena Horne in Hollywood, and he probably had the clout to get Bill a part in *Show Boat*. Whether Bill ever auditioned for the part is not known. *Show Boat,* with music by Jerome Kern, opened on Broadway in 1927 and was a major success, spawning two films and numerous revivals. But Bill remained on the vaudeville circuits.

It is possible that he himself was loath to leave vaudeville, in spite of the greater fame that appearing on Broadway might entail. For all its trials, he was comfortable on the circuits. He knew the circuit managers and he knew the theater managers and police superintendents in every town, not to mention the poolhall operators and crapshooters. While he believed his talent should be acknowledged, he had no overriding ambition. He was keenly aware of the limits to which a black performer could go. He was content with his life and asked only for enough money to feed his gambling habit, maintain his natty style, and keep Fannie at bay, plus get a few headlines now and then.

But Marty Forkins understood that soon Bill would not have a choice. For some years Hollywood and vaudeville had been vying for audiences, and when *The Jazz Singer,* the first talking picture, was released in 1927, a smart manager like Forkins could see which way the wind was blowing. He foresaw that nightclubs would soon be the only stage left on which Bill could perform, unless he could break into Broadway or the movies. Unfortunately, he was little known, if at all, in either venue. Thus, when the opportunity arose for Bill to appear in Lew Leslie's *Blackbirds of 1928,* Forkins jumped at it.

Lew Leslie saw that the time was ripe for the kind of black revue that would click. He also wanted Florence Mills to star again in his show, but in late 1927, Florence Mills died of a ruptured appendix. Florence was buried in a five-thousand-dollar bronze replica of

Rudolph Valentino's coffin. Earl Dancer, Ethel Waters's husband, took over the funeral arrangements from Kid Thompson, who became distraught. Florence's funeral was the largest that New York had ever seen, but that didn't help Lew Leslie.

According to Rae Samuels, Bill joined the cast of the show as a favor to Lew Leslie, having no idea that it would make him a star. But Marty Forkins saw the move as a favor to Bill's career, and in just two years he would come to regard the move as a favor to himself as well: In 1929 the great Keith-Albee-Orpheum chain, which had merged in order to stay alive, became the RKO (Radio-Keith-Orpheum) motion picture theater chain. Thus Forkins, who in the closing years of vaudeville handled 200 acts and held the all-time record for the Keith Circuit—215 acts booked in one week in 1928—would have been forced out. But thanks to Bill, he moved easily into the newer entertainment areas.

Blackbirds of 1928 was Lew Leslie's big gamble. He wanted to rival the success of *Shuffle Along,* something that no other black revue had even come close to doing, though there had been several notable recent efforts. Nineteen twenty-seven was a watershed year for black musicals. There was *Bottomland,* with singer Eva Taylor and music by Clarence Williams but no prominent dancers. It ran for twenty-one performances. *Africana* starred Ethel Waters, who got her start as a favorite of the mob in Chicago. This show was heavy on dancing, and helped to focus the critics' attention on tap and "eccentric dancing" as presented by Glen and Jenkins, Eddie and Sonny, and "The Two Black Dots" (Taylor and Johnson). Prior to the opening of *Africana,* white critics approached black shows from a very biased viewpoint: The shows either had to be "racial," which meant replete with watermelons and razor fights, or derivative of white shows. These critics were unable to comprehend a black show that, for example, featured dancing that was particularly representative of black idioms.

Lew Leslie cast Adelaide Hall in the part he had planned for Florence. *Blackbirds* would be Hall's Broadway debut. Leslie also cast Aida Ward, another singer, who was no stranger to Florence and her husband, Kid Thompson, who said, "I put her in show business. She used to be a piano player in the pit. Her father was the principal of a school in Kansas City, Kansas—Bendare College. Aida used to play the piano in the theater in Kansas City and I was playing there—doing stock. Every week you used to change your act. You get to be a favorite and they kept you there. I got to be a big favorite in Kansas. They had a colored theater and it was packed. Aida became a big favorite, too. Then a producer, a man named Adams, took her, made her black up to do a blackface act. From then on she was a star."

Tim Moore, an ex-prizefighter and comedian (who later gained greater fame playing the Kingfish on *Amos 'n' Andy*), was teamed with George W. Cooper, Bill Robinson's former vaudeville partner. Cooper played straight man to Moore. In the years since splitting up with Bill, Cooper had worked with Eddie Hunter and been part of the team called Cooper and Smith with Chris Smith, who wrote such song hits as "Ballin' the Jack" and "Shimmy-Sha-Wobble." Cooper had also worked with his son for a while, but George was confined to the small-time circuits.

While Leslie had enjoyed some success with his revues in Europe and New York, he did not have a lot of capital to invest in the new show. Still, he knew that what money he did have would be well spent on talented songwriters. *Blackbirds of 1928* had the first complete score written by the songwriting team of Dorothy Fields (lyricist) and Jimmy McHugh (composer).

McHugh, a native of Boston, was already well known. When the whites-only Cotton Club had opened in Harlem in 1923, he was its resident composer. In the early years of the club, he introduced such songs as "I Can't Believe That You're in Love with Me" and "When My Sugar Walks Down the Street." For part of the fall 1927 Cotton Club show, he had collaborated with Dorothy Fields, who was just twenty-three at the time. As daughter of Lew Fields of the famous Weber and Fields vaudeville team, Dorothy came naturally by her interest in show business, but her father was adamantly against any of his children going into the profession.

Dorothy began writing songs with McHugh in early 1927, and worked with him on the score of *Harry Delmar's Revels,* a show that folded in two weeks. She was, therefore, grateful when he asked her to work with him on the new Cotton Club show, but she did not tell her father. She had no illusions about his reaction to her working for a club operated by gangsters. When he found out about her latest project, she hastened to assure him that the mobsters at the club were perfect gentlemen. At the opening her father was a proud member of the audience. It was Dorothy who was mortified when the singer of a song whose lyrics she had written gave those lyrics a decidedly blue tint. She complained to Lew Fields, who in turn went to the Cotton Club management and made sure that his daughter's name was not associated with the song. But this experience did not drive Dorothy Fields out of show business or away from the Cotton Club. She and McHugh went on to write some of the club's most memorable shows.

The partners created a fine score for *Blackbirds of 1928,* including the song "Diga Diga Doo," which Adelaide Hall sang, backed by a chorus line of girls in red sequins and feathers who did a frenetic "Zulu" dance following the song. "I Can't Give You Anything But Love, Baby" was the other big hit of the show. Fields and McHugh got the idea for the song one day when they were standing outside Tiffany's on Fifth Avenue and overheard a fellow tell his girl, "Gee, honey, I can't give you nothin' but love." They had first presented the song in the ill-fated *Harry Delmar's Revels* (Patsy Kelly sang it in that show), but were so convinced of its possibilities that they tried it again in *Blackbirds.* Sung by Adelaide Hall and Bill Robinson, who blew some of the lyrics on opening night, it was a great success.[2]

Though Leslie had a talented songwriting team and a talented cast, he was unhappy as he watched the early rehearsals. Something was missing. He had beauty and, in the person of fat, toothy Tim Moore, he had comedy. He had the requisite interpretations of currently popular novels. But he did not have enough showstopping numbers. It was then, according to Rae Samuels, that he got in touch with Bill Robinson. As a favor to Leslie, Bill agreed to join the *Blackbirds* cast. It would be the first time he had worked in the same show with George Cooper since they had split up. For Cooper it must have been a painful reminder of what might have been.

By the time the show opened at the Liberty Theater on May 9, 1928, *Blackbirds of 1928* was polished, and though it broke no new ground in terms of stock situations—it contained stereotypes of black children eating watermelon, for example—it was marked not just by the talent of the performers and songwriters but by the excellence of its staging. The first-act finale, a tribute to the DuBose Heyward novel *Porgy,* featured a huge black screen on which were reflected the magnified shadows of the performers. The first production of the George Gershwin opera *Porgy and Bess* several years later featured a similar stage effect, though it is not known whether director Rouben Mamoulian consciously copied the *Blackbirds* segment.[3]

Bill Robinson did not appear until the second act, but from the moment he came on the stage he seemed to electrify it. His routine was similar to his vaudeville act: He sang and danced to a number titled "Doin' the New Low Down" (later to become his radio theme song). He tapped up and down a flight of five steps. He flashed his infectious smile. He very cleverly made the audience pay attention to his feet by watching them himself, thereby commanding the audience to do the same. For the first time, the "downtown ofays" began to appreciate the finer points of tap. The audience for Broadway shows, often called the "carriage trade," was different from that for vaudeville, but it responded to Bill in the same way: They were enraptured.[4] The reviews of the show were almost uniformly glowing. And as had become the custom in his vaudeville appearances, Bill garnered the greatest number of plaudits. Mary Austin, a writer for *The Nation,* said that no other dancer in the world could compare with him. He was established as a Broadway headliner.

Walter Winchell, in the *Graphic* (May 10, 1928), wrote:

> Forty-second Street went Harlem again last night, via the Liberty Theatre, where Lew Leslie fetched his sepia-shaded specialists.
>
> Aida Ward rendered an impersonation of the departed favorite, Florence Mills.

Ibee, in *Variety* (May 18, 1928), wrote:

> In addition to Miss Ward's physical charms she has a voice that rates her an embryo Florence Mills. Those curious high notes are not as lusty but with training she could become the successor, from the present colored field, to Miss Mills, the leading musical comedy actress of her race.
>
> Just before the finale Miss Ward came on in immaculate male evening clothes—no actress ever looked better in them. The bit was billed "A Memory of 1927," an impersonation of Miss Mills without her name mentioned. In the departed star's favorite togs she sang her favorite number, "Mandy Make Up Your Mind," while the chorus bent eyes stageward. It was a sentimental gesture, one appreciated by the first nighters finely accomplished by the Ward girl.
>
> Robinson led the good looking chorus of high browns in "Doin' the New Low Down," but one of the specialists, Earl Tucker (Snakehips), in his low down, is a caution. Has he got snake hips—and how! Tucker is a marvel in his way, for no such weaving of the hips has yet been shown. That boy certainly smacked them hard.[5]

Broadway was not much different from vaudeville, Bill thought, as he publicly expressed his gratitude to "Mr. Leslie" for giving him a chance, keeping to himself the knowledge that it was he who had agreed to help Leslie. Still, he was ebullient at having conquered the Great White Way, and for a brief time he seemed to let down his guard around "white folks." Asked by W. A. Roberts of the *New York World Telegram* how he had developed his dancing style, Bill obliged by showing the reporter some complicated steps, then said, "All these have been supposed to be white tap dances which I adapted and ragged. But the truth is . . . I never consciously imitated a white performer."[6] As a rule, Bill was careful to give most of the credit for his dancing to white influences.

Blackbirds ran on Broadway for 518 performances (sixty weeks), only one of which was marred by unruly members of the audience. According to U. S. Thompson, "They were making fun of the girls—'I'll take this one and that one's got pretty—and that one's got skinny—and I don't like that one and—' They were making a lot of noise and interrupting the performance. So when Bill came on—he was way down in the last part of the show—he told the orchestra to stop. And he told those fellows, 'Now, you wouldn't do that at Ziegfeld's and you ain't gonna do it here no more! If you do, then I'm putting you out.' They started making noise again, and Bill jumped down off the stage and carried them out. When he got back, he told the orchestra to begin again, and they did."

At the age of fifty, Bill Robinson had hit the big time at last. Suddenly, as Ethel Waters wrote in her autobiography, "Harlem was crazy about Bojangles. They would yell, 'Bo, Bo!' whenever they saw him. . . . Everybody in Harlem said Bojangles was a magnificent dancer and they were certainly right."[7] But if he was the most famous name in Harlem, he had also become a target. On September 23, 1928, Casper Holstein, credited as the inventor of "the numbers" and Harlem's chief black racketeer, was kidnapped and released only after payment of a hefty ransom. His kidnappers were later caught and found to be in possession of a list of "future prospects." Holstein's name was first, Bill's was second.[8] Not long afterward, the men of the 132nd Precinct in Harlem presented Bill with a pearl-handled, gold-plated revolver and a magazine filled with gold bullets. It was, in Bill's opinion, the greatest honor he had ever received. In the opinion of Rae Samuels, it was a mistake: "Now, to give him a gold gun was like putting a knife in the hands of a maniac."

He was asked to do benefits for an even larger assortment of causes and acceded to most requests, including the honor of being a charter member of the Grand Street Boys' Club. Meanwhile, Fannie was seeing to it that some of the "benefits" of her husband's stardom accrued to him, and to her, and that they would live in an apartment that befitted his star status. When the Dunbar Apartments opened in Harlem in 1928, the Robinsons were among its many illustrious tenants.

Begun in 1927, the five-acre, 511-unit complex, bounded by Seventh and Eighth avenues, 149th to 150th streets, had won first prize for design from the New York chapter of the American Institute of Architects. The complex was financed by the Rockefeller family and operated on a preter–co-op model—after twenty-two years the tenants would own their apartments. The rents were designed for people whose median monthly income was about $150, about $40 higher than the average Harlem family's, and the Robinsons were in elite company. Among the other tenants were W.E.B. DuBois and his wife, Shirley Graham DuBois (they had two apartments); the cartoonist E. Simms Campbell; bandleader Fletcher Henderson; entertainer Lucille Randolph and her husband, Asa; Paul and Essie Robeson; and actor Leigh Whipper.[9]

While the average observer would not have considered it a triumph for Bill and Fannie to be among the Dunbar's tenants, insiders knew it was a great triumph for Fannie. If she hadn't saved some of the money he made, they could not have afforded to live there. Bill would have also been in trouble with the government over nonpayment of taxes. "She had a hard life with him," said Rae Samuels. "Don't think she didn't." He expected her to manage finances and file his income-tax returns correctly and promptly—he didn't want any trouble with the law at any time—but she was forced to nag him constantly for the money to do it.

Bill was now making big money. Marty Forkins booked him into presentation houses at double his vaudeville salary. He declined to go on tour with *Blackbirds* because Lew Leslie didn't offer enough money. He was replaced by Eddie Rector, whom Leslie wanted to do a stair dance. Bill sent Rector a telegram: DO MY STAIR DANCE AND YOU DIE. Leslie insisted that the stair dance be used, and it was. Bill was furious with Leslie, and most sources say that this was the incident that started a long feud between them. Marty Forkins had his turn at the screw when he arranged to book Bill against *Blackbirds* in each town it played, and everywhere, Bill outdrew the show. Years later, Bill also got back at Eddie Rector, who was famous for dancing on drums. In the film *Stormy Weather,* he imitated Rector by dancing up and down a staircase of huge drums.

Bill did return to vaudeville. Though he appeared in *Hot Chocolates* at Connie's Inn in Harlem, he declined to move downtown with the show in 1929, pleading vaudeville commitments. He was not at all sure that he wanted to stay in one place for any length of time. In the course of his 518 performances with *Blackbirds,* Bill had the uncommon experience of going home to the same place for weeks on end, and seeing the same fellow gamblers for weeks on end—not always, in his experience, a good situation. He missed seeing his friends, and fellow gamblers, and the police chiefs in the far-flung stops of the vaudeville circuits. He missed the rhythm of the road. But he was fifty years old, and had to consider the toll all that traveling took on his body, particularly on his feet. His foot doctor was in New York—he'd been going to Dr. William J. Carter, with offices at 213 West 138th Street, and when he was on the road, he wired him the moment his feet bothered him the least bit.

For a while, Bill chose the happy compromise of remaining in vaudeville, but playing primarily in New York City and on the East Coast. He was practically an artist-in-residence at the Palace, where he appeared in late May, July, and October. In fact, he was "pleasing the Palace audience" when the stock market crashed. But the collapse of the market meant little to Bill, whose idea of a commodity was a piece of gold jewelry. Yes, he lost a great deal of money, but by giving it away to those in need.

Having the position of being the top-paid Negro entertainer in the world carried certain responsibilities. Bo knew he could not enjoy his financial success without first helping his brothers and sisters, who were being pushed out onto the street as casualties of the Depression. Though he didn't publicize it, he was probably one of the greatest contributors to many of Harlem's relief programs. In a sense, he was a one-man recovery act. If he saw a family being dispossessed, when he could he would pay their back rent, pay some street men to carry their belongings back into their apartment, and move them back into shelter. Then he might also fill up their cabinets so the mother could feed her family. Strangers wrote to him for money. Some asked for a few dollars. Some asked for enough money to start a business so they could support their families again and gain a feeling of self-respect. Fannie read all the letters and related the most worthy to Bill. He decided if something was to be sent. She decided on what was sent. If a child was involved, she might send money for food, or a particular item of clothing that she would pick out herself.

When Bill and Fannie weren't giving their own money away, they were freely giving up their time. Fannie, Bo, and Marty all put in countless hours to help organize benefits, and to make sure Bill would take the time to appear at a benefit. When Bojangles performed, the house was filled. And a packed house meant more money for whatever charitable cause they were trying to help.

Ed Sullivan said in an interview:

> Bill was tremendous with his race. He loaned money to them and he was always kind to them. They would always come backstage when he was in my revues and I'd say, "Bill, Christ, they're downstairs again and they want money." He said, "Old Bojangles has to help them out because I once was in the same spot myself." He was a fine, fine gentleman.

The Depression seemed to mean little to most well-to-do New Yorkers, who partied on as before, and during those years Bill was in great demand as an entertainer at private parties; though Ethel Waters remembers him being the rage of Harlem, he was also exceptionally popular downtown. Tap dancing was suddenly "in" among society types, and he not only taught afternoon classes to debutantes, among them tobacco heiress Doris Duke, but also entertained their parents after his shows at night. "He would take Little Bo," according to Lillian Alpert Wolf, Marty Forkins's assistant. "Mr. Forkins saw to that because he didn't want Bill to be mixing with the white people, because it would cause some talk if they saw Bill talking to the white folks. If his wife was there, then everything was all right, that made it kosher. . . . And do you know what those society girls would do? They would sit around on the floor and watch his feet. They made a big fuss about it. He played a lot of those parties." Ed Sullivan, then a noted Broadway columnist, recalled being at many of those parties and noted the particular relationship shared by Robinson and Marty Forkins:

> Marty Forkins was a very smart man and he and Bill were very attached to each other. If Marty was having a theatrical party or going to attend a theatrical party he would always bring Bill along. If anybody said anything about Bill or about blacks or whites . . . you know you always forget—there are just as many white bastards as there are black bastards. The blacks have been singled out. The people forget or don't remember vividly enough the great blacks. The Paul Robesons and other people. When I was a kid writing sports up in Port Chester, New York, there were a tremendous number of these people.

Bill generally observed the social conventions that he felt he could not change. Lillian Alpert Wolf recalled in 1974 that Bill would sometimes ask her to accompany him to buy gifts. He would keep them in the safe in the Forkins's New York office to have on hand when he felt like giving someone a present:

> He wanted me to go with him to Nat Lewis', which was a very famous haberdashery—catered to all the theatrical people. He wanted me to help pick out girly things. Well, as soon as we got out onto the street, he started running. I couldn't catch him, because he was a sprinter. I called out that I couldn't keep up with him. He called back, "You can't walk with me on Broadway. I'm a black man and you're a white lady. You meet me at Nat Lewis'." He knew his place. He loved to be with white people, but he knew how far to go.

He loved to take me and the other girls in the office out to lunch. We'd go to the Brass Rail. He couldn't sit with us, so he stood at the bar and had his steak sandwich with a glass of milk. We sat at a table and had a lovely lunch, and he picked up the tab and he was the happiest man on Broadway.

Invited to the Stork Club, Bill refused to go. He avoided white hotels except when he entertained at private parties. He realized that the key to his success was not merely his talent but his behavior in the increasingly white world in which he found himself after the success of *Blackbirds of 1928*.

On May 8, 1930, *The New York Times* announced: "Bill Robinson, Negro tap dancer, who was featured last season in *Blackbirds,* has been engaged by Florenz Ziegfeld as one of the principals of the new *Follies,* scheduled in New York during the Summer. Mr. Robinson has been seen frequently in vaudeville here this season."[10]

On May 14, 1930, *The New York Times* declared: "Florenz Ziegfeld's announcement that he had engaged Bill Robinson for the forthcoming *Follies* was denied yesterday. . . . Mr. Robinson has signed a contract to appear under the management of Marty Forkins, a vaudeville agent, in a Negro musical comedy scheduled for next season. This arrangement was confirmed by Mr. Forkins who declared that he is planning to put the show in rehearsal in July, with Adelaide Hall also in the cast.

"Stanley Sharpe of the Ziegfeld office insisted that Mr. Robinson is under contract to Mr. Ziegfeld."[11]

When you consider that Forkins reviewed, often wrote, all Bill's contracts, the *Times* announcement couldn't have been any more than wishful thinking on the part of the Ziegfeld office.

Brown Buddies, the new musical revue in which Bill was to star, was produced by Marty Forkins, his first venture into the form. The book was written by Carl Richman, the music by Joe Jordan and Millart Thomas; the staging was done by Ralph Rose. In addition to Bill and Adelaide Hall, the show featured Ada Brown, Putney Dandridge, and the comedy tap-dancing team of Red and Struggy. It was heavy on tap and light on story line. As customary, the show was rehearsed in New York, then tried out elsewhere before being taken to Broadway. On September 15 it opened at the Apollo Theater in Atlantic City. At the end of the month it played a week in Pittsburgh. There, on October 5, two days before the show was scheduled to open at the Liberty Theater in New York, Bill received another bullet wound.

He had left his hotel and was hailing a taxi to take him to the train station when he heard the screams of Mrs. Annie Bies. The white woman pointed after a fleeing black youth, who had her purse in his hand. Bill dropped his bags and gave chase, calling to the boy to stop. When the youth kept running, Bill pulled his gold-plated revolver and fired. He missed the youth. Patrolman Michael Horan heard the shots, ran in their direction, and seeing a black man with a gun, fired. Bill dropped. The purse-snatcher escaped, and Bill was taken to Mercy Hospital. Treated for a superficial wound in the left arm, Bill was released and resumed his journey to New York. Two days later he opened in *Brown Buddies* as scheduled, with his arm in a white satin sling, and managed to carry on until the finale, when suddenly he felt faint. He whispered to his fellow cast members, "Get me off." Leaning on the arm of a large male dancer, he reached the wings and collapsed. But he went on as scheduled the following night. Asked how he felt about being shot while trying to help the woman who'd lost her purse, Bill stated he felt no rancor toward Officer Horan, which further endeared him to police departments all over the country.

Brown Buddies received cool reviews. The critical consensus was that the talents of the performers were wasted in a show where the music was not so much music as "din" and the book and staging hopelessly imitative. The *Tribune* called it "a cheaply pretentious . . . imitation opera," and the *World,* referring to the black performers, pronounced, "How near they are to a Broadway which used to copy them, but which they now copy in return." Such critics had little awareness of, or sensitivity to, the historical problems of blacks on the stage. Just as minstrelsy, originally a white imitation of antebellum black music and dance, had become so standardized that by the time blacks were allowed to perform in the shows they had to do so in blackface, the same sort of thing was happening in musical comedy. Salem Tutt-Whitney of the *Chicago Defender* was tired of hearing the charge of imitativeness: "Most of our shows are financed, staged and directed by white men," he pointed out, "and most of these white men arrogate the right to tell us when and how. Under the circumstances, I don't see how we miss being colored so often."[12]

Despite the lukewarm critical reception, *Brown Buddies* ran for 113 performances, and Bill Robinson received universal rave reviews. Wrote the reviewer for the *New York World Telegram,* October 8, 1930: "A few days ago Bill Robinson chased a thief in Pittsburgh and was winged by an unobservant and ungrateful cop. So last night he appeared with his left arm in a sling, which, if anything, made his feet even more subtly talkative than usual. When Robinson hushed those miraculous tap steps of his to a whisper you could hear the whole house holding its breath." In fact, the show was a personal triumph for Bill. The *Tribune* reported that the applause for him "has not been equalled since the first night of *The Merry Widow.*" George Jean Nathan, preeminent critic of the day, pointed out that Bill was a fine actor as well as dancer; and no doubt this review helped launch his film career.

After 1930 there were few opportunities for him to appear in black musical revues on Broadway. The first year of the new decade was also the last year when a major black revue opened. The genre had lasted ten years, beginning with the success of *Shuffle Along* in 1921, but no subsequent show had been able to capture the imagination of downtown theatergoers as that seminal revue had done. The last noteworthy black musical, *Blackbirds of 1930,* starring Ethel Waters, ran sixty-two performances. A new edition of *Blackbirds* in 1933, starring Bill, lasted a month. By that time, most people talked about "colored revues on Broadway" as a thing of the past.

In *Jazz Dance* Marshall and Jean Stearns cite several causes for the death of the Negro musical and of "vernacular dancing" on Broadway: "The immediate causes were careless presentation, overexposure, and the Depression. The most crushing blow came from within. In 1936 *On Your Toes* featured the widely acclaimed ballet sequence *Slaughter on Tenth Avenue,* choreographed by George Balanchine, and any comeback that tap dancing might have staged was nipped in the bud. With the appearance of *Oklahoma* (1943), the process was irreversible. Ballet was the rage, and 'ballet,' says George Balanchine, 'is woman.'"[13]

By that time, however, Bill Robinson's stardom was not dependent upon the vagaries of public taste in dance or even race. U. S. Thompson believed that the key to Bill's fame was his personality:

> Bill Robinson was the best box office, we'll put it like that. There was no other dancer who could get the money and get the people in like Bill Robinson. There were hundreds of guys who could beat him step for step—John Bubbles, Eddie Rector, Rastus Brown, Willie Covan—they all did five or six routines. Bill Robinson did only about three routines—same steps, same routines, couldn't teach him a step 'cause if he didn't create it himself he wouldn't do it. He was a good dancer—you can't take that away from him—but he was a great promoter. Bill Robinson had sense enough to get out to the streets and run backwards and all that stuff. And fight and raise hell and then send the sheriff tickets. Box office: No other dancer was a public relations man like he was.

8

Mayor
of Harlem

By the time the *Brown Buddies* run ended, Bill Robinson's fame had reached almost mythical proportions. Among blacks especially, his name was a household word, though he was not regarded as a hero in some black households. There was more than a little jealousy and carping about his close relationship with whites. Bill had achieved such success, had advanced so far beyond even the wildest dreams of most black Americans, that some people could not justify it except to suggest that he had arrived at it in a somehow unethical way—e.g., by turning his back on his own people and kowtowing to whites. If challenged to prove such assertions, however, most of his critics would have been hard put to do so. As U. S. Thompson said, "He proved he was no Uncle Tom because Uncle Tom didn't fight. But Bill, if you made him mad, he'd fight at the drop of a hat." Bill's critics would have had particular difficulty citing evidence that he had turned his back on his own people. And no other successful black artist was as willing to do benefit performances, or as proud to display the awards and other tokens he received in lieu of pay.

It galled Fannie Robinson to hear of attacks on Bill's racial pride. Anyone who knew Bill Robinson knew he was quick-tempered and fast to fight. When it came to injustice, his friends and associates were fighters also. Bert Williams used a song. Jackie Robinson played ball. Joe Louis used his fists. Bill Robinson used his feet, his gun, his fists, his smile, his charm, and anything else at his disposal. Almost nothing stood in his way of demonstrating his demand for social justice, or arguing against injustice. He was consistent in this pattern. He did not stand up for a cause only when it was in the public limelight. Bojangles, Marty Forkins, and Fannie quietly formed their own crusade to demonstrate that when whites and blacks worked together, both sides could see things differently and changes could be made in the course of black history. By taking a few small steps, they formed small cracks in social barriers. On a few occasions, those cracks opened the way to positive accomplishments.

At benefits, if a white-only audience were scheduled, Bo would ask that blacks be allowed to attend. The same would hold true if the reverse audience applied. Bo would be just as angry seeing prejudice coming from a black man as coming from a white man.

In her 1953 *Ebony* article, Fannie wrote about how Bo's actions caused a considerable change in the lives of many people from Dallas, Texas, where he was about to play a benefit.

Bo and Fannie were at a gathering with Bill and the powerful Dallas citizens who had organized the affair. Bill casually asked if a few of his acquaintances could join his wife in the audience. There is no record of it, but the room must have fallen silent, except for the sound of mouths dropping open in surprise. Though today one might view this as a modest request, at the time it represented a major concession contrary to the standard Dallas policy. The organizers agreed, thinking this little action wouldn't lead to anything. But it did.

A few days after the successful benefit, Bill and Fannie had to get back to New York quickly for the Joe Louis fight. The only way they could make it back on time was by riding the usually all-white train. They faced a few problems: first, getting on the train; second, staying safe after leaving Dallas and riding through many small country towns prior to northern territory.

To accomplish part one, Bill went back to some of the benefit organizers and asked for help. They agreed and called some of their friends. Before they knew it, Bill and Fannie were on board an all-white train headed back to New York. Fannie wrote how she was tense and anxious about an incident. Sure enough, there was an incident. One that changed life in Dallas.

It seems that when word got out that Bill Robinson was on the train, every little boy and girl rushed to see him. Their parents followed close behind. Bill, without much persuasion, wound up doing an impromptu show that lasted for hours. Of course, he asked for no payment, but he wound up with a bunch of hugs and kisses from the kids, and respect and many thanks from their parents.

Weeks later, there was a second unexpected payoff.

Bill and Fannie were notified that for the first time in Dallas history, a number of Negro officers were hired to work the Negro section of town. It was a new, small, positive step that Bill didn't have to stand on a soapbox to accomplish. He didn't scream that action be taken. He just did what he did best. He danced for himself and his friends. He fought with action and example. He tried to demonstrate how things could and should be—people working, living, and laughing together. By dancing at the right place and at the right time, a few whites and blacks in Dallas changed their attitudes. A few more people got a small taste of justice and dignity. Bill knew that he, Fannie, and Marty could not conquer social injustice, but each small step was a personal victory, and one of the few things he didn't brag about.

That Bill traveled, at least professionally, in increasingly white circles was not so much a matter of choice as one of reality: There were few others of his complexion who were in his star position. His field of choice, even on the stage, was now narrowed considerably, due in part to the Depression. In 1931 two thirds of Manhattan's theaters were shut down, putting hundreds of writers, directors, set designers, prop and lighting men, and orchestra members out of work. In the winter of 1931, *Variety* reported that there were twenty-five thousand unemployed theatrical people in all areas of the profession (three thousand of these were black, this figure representing nearly all the blacks in the profession at that time).

The Depression, however, was not Bill's main problem. His real problem, by 1931–1932, was that he was too big a star to return to the vaudeville circuits. A per-

former of his caliber could play only at the Palace and
similarly illustrious venues, which were few and far between. During 1930 and 1931, he made his first forays
into filmdom, which seemed the logical next step after
Broadway. Opportunities in films for blacks, however,
were limited.

Bill's first film had been released in the summer of
1930. Titled *Dixiana,* it was an RKO release and thus
very much in the family. In RKO's first decade of existence, its pictures had experienced severe financial diffi-
culties and contained little of substance. *Dixiana,*
starring Bebe Daniels and featuring the comedians
Wheeler and Woolsey, was an obvious imitation of the
highly popular *Rio Rita.* The cast was predominantly
white; Bill did a "specialty number," a role that was familiar to black entertainers in the early days of film—
and in later days as well. No all-black film had ever been
produced by a major white studio, and black parts in
the otherwise white films fell into two general catego-
ries: In dramas, blacks played servants or jungle natives;
in musicals, they did specialty acts. Since black entertainers might be viewed as real people, their specialty
numbers were always easily excised by southern censors,
who would not allow black screen images other than
servants or jungle natives. Richard Watts, Jr., of the
New York Herald Tribune wrote, "The most interesting
episode of the film is contributed by the incomparable
Bill Robinson, in his equally incomparable staircase
dance." But southern reviewers never even saw that segment of the film. (While *Dixiana* made little difference
in RKO's fortunes, there were high times ahead for the
company. In 1931 RKO produced *Cimarron,* from the

novel by Edna Ferber, and in 1933 it hit the jackpot with *King Kong*.)

In 1933, Bill appeared in the first all-black film ever made. *Harlem Is Heaven,* a Herald Pictures, Inc., release (the company was organized by two white brothers, Jack and Dave Goldberg), featured Anise Boyer, Jimmy Baskette, Henri Wessel, and Eubie Blake's orchestra. Actually released to theaters in 1932, the film played in northern black theaters and southern black churches. It did not advance Bill's film career to any appreciable extent.

Cut off from the regular vaudeville circuits by his fame, from Broadway by the demise of the popularity of black musical revues, "vernacular dancing," and the Depression, and from work in major films by racism in both Hollywood and the South, Bill Robinson and Marty Forkins found few avenues available to them. One of the few was a vaudeville musical revue, a road show that could travel from theater to theater around the country. There was precedent for such a black traveling revue—Sissieretta Jones had been highly successful with her *Black Patti Troubadours* show around the turn of the century—so Bill and Forkins decided to try one of their own.

It was easy to gather personnel. The singers and dancers from *Blackbirds, Brown Buddies,* and other black Broadway revues weren't exactly in demand elsewhere. Ada Brown, called the "Sophie Tucker of the Colored Race," had starred with Bill in *Brown Buddies* and was happy to work with him again. Born Ada Scott in Junction City, Kansas, she learned to play the piano for her father, a circuit-riding preacher, and soon graduated to movie-house pits. She added singing to her repertoire and later went to Chicago to entertain in cabarets. She had done vaudeville and recorded "mammy songs" before reaching the Broadway stage. Having left school at the age of fourteen to go on the road, Ada was keenly aware of her lack of education and was a voracious reader. Her most prized possession was a small leather-bound volume of essays by Thackeray, Scott, Lamb, Tennyson, and Lincoln, and it traveled with her wherever she went. The chorus girls and boys and the specialty dancers changed with the season. In the cast of an early edition of the revue were the Brown Buddies Chorus, the Russell Wooding Choir, Shorty and Gay (lindy hoppers), Swan and Lee (intricate team dancers), Pearl Baine, Jimmy Baskette, and Harry Swanagan.

Robinson and Forkins chose as their model for the revue a show with which white singer Kate Smith was currently touring. The Robinson revue, called *Hot from Harlem*, opened on February 13, 1932, at the premier vaudeville showcase, the Palace, and shared a bill with "Red Hot Mama" Sophie Tucker, Smith and Dale, Jack Whiting, "The Four Golden Blondes," and Bernice and Emily. According to the reviewer for *The New York Times*, "From the intermission to the end, the show belongs to Mr. Robinson, of the restive feet and his company of twenty-five from up Lenox Avenue way. When the old master himself is not on the stage, observing with detachment the behavior of his tapping toes, his friends are exceedingly busy. A chorus of six of his feminine students dance with what can accurately be called abandon. A scarlet-coated young man skips rope to music, and a girl, who can be identified as having a voice like a copper gong, sings one called 'Tragedy, Tragedy.' John Mason, of 'Brown Buddies' memories, conducts a revival meeting, and when they have all explored the deep South pretty fully Mr. Robinson comes back for some more of his insinuating stepping."[1]

While such reviews pleased him, Bill was his own company's strongest critic, and he demanded perfection. He would detain the chorus girls until late at night to ensure that their performance would be right for the following day. He was unsympathetic to their pleas of exhaustion, for he required only four hours of sleep a night.

One night Bill, who was a great fan of Smith and Dale, was in their dressing room watching them rehearse some new steps while awaiting their turn to go on. Suddenly, Fannie burst into the dressing room screaming, "The theater's on fire! Get out, get out!" The men thought she was just kidding. Meanwhile, Bill went over to the wings to watch Sophie Tucker, who was finishing her act just before intermission. He did not notice when a tongue of flame appeared near the electrician's switchboard at stage left. It ran up the traveling curtain and showered sparks over the stage and the first few rows of the orchestra. Tucker, a true professional, kept right on singing until a property boy pulled her off the stage and the asbestos curtain was rung down. Then the ushers went into action, quickly but calmly escorting the audience to the exits. Meanwhile, backstage, the performers were hustled outside, most of them in states of undress. At first, Bill was not among them. Overcome by smoke, he had passed out in the wings, but later he revived and eventually joined his fellow troupers outside.

His was the only "injury." He also suffered the most

property damage. Though firemen quickly put out the blaze, they were unable to save most of his revue's scenery. His suits were permeated with smoke, and his shoes thoroughly soaked by water from the firemen's hoses. Still, he made it to a scheduled appearance at a benefit for disabled veterans. And the Palace did not miss a single show.

Reporting on the fire, the newspapers could not resist running headlines like RED-HOT MAMA BURNS UP PALACE THEATRE.[2]

Bill replaced his suits and shoes and got more scenery for his revue, and went on as before, playing major theaters on the RKO-Orpheum Circuit. In June they were in Los Angeles; in August in New York again, at the Palace. In January 1933 they were at Loews State in New York; in August at the Academy Theater in New York. During that run Bill was in the middle of a dance onstage when a rat walked down the extreme left aisle and climbed the steps to the stage. The audience was unaware of the visitor, which Bill later described as "smaller than a cat, but bigger than a kitten," and he hoped that it would just go along backstage. He kept dancing, but slowed his steps so as not to alarm the creature. Unfortunately, some people in the front rows saw the rat. They began to squirm, a woman let out a low scream. Realizing that soon the whole audience would be thrown into a panic, Bill darted into the wings and in an instant reemerged with a block of wood used to support scenery. Waving the piece of wood reassuringly at the audience, he danced slowly toward the rat, using a shuffling, sliding step. Over on the left side of the stage, the rat, intrigued, sat up like a squirrel and watched the dancer. As he reached center stage, Bill let fly the block of wood, which hit the rat squarely in the chest. Bill ran over, picked up the piece of wood, and crowned the rodent. The orchestra responded with a long drumroll and an exultant clash of cymbals. Bill was a publicity hound, but there were times when publicity came to him unbidden. The papers had a field day with the story.

During the second year of the run, the name of the revue was changed from *Hot from Harlem* to *Goin' to Town*. The change was the result of the demise of Harlem as a playground, the inevitable result of the deepening Depression and the repeal of Prohibition. Harlem, home of "last-hired, first-fired" blacks, showed the effects of the Depression in stark relief by the middle of 1932. Even the most insensitive revelers at exclusive clubs like Connie's Inn and the Cotton Club could not ignore the long lines outside hastily organized soup kitchens and the look of despair on the faces of Harlemites. More compelling was the air of violence in the streets as fat-cat mobsters faced the fact that their primary source of revenue had ceased to exist. Mob violence had increased, and innocent bystanders had been killed by stray bullets. While the repeal of the Volstead Act was not officially ratified by the required number of states until December 1933, the proposed constitutional amendment to repeal Prohibition was submitted to the states in January 1933 and confirmation was so certain that beer was legalized the following month. Connie's Inn, a Harlem institution, moved downtown that year. The mob-run clubs that remained became increasingly jittery business propositions, for their primary source of income—illegal liquor—was about to become legal again, and their primary attraction—forbidden black fruit—had begun to pale. The Cotton Club, the premier exclusive establishment, would hold on until 1936, but in 1933 even its presence in Harlem was not enough to dissuade Robinson and Forkins from getting rid of the Harlem association in the name of their revue. They did not, however, change its flavor.

PROGRAM

BILL ROBINSON
The Dancing Master
In
"GOIN' TO TOWN"

1.	A Dixie Rhapsody	
2.	There Goes My Headache	Pearl Baine
3.	Voodoo	Swan & Lee and Jimmy Baskette
4.	Happy As The Day Is Long	Bill Robinson, Pearl Baine, and Girls
5.	Specialty	Ada Brown
6.	Breaking Out	Swan & Lee & Co.
7.	Stormy Weather	Ada Brown, Jimmy Baskette, Russell Wooding Choir and Girls
8.	Still Goin' To Town	Bill Robinson
9.	Black Eyed Susan Brown	Swan & Lee and Entire Co., Featuring Shorty & Gay

The shows combined a bit of the exotic, some comedy, a bit of the old plantation, lots of dancing, and at least one currently popular number. On this program that number was "Stormy Weather," which had been the hit song of the spring 1933 Cotton Club revue. Written by Harold Arlen and Ted Koehler, and sung by Ethel Waters at the club, the song was the talk of New York. Its impact was so great, in fact, that it had obscured the rest of that revue, which forever after was called the "Stormy Weather Show." Waters's career took off, and she always credited the song as the turning point for her.

Bill Robinson's *Goin' to Town* revue, featuring "Stormy Weather," hit the vaudeville circuits with great fanfare. The exploitation tips supplied by Forkins's office included promises that Bill would give free dance lessons to "local kiddies," run backward against any forward-running challengers, and feature contests for local tap dancers as part of the show. Here was another suggestion:

THE MECHANICAL DANCING SAMBO is still a standard mechanical toy. You know the colored fellow who steps when he is wound up. Get one of your stores to make a window display of these mechanical toys with a sign in the window reading in effect "THESE FELLOWS CAN DANCE, BUT YOU OUGHT TO SEE BILL ROBINSON AT THE RKO THEATRE."[3]

In 1933, Bill returned to Richmond, Virginia, which he visited as often as he could. He also frequently wired money back to his hometown for charities and worthy causes. He looked up his childhood friend, Lemmeul Eggleston, and Eggie invited him to dinner. "We just talked about dancing and things like that and told a whole lot of jokes. We stayed up one night to half past two o'clock, to see who could tell the best jokes or how many. I think I beat Bill some way or another," Eggleston later recalled. During his visit Bill noticed that there were no traffic lights at the intersection of Leigh and Adams streets. Actually, there were no traffic lights north of Broad Street, where the black section of town began, but this particular intersection was heavily trafficked, and Bill decided that it was dangerous for the schoolchildren. On his return to New York, he sent $1,240.70 to Richmond to purchase four traffic lights for that intersection.[4] Vaudeville performer Leigh Whipper recalled that Bill's brother, Percy, was also "instrumental in putting up the street light in Richmond."

The city of Richmond invited Bill to dedicate the traffic lights when they were installed, put a bronze tablet on one of them stating that he'd given them "for love of the city which gave him birth," and gave him a gold key that would unlock the police signal control box containing the switch for the lights. Henceforth, he always carried the key in his upper left vest pocket.

What endeared Bill to many people was his obviously genuine delight in these tokens of appreciation. In the fall of 1934, St. Clair McKelway of *The New Yorker* did a two-part profile on Bill, in the course of which his pride in such things was described in inimitable *New Yorker* style:

"He is a Special Deputy Sheriff of New York County

and carries the gold badge in a diamond-studded case which fits his upper right vest pocket. Twice threatened by kidnappers, he was presented with a gold-inlaid, pearl-handled, thirty-two-calibre revolver some years ago by the police of the Harlem station, and he always carries it in an alligator-skin holster on his right hip. He is one of the two honorary members of the Grand Street Boys' Association; the other is Patrick Cardinal Hayes. He is a Special Inspector of Motor Vehicles for the State of New York, and wears the gold badge, No. X-298, under the lapel of his coat. In his left pocket, he carries a morocco-leather case containing his pistol permit, an American Legion membership card, his credentials as an Admiral in the Great Navy of the State of Nebraska (a celebrity-catching organization), and documents establishing his personal friendship with the police chiefs of all the larger American cities, with former Governor Pollard of Virginia, and with Edward P. Mulrooney [Chief Inspector, N.Y.]. He possesses a scroll identifying him as the honorary mascot of the New York Giants, but that is too cumbersome to carry. . . ."[5]

In 1933 he was named "Mayor of Harlem," and joined the roster of "locality mayors," an unofficial title conferred on men of importance in various areas of the city. Most of the locality mayors received their appointments as political favors and were not well known in their communities. Bill Robinson had been Mayor of Harlem, in effect, for years. Bill took his honorary position seriously. One of his most popular official acts was saving Harlem's famous Tree of Hope. The old elm, which stood at Seventh Avenue and 131st Street, over the years had become known among Harlem show people as a sort of living Aladdin's lamp, for it was believed that if people rubbed its bark and made a wish, the wish would come true. At one time or another, almost every actor, singer, or musician in Harlem had taken up vigil under the Tree of Hope. Unfortunately, the tree was in poor health. In 1934 plans to widen Seventh Avenue included cutting down the tree, and the community was desperate to save it, to no avail. Bill managed to preserve the stump and stored it temporarily at the stage entrance to the Lafayette Theater. Then he appealed to Mayor Fiorello H. La Guardia for help. After Seventh Avenue was widened, in a special ceremony, a new tree was planted. Mounted next to it was the stump of the old tree, together with a plaque that read "The Original Tree of Hope Beloved by the Citizens of Harlem. You Asked for a Tree of Hope, So Here 'Tis and Best Wishes—Bill Robinson."[6]

By one count, Bill performed at over three thousand benefits in the course of his career.[7] Ed Sullivan recalled that he "used to be ashamed to call him up so often for benefit shows. I'd call up Marty Forkins and say, 'Marty, I'm ashamed to keep calling this way, but there is a benefit show coming up and I'm one of the sponsors and I'll be emceeing it.' So Marty would say, 'Wait till I look at his schedule, Ed.' He'd say, 'Yes, he's going to be there then. He'll be there for eight days, so just put him down. He'll be there.'"

Bill helped hundreds of unorganized charities and individuals. As the Depression cast its lengthening shadow over Harlem, the 132nd Precinct station began to keep a list of well-to-do people to be contacted when the officers found a particularly destitute family. Bill's name was at the top of the list, for he never failed to respond with a bag of groceries or money to pay for a funeral or for the care of a sick child. The biggest free kitchen in Harlem was run by the Cotton Club. Bill often showed up to hand out groceries. In the winter of 1933–1934, it occurred to him that people would enjoy receiving packages of food that he had wrapped personally. Unfortunately, he soon had to stop the practice, for some people protested that they were being slighted when they were handed food packages *not* wrapped by Bill.[8] At home, Bill had to have a "look-see" slot installed in his door, an item unfamiliar to those who had never frequented the old speakeasies. His doorbell rang constantly, and neither he nor Fannie nor their maid, Carrie, could ever be sure who was on the other side of the door. His telephone rang incessantly, and the majority of callers wanted money.

To these people, Bill was unimaginably rich, and by most standards he was. He bought diamonds for Fannie by the handfuls, though she never wore more than one at a time. In the fall of 1931, he bought her a sable coat that cost $4,750. In early 1934 he bought his first automobile, a $17,500 Duesenberg limousine, license plate BR6, and hired a chauffeur to drive it. Yet, he was frequently broke. What with his love of luxury, his extreme generosity, and his undiminished penchant for gambling, Bill Robinson often hadn't a dime in his pocket. And so he habitually borrowed money.

"It was always 'Mr. Marty, take care of that, please.'" according to Rae Samuels. "That's why we had our phone unlisted. He was a rascal, very trying." But

Lillian Alpert Wolf had the Forkinses' telephone number, and Bill would appeal to her. "He was playing at the Loews State, and one morning he called me at the office. 'Buddy (he always called me that after *Brown Buddies*), I'm in trouble. Come right down.' Well, I closed the office and went right down. Mr. Forkins didn't come in until about noon and it was about ten-thirty A.M. Bill was walking up and down in his dressing room. 'Buddy, call Miss Samuels. I need seven hundred fifty dollars right away.' I told him I wouldn't call Mrs. Forkins at that hour; they were probably asleep. They kept terrible hours and probably hadn't even gotten to bed until four or five that morning. So Bo said, 'Here, take my jewelry.' He took off fifteen thousand dollars' worth of jewelry and told me to go to Nat Lewis or to I. Miller and give them the jewelry. 'They'll know it's mine,' he said. 'They'll give you the money for me.'

"To make a long story short, I got the money from Schimill after Miller and Lewis turned me down. When I got back, Bo said it wasn't enough money. I was scared stiff. He said, "Oh, that Little Bo. She's a bad girl today. She won't give me any money.' I wanted to know if he needed it for gambling, but he said no, he needed it for some club. They needed money for apparel. He was really mad. So I told him to go down to the box office and get an advance and, sure enough, he did. He got another two hundred fifty dollars for walking-around or ice-cream money. I think he'd already gotten some from them before. Little Bo held onto the money, and I don't blame her.

"Another day, Bo came to me and borrowed five hundred dollars. He even borrowed five hundred dollars from my brother one day. I had to write to Mr. Forkins when they were on the road to get my brother's money back for him. Bill wired back the money, saying, 'Here 'tis.' He always paid you."

The one thing money could not buy for Bill Robinson was protection from the indignities of racism. Nor could he count on his considerable fame to protect him everywhere he went. What was perhaps hardest for him to deal with was the awareness that an incident could occur at any moment, and every certificate and key and license he made sure to carry on his person made no difference to another person who didn't like the color of his skin and acted on that prejudice. Though he was constantly on the lookout for trouble, he could not be eternally vigilant, and when he was unpleasantly surprised, his first reaction was unbridled fury.

"This is a true story," confided U. S. Thompson in 1975. "He and his wife were on a train once, going from Chicago to St. Louis, and when it was time to eat they went into the dining car. [Ordinarily, Bill and Fannie waited until all the other diners had left, but this particular morning they knew that the dining car was being dropped off early. There was one white man still eating and, when asked, he said he did not mind if they sat down and ate.]⁹ Just as his wife was going to sit down, the steward said, 'This table is reserved,' and pulled the chair out from under her. She sat right down on the floor. Bill went wild. I think he knocked the man down, and he pulled out his pistol. The conductor on the train didn't know who Bill Robinson was, so he telegraphed ahead to the next stop, Decatur, that there was a bad man with a pistol in the dining car. Now, Bill had played Decatur just a couple of weeks before, and they all knew and loved him, but he wasn't taking any chances. He slipped the gun to the cook in the kitchen.

"When the train pulled into Decatur, the sheriff got on, and when he saw who they were talking about he said, 'Why, he's Bill Robinson. Everybody knows Bill Robinson.' Then he said, 'Bill, do you have a gun?' Bill said, 'No, I don't have no gun!' The sheriff said to the conductor, 'Well, what can I do about this? He don't have no gun. Everybody knows Bill. He ain't gonna bother nobody.' He didn't arrest him or even take him off the train.

"When the train got to St. Louis, Bill went to the railroad manager and made a complaint against the steward. They said they would fire the fellow. But Bill didn't want the man to lose his job. So he said, 'I'm playing at the Orpheum Theater. If he wants to come down and apologize to me, I won't force this charge against him.' So, the fellow went down and apologized to save his job and a lot of trouble. I know that as a fact."

In February 1934 the New York Society of Teachers of Dancing held an entertainment and ball at the Waldorf-Astoria for the benefit of unemployed dancers. Bill was invited to participate and agreed to take part in the gala. As a rule, his hosts at such events were careful to inform the hotel or apartment-house staff that Bill was expected. But apparently no one at the Society of Teachers of Dancing convention had been delegated to take care of that task. Thus, when Bill arrived with his dancing shoes, the elevator man would not let him on.

In a rare public display of anger at such discrimination, Bill socked the man in the face, saying, "I'm Bill Robinson and I came here to teach all your white teachers to dance." Some time later, he took a different tack. Rae Samuels was invited to perform at a luncheon at the Uplifters Club in Los Angeles, which was headed by Hal Roach. Rae invited Bill to appear, too, and was puzzled when he did not show up, for he was ordinarily very punctual and always appeared as promised. The luncheon was almost over when he was discovered downstairs in the kitchen. He had refused to go up to the luncheon in the "white" elevator.

Not long after that, and some four months after the incident at the Waldorf-Astoria, Bill attended a performance of *Stevedore,* a play in the Group Theater mold that was popular at the time. Written by Paul Peters and George Sklar, it told the story of a determined black dock worker who stands up to the white bosses and unites black and white workers behind him. It was a powerful play and contained a climactic scene in which the blacks barricade themselves behind barrels and mattresses and engage in brick-throwing and shooting with a group of white thugs. The cast at the Civic Repertory Theater in New York City got very emotionally involved in the scene and were in the habit of ad-libbing about two hundred more expletives than the script contained, but they were unprepared for the involvement of the audience. One Tuesday matinee in late June, Bill was at the theater and obviously became caught up in the drama. At the point in the third-act battle scene when the blacks were losing ground, he leaped out of his seat, took the stage steps three at a time, got behind the barricades, and started hurling bricks with the rest of them. The actors, aghast, stopped in mid-hurl; and Bill, suddenly aware of where he was, left the stage and returned to his seat. When the play was over, he was called back to the stage. He explained that he had "no conscious notion" of what had happened. He did not apologize.[10]

Two others remembered how Bill used to get caught up in the drama of racial indignity. Olivette Miller-Briggs, wife of Bunny Briggs (a famous dancer and Bill's former dancing protégé), and Patrick Forkins, son of Marty and Rae, recalled how Bill handled one of these incidents in Sioux Falls, South Dakota. There was a life-threatening blizzard under way when Olivette Miller and her troupe arrived in town to play a concert. Their lodgings, which had been prearranged, were not honored when the manager saw the complexions of the troupe. The manager insisted they leave and return to the blizzard to find other living quarters, although the manager knew there were none. Olivette knew that Bill was playing at a theater in town, so she went to him for assistance. Bo was angry and determined to help. He called the president of the Pennsylvania Railroad and made arrangements to staff, heat, and fully service the dining and drawing-room cars. Pat Forkins recalled in 1987, "Bo was so furious at how those people could be so inconsiderate to other human beings." Olivette remembered, also in 1987, that Bo said, "You can't do this to these people." She told how "Bill pulled out his gun and was ready to shoot anyone who would deny us help."

The poverty and suffering of black people weighed

heavily on Bill's mind at that time. He saw it every day in Harlem. He heard about it from unemployed black performers at the clubs he frequented. He tried to do his part to alleviate the suffering, but there was only so much that a single individual could do, no matter how wealthy he was. He placed great hope in President Franklin D. Roosevelt's New Deal and, when he had the opportunity to meet the president, took the occasion to put in a word for his people.

"Roosevelt was crazy about him," according to Rae Samuels, "and Bill was playing at some big newspaper thing that was being held in Washington. They brought Roosevelt in there, in the chair. [Bob] Hope and everybody else was there, and they were going up to Roosevelt and shaking hands. Roosevelt said, 'Where's Bill? Go get Bill. I want to see him.' So Bill came down and bowed to the president, saying, 'Yes sir, yes sir, Mr. President. How are you today?' He knew how to put it on for him. Then he said, 'By the way, Mr. President, I see you got some kind of New Deal going. Just remember, Mr. President, when you shuffle those cards, just don't overlook those spades.' That's the truth. He really did say that." Rae Samuels believed that it was Bill's lack of education that caused him to be so open and "regular" with the rich and powerful: "If he had been educated, I don't think he'd have been as clever as he was; he would have been hesitant about things he did." But it was not simply a question of education. Bill knew who he was, and knew that in spite of the barriers put in his way that he could not remove, no man was better than he was.

*   *   *

Between 1930 and 1931, when he appeared in RKO's *Dixiana* and Herald Pictures' *Harlem Is Heaven,* and 1935, Bill had only one opportunity to be in a film. In the spring of 1934, he made a Vitaphone short called *Black Orchids,* produced in Brooklyn as part of a series of shorts called "Broadway Brevities." However, Marty Forkins had been working hard to promote Bill in Hollywood, along with Will Rogers and other clients, so it came as no surprise when Bill returned to Hollywood in 1934 at the invitation of Twentieth Century-Fox.

The story goes that while Bill was playing the Paramount in New York (at three thousand dollars a week), Marty Forkins got in touch with Winnie Sheehan, a producer with Fox. Over lunch, Forkins pressed Sheehan to put Bill in a picture. "He's a dancer," said Sheehan. "He can't act." "He can act," said Forkins, "or we don't get a dollar." Sheehan didn't make any commitments then, but a few days later he was back in touch with Forkins. "What do you want for your man?" he wanted to know. "For how long?" Forkins asked. "Four weeks." "Twelve thousand dollars and transportation," said Forkins. Sheehan agreed and said that he hoped that in Bill Robinson he had found the right black star to appear with Shirley Temple, whom the studio wanted to present in a more humanized role than in her earlier films.[11]

Little Shirley Temple, born April 23, 1928, had burst onto the silver screen in 1934, appearing or starring in no fewer than five movies: *Stand Up and Cheer, Little Miss Marker, Baby Take a Bow, Now and Forever,* and *Bright Eyes.* According to film historian Donald Bogle, she was a true Depression heroine who was always as much a victim of hard times as anyone else. The circumstances of her victimization usually brought her into association with down-and-out or low-life types, with whom she enjoyed a sense of community, and from the beginning this group included blacks. Stepin Fetchit and Willie Best were both featured in *Stand Up and Cheer,* playing shuffling, inarticulate servant types, and this pattern was to be repeated so often that there was an inside Hollywood joke that a Temple picture was incomplete without at least one darky.[12] Both Stepin Fetchit and Willie Best would play similar roles in later Temple films. But by late 1934–early 1935, a barely perceptible trend toward more sympathetic and less racist portrayals of blacks had begun in Hollywood, and when the task of casting Temple's next film, *The Little Colonel,* presented itself, the people at Fox felt they had to search beyond the small colony of black actors in Hollywood. They needed an actor who knew his place but had a little dignity. Bill Robinson seemed to fit the part. In mid-November 1934 it was announced that he would co-star with Shirley Temple in her next movie.

When Lena Horne arrived in Hollywood from New York eight years later, she was greeted with antipathy by the black actors there; they considered her an eastern usurper. Bill Robinson experienced no similarly cold reception. He had an advantage over Lena in that during his years on the vaudeville circuits, he'd made many friends in Hollywood and environs. If there was resentment against Bill Robinson among blacks in the film colony, it was not publicly aired.

The plot of *The Little Colonel* was standard if not

downright tired. A little child succeeds in bringing to-gether her curmudgeon grandfather and her mother, who has been disowned for marrying an unacceptable man. The setting is the postbellum South, and the bone of contention is that the husband is a Yankee. Bill was cast in the role of Shirley's favorite old family retainer, who danced for her whenever she asked and who com-forted her while she tried to bring peace to the family. The grand staircase of the mansion was an ideal setting for Bill's stair dance, and as soon as Bill was signed to do the picture, the stair dance was written into the script.

The staircase of a Colonial mansion was vastly dif-ferent from Bill's custom-made stage stairs, and he had to do a considerable amount of practicing to make the transition to the movie set's stairs. While he worked to rearrange his steps, someone on the set had the bright idea to have little Shirley join him at the end of the dance. Everyone else liked the idea, including Bill, but he realized it was up to him to make it work. He would have to teach the child the steps, and the film's shooting schedule did not give him much time.

After thirty-plus years of stair dancing, Bill found himself having to look at that dance in an entirely dif-ferent way. He had to find a simple key, one that a seven-year-old could understand. He realized that he could not teach her the basics of tap in a few days, but he discovered that he could get the necessary extra-tap-per-step sound from her feet by teaching her to kick the face of the step with her toe. It took him three days to make her understand why she had to keep her steps close and precise, and why she must tap the riser instead of trying to get the same effect on the step itself. Once she had mastered it, she worked with all the concentration she could muster, and in two more days she was ready. The highlight of the film was Bill's stair dance, with Shirley joining in at the end.

With his success in *The Little Colonel,* Bill's Hollywood career was launched. But there were few dramatic roles for blacks, and so Bill free-lanced. He did a specialty number in *Hooray for Love* (RKO, 1935), starring Ann Sothern and Gene Raymond; he was formally crowned Mayor of Harlem in this film. He did another specialty number in *The Big Broadcast of 1937* (Paramount, 1935), starring Jack Oakie and, from the old vaudeville days, George Burns and Gracie Allen. He had a more substantial role as Will Rogers's servant in *In Old Kentucky* (Fox, 1935), no doubt because Rogers was also a client of Marty Forkins's, and because Rogers liked Bill very much. In the role, Bill teaches his employer to dance, and though it was nominally a story about horse racing, there was an important subplot regarding the history of tap. Bill introduced a completely new routine, setting a table as he tapped out a dance, using the sounds of the dishes and flatware placed on the table as a rhythmic accompaniment. In the end, he helps Rogers escape from jail, for Rogers blacks up and imitates Robinson's dancing. (One wonders if the creators of the Mel Brooks–Richard Pryor film *Stir Crazy* were influenced by this film.) This was the last film Will Rogers made, since he died in a plane crash in August 1935. Bill's fear of flying may have been due to the accident, and he once said that Rogers's death was the saddest moment of his life. After that, Bill contracted with

MGM to do *The Great Ziegfeld*, in which he was to play the legendary Bert Williams. The picture was held up in production, and eventually Bill's part was written out, but by the terms of the contract of purchase, MGM still had to pay Bill twenty-five thousand dollars. Marty Forkins was getting very good at playing the game of Hollywood high finance.[13]

However, as good as Marty was at this, he knew he could push his client only so far on-screen. Racism, though not often discussed on or off the set, played a major role in how far Bill's screen career could advance.

When the young Eleanor Powell arrived in Hollywood to begin her dancing career, she was attracted to Bill as a teacher and friend. He took her under his dancing wing, just as he had loved to help Florence Mills (he called her "Kid Florence"), Fred Astaire, little Shirley Temple, and countless others. It hurt Eleanor Powell when Bo was hurt by racism, and she harbored those emotions for decades. Like every other good studio performer, she was taught not to discuss Hollywood's family problems in the press. However, shortly before she died, in an interview by David Galligan, Eleanor Powell released her hurt emotions the moment Bill Robinson's name was mentioned. She said, "Blacks—though they were called *colored people* in my time, were not allowed to be on stage with a white person unless they were in a subservient position—like a janitor or a maid or a washlady or something like that."

Bill Robinson, though he was known on Broadway for his top hat and tails image, was constantly being cast in a butler-type role. But offstage, Bill took every opportunity he could to wear his tails proudly. Eleanor Powell was invited by Bill to work up a dance routine they could perform together at private high society parties at a salary of one hundred dollars each. When Eleanor Powell was told that only she was allowed up the front elevator and Bill would have to use the freight elevator, she responded, "In that case, I will ride with Mr. Robinson in the freight elevator."

On one occasion, after a performance, the two were offered something to drink. Eleanor Powell told the butler she would enjoy a glass of water, but only if Bill could have one also. The butler obliged and both were served. When they finished, Bill broke his glass, then offered to pay for it. According to Eleanor Powell, "The reason he did, he told me, was because he knew no one was going to drink out of that glass after him. He realized that. Most of the time it was a crystal glass, too, and they'd take his money."[14]

Bill's hardest role in Hollywood was not on the set, but off. His temper, which usually didn't take much to evoke, had to be restrained. That was not easy. He was living under the pressure of knowing that if Bojangles ever tarnished his image as America's favorite colored performer, the consequences could trickle down to every other black person from Harlem to Hollywood. He may have thought of quitting and shedding his subservient Hollywood rags for his top hat and tails. But he couldn't quit. The money was good, but he could have gotten along without the Hollywood income. He couldn't quit because he knew he was breaking down doors. His rule for learning how to dance on stairs was the same rule he employed for living: small steps.

*   *   *

Bill and Fannie returned to New York for the summer of 1935, but they were quite certain that Bill would be called back to the West Coast soon. Fannie was already looking for a house in Los Angeles. Sure enough, in early September, Marty Forkins announced a new, four-picture deal for Bill with Twentieth Century-Fox. *The Little Colonel* had done so well at the box office that a similar picture starring Shirley Temple and Bill, *The Littlest Rebel,* was already in the works.

This time the setting was the South during the Civil War. In the story, little Shirley's mother dies, and if that isn't enough for the child to bear, the Yankees invade her mansion home during her birthday party, capturing her father and taking him prisoner. The old family retainer, Uncle Billy, becomes Shirley's guardian, and together they make their way to Washington, D.C., financing their trip by dancing, so they can ask President Lincoln to pardon Shirley's father.

In black film history, this was a big step forward, for Bill, as Shirley's guardian, was the first black ever to be made responsible for a white life. Donald Bogle has called Bill Robinson and Shirley Temple "the perfect interracial love match," and Bill's role, that of the quintessential Tom. Bill's acting, according to Bogle, was superficial and unvaried, but his dancing had the same effect on film audiences as it did on live audiences—it was exciting and real. He was successful because he provided a reassuring framework for the film—with Uncle Billy around, little Shirley would be all right. And, Bogle allows, Uncle Billy, articulate and reliable, was a cut above the characters that actors like Stepin Fetchit and Willie Best had traditionally played.

What Bogle failed to recognize, or chose not to deal with in *Toms, Coons, Mulattoes, Mammies and Bucks,* his urbane and witty history of blacks in films, was the genuine affection that developed between Shirley Temple and Bill Robinson. Without it, none of the four movies in which they appeared together would have been as successful. In current Hollywood terms, their effect on each other would be called chemistry, but actually it was just simple caring. While Shirley was treated kindly by most of the adults she encountered in Hollywood, she had a child's ability to see through artifice. Uncle Billy was real. Bill's papers include a telegram, dated July 29, 1936, she sent him at the Palace Theater in Chicago:

DEAR UNCLE BILLY I HOPE YOU HAVE A NICE TIME PLAYING AT THE PALACE THIS WEEK. MOTHER AND DAD AND I ARE LEAVING ON VACATION AND WILL MISS YOU LOTS OF LUCK AND LOVE SHIRLEY TEMPLE [15]

For his part, Bill genuinely loved Shirley—by one account he had seventeen pictures of her in his New York apartment in 1936—and treated her like a real person, as he did most children.

The two kept in touch long after they stopped working together. "He was a good friend," Shirley said to Hans J. Massaquoi in an interview in *Ebony* in March 1976. "When I got married the first time [to film actor John Agar], he told my ex-husband, 'If you ever hurt this girl, I'm gonna cut you.'" And in *The Shirley Temple Story* (1984) Lester and Irene David report that when Shirley was seriously ill with complications after the birth of her first child, in her delirium she saw the face of the dead Robinson:

> "Come on up, Shirley," the dancer seemed to be saying, "it's just wonderful up here. Come on up and we'll have a real good time." Shirley called for the nurse and begged not to be left alone.

In 1974, Rae Samuels and Lillian Alpert Wolf spoke of Bill and Shirley's relationship:

SAMUELS: Did Bill ever tell you, Lillian, that they were called "One-Shot Temple and Robinson"? They never had to do it twice. One day, she kind of missed. They had to start the dialogue before they got to the steps, and she couldn't do it. Bo stopped the rehearsal. He said, "Why don't you let that child alone? She's hungry and she's tired." He said to her, "Come on, Shirley," and they went over for a rest. She was getting a little chubby by then, and she wasn't allowed to eat ice cream. She and Bill used to love to eat ice cream together, but now he had to eat it by himself. So the kid was sitting there, and the mother was right nearby. They had about a fifteen-minute rest and Bill's quart of ice cream was brought to him. He got busy eating the ice cream and, when nobody was looking, he handed it down to her.

WOLF: He bought her a little electric automobile for the studio. She used to ride it around the lot. He adored that child.

SAMUELS: The last thing he bought her was a whole outfit for her baby—a little ermine coat and bonnet. Little
Bo picked it out. They [the furriers] made it up and sent
it to Shirley Temple. Bo told her, "I just want to live
long enough for this child to get big enough so I can
make her dance like you did."

9

The Hot Mikado

In January 1936, after recurring attacks of appendicitis, Bill entered a Hollywood hospital and had the offending organ removed. Whether or not the surfeit of ice cream had anything to do with his medical problem, he was denied ice cream for the duration of his stay. Since he had been accustomed to eating anywhere from four to eight quarts of vanilla ice cream per day, this was serious deprivation. Otherwise, fifty-seven-year-old Bill Robinson was in remarkably good health. His legs, according to his longtime podiatrist, Dr. Carter, were like those of a sixteen-year-old. His energy level was that of a man half his age. He had an amazing recuperative ability. When smoke from the Palace Theater fire briefly rendered him unconscious, he had revived by himself. While filming *The Littlest Colonel* the previous October, he and actor John Boles had fallen from a log in a studio-created stream and been trapped underwater by its branches. Bill had struck his head on the log in the fall and had to be pulled, unconscious, from the water by a sound man. But he quickly recovered from that accident. Now, the mere removal of an appendix was not about to slow him down.

That year marked his fiftieth in show business, and his schedule was as demanding as it had been twenty years earlier. He and Fannie lived a bicoastal existence now, spending several months in Hollywood. Fannie had been putting aside money to build a house, not having found one that she liked in a neighborhood where they would be allowed to live. According to U. S. Thompson, putting aside that money was no small accomplishment on Fannie's part: "When he worked with Shirley Temple, Fannie got the money in advance, collected it all before Bill could get it. Bill used to have those cardplayers come and sit there in his dressing room while he was making a picture, playing for big money, so Fannie had to be smart to get that money before Bill got it. She catched him in a good humor, I guess."

They returned to New York primarily for "vacations," which for Bill usually meant a round of benefits and baseball games. He always tried to be in New York as much as possible during baseball season, for he was still a rabid Yankees fan. "He loved DiMaggio," Rae Samuels recalled in 1974. "He gave DiMaggio a gorgeous gold watch that he wears to this day. Ed Barrel, who was president of the Yankee ball club, was crazy about Bill and whenever they had those big tadoos they'd have Bill down there to entertain them. He would tell them stories he would never tell on the stage. One thing about Bill Robinson, he never did an unclean thing on the stage, never, he thought that was terrible. But what he did when he was with those men in the ball club . . . They told me they had a governor's club and there was a big fat man who they thought was going to die because he was laughing so hard. He pleaded with Bo to let him alone. They had to take him out."

In the fall of 1936, Bill got the opportunity to attend Yankee games *and* work in New York for pay: He had the honor of opening the new downtown Cotton Club.

The Cotton Club had held out in Harlem as long as it could, but by the mid-1930s the capital of black America could not by any stretch of the imagination be called an exotic playground. Poverty and destitution were everywhere in evidence—by one assessment in 1934, 80 percent of Harlem's residents were on relief. The sense of hopelessness had spawned a new militancy among Harlem blacks, articulated most effectively by young Reverend Adam Clayton Powell, Jr., whose column, "Soap Box," in the *New York Amsterdam News* dealt with the seemingly limitless areas in which blacks were exploited or discriminated against. Evidence that this militancy was percolating down even to black children was the comeuppance Bill got from a black youngster in that era. According to Cab Calloway, once when he and Bill were rehearsing together at the Cotton Club, a young black boy approached Calloway for his autograph. Calloway dismissed the boy. Robinson saw the incident and introduced himself to the youngster, calling him a "cute little pickaninny." Furious, the boy shouted, "My granddaddy was a pickaninny and you was, but don't never call me that."

Black anger and resentment increased against white Harlem store owners who would not hire them and whose prices were too high for them to afford, and on March 19, 1935, this resentment exploded. Lino Rivera, a sixteen-year-old black Puerto Rican, was caught trying to steal a ten-cent knife at the Kress department store on 125th Street. As he wrestled with his captor, a crowd gathered, and the rumor quickly spread that a black youth was being beaten by a white man. When the people in the area heard an ambulance siren, some were certain that the rumor was true. Actually, Rivera had bitten his captor's finger, and the ambulance had been summoned for the older man. But that fact was lost when someone threw a brick and Harlem went wild.

The riot in 1935 was one of several reasons why Harlem lost its exotic playground image. That image was more than a decade old, no longer exciting and different. Nor was the "New Negro," who had been celebrated during the Harlem Renaissance, new any longer; as Langston Hughes put it, "We were no longer in vogue." The Cotton Club, however, had acquired a solid reputation for glamour, and its operators saw no reason why they could not transplant that glamour downtown. By the time the Harlem Cotton Club closed its doors for good on February 16, 1936, manager Herman Stark was already negotiating a lease for the top floor of a building on Broadway and Forty-eighth Street, in the heart of the theater district, and planning a smash-hit opening in the fall.[1]

As the top black star in the nation, Bill Robinson was a must-have for the show; and now that the club was downtown its traditional policy of featuring only "tan" performers did not hold. Actually, the club had relaxed its color barrier for a few performers years earlier—in 1932, Lucille Wilson, later Mrs. Louis Armstrong, had been the first dark-skinned chorus girl hired, but the darker-skinned Armstrong would not play the club until he headlined with Bill in 1939. Originally barred from performing at the club because of his dark skin, Bill may not have been deliberately snubbed in more recent years. Rather, the reason he had not appeared at the club earlier might have been due to his film schedule, and perhaps also to Marty Forkins's hefty salary requirements.

For the Cotton Club's grand opening downtown, Bill and Cab Calloway shared top billing, and 130 other performers appeared in the most lavish revue yet. Bill introduced a new dance, "The Suzi-Q." Lured by advance publicity and the more accessible downtown location, crowds flocked to the club, which officially opened on September 24; and on November 18, Stark announced that the downtown club had hosted a total of 100,000 patrons. Hoping to maintain the flow of customers through the traditionally slack December holiday period, Stark negotiated with Forkins to keep Bill on through New Year's Eve, offering as an inducement a gala celebration of Bill's fiftieth year in show business.

Dan Healy and Cab Calloway co-hosted the event, though Calloway's heart really wasn't in it. He had found it difficult to share top billing with Bo: "It was the 'I am the star routine,'" says Calloway. "'Nobody gets a bigger hand than me. It's me all the way.'" The chorus girls also grumbled, for Bill had a habit of fining them a dollar for talking during performances, a levy he was in a position to impose because during his tenure at the club he had demanded the job of stage manager and the twenty-dollar salary it paid per week.[2] Both Calloway and the girls were far too professional to balk publicly, however, and anyone who witnessed the Bill Robinson tribute could not have detected any ill feeling.

During the gala Marty Forkins recalled the old days of vaudeville. Johnson and Dean, who had introduced the cakewalk to New York at Hammerstein's Theater in 1891, re-created the event. James Barton, a white Virginian musical comedy star who had been an early idol of Bill's, did a buck-and-wing to "Annabel Lee." Ray Bolger did a hilarious imitation of Bill's stair dance. Ethel Merman sang. Jimmie Braddock and Max Schmeling, current and former heavyweight boxing champions, respectively, swapped playful punches with Bill. A host of other personalities paid tribute. Telegrams were read from Darryl Zanuck, president of Twentieth Century-Fox, Shirley Temple, Alfred Lunt, Noël Coward, Fred Astaire, and Mayor La Guardia. Then the Cotton Club Girls and Boys presented Bill and Fannie with gifts they had bought especially for them. Finally, at 3:45 A.M., Bill was called to the microphone. As he began to speak, the famous smile faded and tears welled up in his eyes. "What success I achieved in the theater," he said, "is due to the fact that I have always worked just as hard when there were ten people in the house as when there were thousands. Just as hard in Springfield, Illinois, as on Broadway."[3] By the time he finished his short speech, tears were streaming down his cheeks, and he walked off the floor with a handkerchief to his eyes. There were few dry eyes in the place, for even those who resented his high-handedness realized that he was a consummate professional and respected his longevity on the stage. The chorus girls and others whose livelihood was dependent on the success of the club also had another reason to fete Bill Robinson: In fourteen weeks he pulled $500,000 into the club, and in the ordinarily slow two weeks before Christmas, the club grossed $35,000 each week. When Christmas came, Bill spent close to $2,000 on gifts for every employee, from Cab Calloway to the janitors. He gave Fannie five brand-new $1,000 bills and bought twelve suits for himself.

By that time, Bill had won Cab Calloway over. While doing a benefit up at Sing Sing (Cotton Club performers played numerous benefits at the prison throughout the club's long existence), Bill had invited Cab to lunch and suggested that they be friends. Calloway accepted both the invitation and the suggestion.

Delays at Twentieth Century-Fox while the new movie was being prepared enabled Bill to remain at the Cotton Club until late January, when an urgent call from Hollywood sent him and Fannie hurrying to the West Coast. Dancer Bill Bailey, Pearl Bailey's brother, took over for him at the club. Bill and Fannie traveled by train, as Bill hated to fly and would not take a plane even when his presence in Hollywood was urgently requested. He once explained, "They say to me, 'What does it mattah where you are? When your day comes you're goin' anyhow.' And I say to them, 'That's all right. But I don't plan to be up there on the pilot's day.'"4 In fact, the only time Bill ever flew was when his friend Mayor La Guardia asked him to as a favor. La Guardia was facing a tough reelection campaign and decided he needed the help of his "locality mayors." The Mayor of Harlem was in Boston at the time, but at La Guardia's request he flew to New York immediately. Though he obviously lived to tell about the experience, Bill never did.

Arriving in Hollywood, Bill learned that a crucial set for the movie had burned down. All he could do was wait around for it to be rebuilt. The film, *One Mile from Heaven*, was Bill's first dramatic vehicle. He starred opposite Fredi Washington, a sophisticated and beautiful actress who had starred with Paul Robeson in *The Emperor Jones* in 1933, and who had emerged as the archetypal "tragic mulatto" as a result of her portrayal of Peola in *Imitation of Life* in 1934. In *One Mile from Heaven* she played a similar character who discovers a white foundling and wants to raise it as her own, but is foiled by Claire Trevor, a white newspaperwoman who is determined to find the child's real parents. Though Bill played Officer Joe, he still managed to dance in the film. Panned by critics as being too gangster oriented, the film died quickly at the box office. It neither helped nor hurt Bill's film career, but it played havoc with his schedule.

By the spring of 1937, Bill and Marty Forkins were talking about mounting another black revue, but *One Mile from Heaven* took considerably longer to complete than expected, and in July, when the new revue would have opened, Bill was still in Hollywood. When he completed work on the movie in late July, he and Fannie returned immediately to New York, but by then there was no time to launch the revue. So Bill agreed to star in the fall 1937 Cotton Club show, providing he received $3,500 a week *and* that half a dozen of his friends be hired as waiters at the club (his personal effort to reduce black unemployment). Herman Stark agreed to these conditions and also went through the necessary details of making special arrangements with Twentieth Century-Fox to get Bill. Then, at the last minute, the movie company changed its mind. One week before the new Cotton Club show was scheduled to open with Bill as star, he was called back to Hollywood to begin filming *Rebecca of Sunnybrook Farm* with Shirley Temple. Such last-minute changes were not at all to Bill's liking, for he had a keen sense of the importance of honoring his commitments. Besides, he had spent weeks practicing for the opening of the revue. But he was under contract to Fox and owed his soul to the company for another year.

The opening of the new Cotton Club show, which had been built largely around Bill, was delayed a couple of weeks while the Nicholas Brothers, tap dancers, rehearsed to take over his spot. The show was the most lavish at the club yet, and did not suffer measurably from Bill's absence. But as soon as he finished filming *Rebecca of Sunnybrook Farm* in mid-November, he returned to New York. There, after rehearsing for a week, he took over from the Nicholas Brothers, and soon had the rest of the cast whipped into shape. Bill Robinson was back, and that meant no fooling around backstage. The Tramp Band got a particularly pointed lesson. One evening while Bill was on, someone dropped a washtub backstage. Worse still, members of the band talked while he was doing his routine. Later, the Tramp Band went on. They pranced out onto the stage, gazookas howling, and wiggled their backsides toward the audience. The leader approached the mike: "Ladies and gennermen," he began. "De next numbah—" Just then, someone started banging a tin platter with a blunt instrument. [Came a voice:] "Peanuts—peanuts." Bill Robinson moved through the audience, grinning, banging the tin plate. The audience broke up laughing, and forgot all about the Tramp Band. Bill had made his point.[5]

To placate Herman Stark, who was still fuming over his sudden exit from the show two months earlier, Bill introduced a new dance. "The Bill Robinson Walk," for which the Cotton Club Girls wore Bill Robinson masks, was, Bill said, the only dance with which he had associated his name in fifty years of show business. While it was an entertaining routine, it was no competition for his stair dance, which was still part of every show.

Bill was unable to perform his dance only once while in the Cotton Club revue, during the second show on the night of January 7. The Strand Billiard Academy, Broadway and Forty-seventh Street, was just across the street from the club. Bill was in the habit of shooting a few rounds of pool between shows, wagering the $200 that Fannie let him have from his $3,500 weekly salary, plus whatever other money he could get from friends or pawnshops. It was about 11:30 P.M. when Bill received a call that he was due to go on soon. Bill started out, but was stopped by a panhandler. He reached into his pocket and pulled out a dollar, gave it to the panhandler, then turned to leave. As he did, he lost his footing and fell, striking his head on a billiard table. He was unconscious for about fifteen minutes. His doctor, Farrow R. Allen, happened to be at the Cotton Club at the time. Summoned to revive Bill, he strongly advised against his doing the second show. But Bill insisted on going onstage, though he realized he was not up to the balancing act the stair dance required. Afterward, all he wanted to talk about was the fact that when he had lost consciousness he had $1,160 in his pocket and that when he woke up it was still there. "It kind of gives me faith in human nature," he said.[6] That faith was further strengthened the following week when he was chosen as the recipient of the 1937 "*Mirror*–Ted Friend Gold Medal." One hundred and two people had been nominated for the award, but the list was quickly narrowed down to eight names—Eddie Davis, Rudy Vallee, Alec Templeton, Paul Draper, Jack White, Cab Calloway, Tommy Dorsey, and Bill. The award was voted him on the basis of ability, personality, and public appeal. His comment, "You know who picked me? A jury of eight white men," overlooked the presence on the panel of W. C. Handy.

It was a season of honors for Bill. In late January, he was named honorary president of the newly formed Negro Actors Guild at installation ceremonies at the Grand Street Boys' Club on West Fifty-fifth Street. The nonhonorary officers were Noble Sissle, president; Duke Ellington, vice-president; Muriel Rahn, recording secretary; Fredi Washington, executive secretary; and Cab Calloway and Elmer Carter, chairman and vice-chairman of the executive board, respectively. For Bill the creation of the N.A.G. was a personal triumph, for he had been trying for years to organize black performers. Fifteen years earlier he had tried unsuccessfully to form a Negro branch of the National Vaudeville Artists. Like Actors Equity and the Catholic and Jewish Actors Guilds, which sent representatives to the N.A.G. installation ceremony, the purpose of the new organization was to provide a unified voice for black actors as well as money to pay funeral and burial expenses for destitute actors. This fund would be composed of membership dues and monies raised through benefit performances and other fund-raising activities. Bill Robinson knew only too well the need for such a fund; he had been digging into his own pocket to pay for the burial of fellow performers for years. Leigh Whipper, another founder of the N.A.G. and a neighbor of Bill's at the Dunbar Apartments, recalled that even though Bill's title was honorary, he played an important role in the work of the guild.

Two months later Bill was again honored at the Grand Street Boys' Club, which he had helped to establish eighteen years earlier with Judge Jonah Goldstein and others. The occasion was his sixtieth-birthday party, held a month and a half early because he was scheduled to be in Hollywood on the anniversary of his actual birth date.

Out in Hollywood that spring, Bill and Fannie visited the home they were having built. A lavish "Hollywood bungalow," it had a round wing containing a playroom that would have a bar and Bill's pool table. The furniture would be brown leather, the walls paneled in bamboo topped by a jungle fresco. According to U. S.

Thompson, "That home cost twenty to thirty thousand dollars—in *those* days. The architect who built it for them was Paul Williams, the same man who built Amos 'n' Andy's home. And Fannie had an interior decorator from one of those big stores, and everything was perfect, even the toilet paper had to match." It was the first piece of real estate that Bill had ever owned, for under the arrangement at the Dunbar Apartments, he would not own his apartment outright for ten to twenty years. Bill had never been big on equity; besides the house, the only substantial assets he had were several large life-insurance policies. But he respected Fannie's desire to have a home and her often futile attempts to keep him "straight." In June, when he returned to Richmond to be honored with a Bill Robinson Day, he gave Fannie much of the credit for his success: "The first thirty-five years of living were very hard," he told the crowd that had assembled for the ceremonies, "but the last twenty-five have been very easy. Why? Because God sent me a real bodyguard, Mrs. Bill Robinson, and as long as I listen to her I can't go wrong." Fannie, who was present at the ceremony, declined to say anything, just smiled and gave a little bow.

A theater at Twenty-ninth and Q streets in Richmond was officially named for Bill that day. The mayor and other notables made speeches. It was the first time that Richmond had ever honored a black man; but that didn't seem as strange to Bill as it would have to many northern liberal whites. "If it hadn't been for Richmond, Virginia," said Bill, "there never would have been no Bill Robinson. I love Richmond and I love the South. There is one thing I have found out and that is,

Southerners are not two-faced. If they don't like you, they'll let you know it, but if they love you, they'll die for you. They won't do like some folks I know up the country, smile in your face, pat you on the shoulder, then knife you in the back first chance they get. California claims Bill Robinson, but Bill Robinson claims Richmond."[7]

Less than three months later, the September 7, 1938, issue of *Variety* carried the official announcement that Darryl F. Zanuck had dropped Bill Robinson and nine others from the contract list of Twentieth Century-Fox. The other players included Claire Trevor, who had appeared with Bill in *One Mile from Heaven,* Ethel Merman, Tom Beck, Dick Baldwin, Paul McVey, Simone Simon, Shirley Deane, Virginia Field, and Helen Westley. Henceforth, Bill would work for the company on a picture-to-picture basis, or so the Fox press release said.

Going on a picture-to-picture basis was the studio publicity department's euphemistic expression for getting fired.

Fox's problem with Bill was that the studio had little work for black actors. His one serious picture had not done well. Except for movies with Shirley Temple, most of his appearances for Fox had been in specialty spots. Shirley Temple was approaching chubby adolescence—within the year she would retire as a child star—and there was no one to replace Bill's major leading lady. For the company, it was not financially feasible to keep him under contract at a guaranteed salary per year when he was needed only for a couple of weeks' work on an occasional picture.

For his part, Bill was not sure he wanted to be associated with Fox at all anymore. He felt as if he had been knifed in the back, and he could not shake off the sense of betrayal. Two weeks after Fox's official announcement that he was being dropped from the contract roster, Bill was involved in a nasty confrontation in which he allowed his resentment to surface publicly.

On the night of September 20, 1938, Bill was driving his brand-new Duesenberg in Los Angeles; his chauffeur was on the front seat beside him. Suddenly a small roadster attempted to wedge itself between the Duesenberg and a truck. The driver of the roadster was Paul Moffat, a two-hundred-pound University of Southern California football player. Bill jumped out and demanded to know what Moffat meant by driving like that. Moffat responded with racial epithets. "He had no reason for talking to me as he did," Bill said later. "No one's going to talk to me that way." Bill pulled out his gun. Moffat went at him with his fists. Bill hit him over the head with the pistol.

By now a threatening crowd had gathered. No one recognized Bill Robinson; they saw a black man who had assaulted a white man. The police rescued him from the crowd and took him to jail. After an hour, Bill was taken into night court and released without bail. Fannie arrived to take him home. Bill's friends rallied to his aid. U. S. Thompson was in Los Angeles at the time and visited Bill several times backstage at the Pantages Theater, where Bill was appearing. During one visit, "Bill showed me a letter from a man who was the district attorney in Richmond, Virginia. It said something like 'Bill Robinson is one of our most beloved citizens, and anything you can do for Bill would be highly appreciated by the city of Richmond.'" No doubt Bill was able to present other such testimonials in his defense.

A week later, a Los Angeles County grand jury cleared him of assault charges, believing his plea that he had acted in self-defense and that "the matter was entirely due to racial prejudice on Moffat's part." Moffat countered by bringing a $15,000 personal-injury suit against Bill, for he had suffered a seven-inch-long wound to his head. He later dropped the suit.[8]

Bill cut down on his usually strenuous schedule for the next few weeks. He was angry and hurt, and deeply depressed over the fact that for all his wealth and fame and good works he was still just a nigger to any young white boy who came along. When he did return to public view, it was back East and on the closest thing to the old vaudeville stages that was still available in the late 1930s: In early December 1938 he played Nixon's Grand in Philadelphia, a house that had been dark on and off for the past five years. He appeared with Louis Armstrong on a bill at the Strand in New York in early January 1939, and at the Palace in Cleveland later that month. The reviewer for *Variety* observed of Bill's performance in Cleveland that he seemed to be "conserving energy" and hinted that the reason was age; but Bill was renewing his psychic energy. At the end of January he signed on with a Cotton Club revue scheduled to open in a month, and to do those two shows a night he had to have plenty of physical energy. Meanwhile, he was about to begin rehearsals for a new Broadway musical, which, if it didn't bomb, would necessitate his commuting from Cotton Club to Broadway theater every night.

The show was a revival of the Gilbert and Sullivan

operetta *The Mikado*—a swing version that had already been tried with some success by the WPA Federal Theater of Chicago. That version had boasted a South Sea island setting with lots of grass skirts and native drums; and it had given a young entertainment entrepreneur named Mike Todd the idea of doing a swing *Mikado* on Broadway. Todd was rich in ideas but poor in capital, and he did a dexterous juggling act to finance the production, which was called *The Hot Mikado*. Casting Bill Robinson in the role of the Mikado was practically step one. According to Rae Samuels, "Nobody had ever heard of Mike Todd yet, so when he went into Marty's office with his idea of a great colored show and boasting that he had plenty of money to put it on, Marty wanted some proof. Todd said the Florsheim Shoe Company was interested. But they wouldn't sign unless he had Bill Robinson's name—he couldn't get the money unless he had Bill." Forkins was persuaded, Bill signed for the show, and Todd proceeded with his grandiose plans for the most elaborate all-Negro show ever to appear on Broadway. He planned to spare no expense and to give Bill whatever he wanted. What Bill wanted, and got, was a specially prepared glazed covering for the stage floor at the Broadhurst Theater. "I never know where I'll finish," he explained to Todd. "I may start at the footlights and finish at the backdrop."[9]

The Hot Mikado was due to open at the Broadhurst the third week of March 1939. Before the opening, it was scheduled for out-of-town tryouts. Bill was rehearsing for both that show and the new Cotton Club Parade (since the move downtown, the club's shows had been called "parades"), whose opening had been delayed.

Somehow, he found time to play a week in Hartford, Connecticut, with Louis Armstrong beginning March 1, and to get involved in another incident, though this time there were no racial overtones. Two black men threatened and pushed their way past Oscar Matarese, the legless doorman at the State Theater, then accosted Bill. He managed to subdue them and relieved one of a pocketknife. As Bill told the story, his part in the incident was aiding the doorman, but with Bill you never knew—the two perpetrators could have been luckless gamblers out for revenge.

The curtain went up on *The Hot Mikado* on the night of March 23, 1939, but not before some last-minute hysterics. It seems Mike Todd had run out of money, and a lot of people, including the costumers, had not been paid. In desperation, Todd went to Marty Forkins, who got the money. "He got that money so fast their heads were swimming," according to Rae Samuels. "He went to the Cotton Club. There was a very rich man connected there—what was his name, Dietz? Dietz said, 'That curtain is going up. Don't bother about that with the costumes. Let her go.'"

Howard Dietz had been director of promotion at Metro-Goldwyn-Mayer since 1924, and he was lyricist, co-scenarist, and co-producer of *Hollywood Party* (MGM, 1934) as well as lyricist for *Under Your Spell* (Fox, 1936). His Broadway credits were even more impressive: Since 1924 he had been lyricist for no fewer than fifteen Broadway shows. He had also produced and directed, as well as collaborated on the lyrics and sketches for, *Flying Colors* in 1932. He knew the Broadway musical business, and he knew a surefire hit when he saw one. With his assistance, the most elaborate all-black show on Broadway opened on schedule. But Mike Todd was so broke that he had to borrow ten dollars from Marty Forkins.

Everyone who was anyone turned out for the premiere, including New York Governor Thomas E. Dewey and FBI Director J. Edgar Hoover, who came up from Washington, D.C., for the occasion (Bill was a black Hoover could understand). On hand as well were several battalions of uniformed policemen, who some in the audience assumed were there to protect Dewey and Hoover. But as they checked their nightsticks, one of the police sergeants informed the hatcheck girl, "We don't expect any trouble. We couldn't get seats so, if nobody minds, we'll just stand around. It wouldn't be fair to Robinson not to have his real pals at an opening."[10] Members of the audience who knew Bill were not surprised to see this army of uniformed fans. Among his favorite unofficial charities was to give benefits for the families of policemen and firemen killed in action. According to U. S. Thompson, "He would get the best names in show business to appear on his program, and they'd turn over the receipts to the widow. That's why he was so well loved. In those days, that was the quick way to the public's heart, to appear on those benefit programs. And Bill used to do as many as three a night." Another quick way to anyone's heart was to remember names, and Bill's memory for names was uncanny. Given enough time, he probably could have introduced personally nearly everyone in that first-night audience, including a goodly number of the police officers. "He always introduced people in the audience, he knew all of them," Ed Sullivan recalled. "I said to him once, 'Bill, for Christ sakes, how do you remember those names? I can't remember two weeks after I meet them.'"

The Hot Mikado proved to be well worth seeing. While the show stuck quite closely to the original Gilbert and Sullivan script, it took marvelously imaginative liberties with scenery, music, and costumes. Nat Karson, who had designed the costumes for the Harlem Federal Theater's production of *Macbeth* (produced by Orson Welles and directed by John Houseman), had swamped the stage with gaily blended colors, suggesting a Japan "as torrid as Fujiyama in eruption," according to one reviewer. Equally stunning was Hassard Short's sense of timing. He had both staged and directed the show and, wrote Robert Coleman of the *New York Daily Mirror,* "piles novelty on novelty. Always manages to bring forth something fresh whenever the swing formula threatens to lose its appeal and pep. Manages to have a surprise and a wallop up his sleeve when it is most needed."

Continued Coleman, "When Mr. Todd cast Bill Robinson as the Emperor, we had our doubts as to the wisdom of the procedure. Bill, it seemed to us, was much too valuable an asset to bring on about the middle of the second act. We thought he ought to be spotted earlier in the evening. But Michael Todd knew what he was about. Bill taps on just when a terrific sock is required for a crescendo finish and delivers comedy and dancing dynamite. The King of colored steppers, assisted by brigades of Jitterbug Girls and Boys and Tap-a-Teers, set the stage ablaze."

The showstopper was Bill's rendition of "My Object All Sublime." The Broadhurst thundered with the applause of eight encores. Standing in the wings while waiting to return to the stage for yet another bow, Bill whispered to the stage manager, "Success at last." But he was not referring to his reception as the Emperor. He was reveling in the achievement of being offered credit at Tiffany's earlier in the day.

The *Mikado* company had decided to buy a watch for Hassard Short, so Bill had picked it out at the Fifth Avenue jewelers' and asked that it be inscribed "In appreciation from the 'Hot Mikado' company, March 23, 1939." That afternoon when he had gone to pick it up, when the time came to pay for it, he discovered he didn't have enough cash. "That's perfectly all right," the salesman had said. "We'll charge it to you. Of course take it with you."[11] To a poor black kid from Richmond, Virginia, *that* was the top of the mountain.

Among the Jitterbug Girls in *Mikado* were Rosetta LeNoire, Bill's goddaughter, and a young dancer from Brooklyn named Elaine Plaines, who used the stage name Sue Dash. Bill had gotten her a place in the chorus, for she had come to occupy a special place in his heart. Elaine's sister, Dot, was a dancer at the Cotton Club, and it was there that Elaine had first met Bill. "Dot loved ice cream, too," Elaine recalled in 1974, "and any holiday Mother would call Breyers and order an ice-cream cake. I remember it was Easter that time, and the cake was a big Easter bunny with pink ears of strawberry ice cream. It cost about twenty-five dollars, which was a lot of money back then. Mama took me to bring this cake over in the afternoon. She sent it to Bill, even though my sister ate most of it. It was sent to Bill for everyone to have. It was the first time I ever saw him backstage. They said, 'This is Dot's little sister' and that kind of stuff."

Nineteen years old, Elaine was extremely shy and carefully protected by her family. At the time, she was working in the chorus line at the Apollo Theater. "My sister used to call up to the Apollo and she'd say, 'You watch out for my kid sister.' My mother used to wait for me every night at the Ralph Avenue [subway] station in Brooklyn. At the Apollo, after each show you had a rehearsal, and anyone who liked me would ask me out for a drink. But I used to say, 'No, no. My mother's waiting for me. I have to go to Brooklyn.' They'd say, 'Brooklyn! Forget about it!'

"One night Bill came up to the Apollo and he was furious. There was a guy on the radio who dedicated records, a white guy named Symphony Sid. He had said, 'This next record is dedicated to the chocolate dolls at the Apollo,' or something to that effect. He didn't mean anything by it, and the girls knew it. He meant it as a term of endearment; in fact later he even married a black girl. But Bill heard it and took it the wrong way. He came to the Apollo raising sand. He came up to the dressing room. He knocked on the door. The radio was still on to the same guy, and Bill said, 'You mean to tell me you're gonna let a white man say something like that about you?' He called them all kinds of names because they accepted it in the way the man had intended it. They knew the man and liked him. I didn't know him. I didn't know a soul. I didn't even know how to put on my lipstick. I was sitting over in a corner and said, 'My

God! It's Bill Robinson!' Well, he stormed out of the dressing room and down the steps. I remember his voice was loud. Loud!

"Then, the next day, he came by and sent someone upstairs: 'Bill Robinson wants to see you.' I was so scared. 'See me?' The girls all said, 'You better go. He could get you fired from here and stop you from working.' All I could say was, 'What does he want me for?' Then I was actually face-to-face with him, and he was actually saying, 'You're Dot's little sister.' That day he started calling me 'Little Sis.' Then he came by one day and asked if I wanted to go up to Small's Paradise. The chorus girls said, 'You better go. He could stop you from working.' I was scared of the man. From the way the girls in the dressing room talked about him, I felt I could be, you know, executed if I didn't listen to what he said. He was the Mayor of Harlem, he was this, he was that. So I went up to Small's with him, but I couldn't eat. That's how it started. But no one ever thought it meant anything. I was just Dot's little sister. I was in awe of him. I went out with him because I didn't know what else to do."

Bill was not sure what he wanted with Elaine. She was more than forty years younger than he was, and painfully shy. He must have sensed that he intimidated her, and was anxious to prove to her that he was not to be feared. But Bill also realized that, painful as it was to admit it, he was hopelessly drawn to her. He had never been a womanizer. Rae Samuels included that in the list of vices he did not have: "He was a man who didn't run after girls. He didn't smoke or drink, ever." He must have felt guilty about the way he thought about Elaine, and how often she entered his thoughts. Perhaps he told himself that she was just a young girl who needed a little help in the tough world of show business and that he was simply giving her that help. That, no doubt, is how he justified seeing her and getting her a job in the chorus of *The Hot Mikado*. Once they were working in the same show, he tried very hard to treat her no differently from the rest of the chorus girls.

The night following the premiere of *The Hot Mikado* Bill opened in the latest Cotton Club Parade with Cab Calloway and his orchestra, gospel singer Sister Rosetta Tharpe, Will Vodery's Choir, and dance team Glen and Jenkins in a show that most critics hailed as fine evidence of the downtown club's continued viability. The way Bill juggled his commitments to both the Cotton Club and *The Hot Mikado* was worthy of its own critical review. He did the 7:30 show at the club, then dashed to the Broadhurst in time for his second-act appearance at 8:40. He then returned to the club for the midnight and 2:00 A.M. shows. It was an eight-hour performing day, and on Wednesdays and Saturdays he also did *Mikado* matinees. How did his feet stand it? His nightly explanation to Cotton Club audiences was transcribed by a local reporter: "Folks, I goes home after dancin' and runs the tub half full of water as hot as I can stand. Then I pours in two quarts of gin. I soaks my feet in it for three hours and then wraps 'em up in cotton battin'. When I gets up in the mornin', 'em feet—they's drunk. They don't know what they're doin'."[12]

Bill missed only two performances that spring, neither for reasons of health. The first time was when he traveled to Washington at the invitation of Mrs. Eleanor

Roosevelt. The Daughters of the American Revolution had barred black singer Marian Anderson from singing at Constitution Hall, so Mrs. Roosevelt and a group of friends had arranged for Anderson to give a concert at the Lincoln Memorial on April 5. Bill was among the seventy-five thousand who attended.

Ironically, the second time Bill had to miss a performance occurred when he believed he had been treated unfairly because he was black. A new animated electric sign had been installed at Forty-seventh Street and Broadway, and among its offerings was a display of Bill's tap steps. One evening on his way to the Cotton Club, Bill joined the crowd that had gathered to watch the sign. Patrolman Thomas Christian came along. He had received orders to keep crowds from congregating on Broadway during theater hours. The 1939 World's Fair had opened on April 30, and city officials wanted to keep Times Square cleared of beggars and pickpockets, and to discourage situations, like large gatherings, where such street denizens did their best work. Everyone but Bill complied with Officer Christian's order to move along. Bill thought he had a right to watch his own steps. According to Officer Christian, he said, "I won't move. Why don't you chase white people?" Bill was arrested for disorderly conduct and taken to the Forty-seventh Street police station. A large crowd followed, many shouting to the police officer that he had arrested Bill "Bojangles" Robinson. Someone offered to post bail, but that proved unnecessary. Bill denied that he had said anything disrespectful to the officer, and Magistrate August Dreyer dismissed the charge. Less than a week later, Bill tapped triumphantly past that same spot, marking his birthday by dancing down Broadway from Sixty-first Street (because he had turned sixty-one) to the Broadhurst Theater at Forty-fourth Street. He also had a nine-man police escort, though it is not known whether Officer Christian was in it. That night the Cotton Club gave him a big birthday party.

The 1939 World's Fair was the first such fair to be held in New York since the Exhibition of the Industries of All Nations at the ill-fated Crystal Palace in 1853–1854, and the city was all abuzz, not just with pride but with dreams of flowing tourist dollars. The Cotton Club remained open that summer with a World's Fair edition of its Parade, and even added Sunday night programs honoring various stars who were in town. Bill was featured in one of those shows: *The Hot Mikado* moved out to Flushing Meadow Park in June with its own, less elaborate World's Fair version. It was so successful that the originally scheduled two shows a day were increased to three—at 5:00, 8:30, and 10:30 P.M.

After the last show, Bill took the Long Island Railroad back to Manhattan, arriving about 12:45 A.M. He then did the 12:30 and 3:00 A.M. shows at the Cotton Club. Home around 5:00 A.M., he usually went to bed at Fannie's insistence ("Some people don't think I get enough sleep," he often grumbled). Up around 10:00 A.M., he had time for interviews and charity work until midafternoon, when he took the Long Island Railroad back to Flushing. He wanted more to do, since he believed he did his best shows when he walked on tired because he "relaxed on his feet."[13]

Elaine Plaines was a member of the *Mikado* company out at Flushing Meadow Park, as was Rosetta LeNoire, Bill's goddaughter. "The first time I ever felt even a little comfortable around him was during the time we played at the World's Fair," Elaine recalled. "He gave me and Rosetta some money—she was the mothering type and always took care of the younger girls—and he told us to go over to some place and eat. It was big money to me—thirty, forty, fifty dollars—and I used to say, 'Wow, look at all that money!' We used to go to eat where he told us to, because he would always stop in to make sure. He said, 'If you don't do anything else decent, make sure you have a decent meal.' He said he'd had a partner named Cooper. Cooper used to save every penny he could. He even saved on his food and used to eat in a dingy place if it was only twenty-five cents for a meal. And one time Cooper got some bad sickness from eating bad food. . . ."

Bill was still being very discreet about his feelings for Elaine. If he wanted to take her out to dinner, he would also take along half the chorus, or at least Lillian Alpert Wolf. He gave her presents that he took from the safe in Marty Forkins's office. But it was obvious to nearly everyone except Elaine that he was in love with her. According to Lillian Alpert Wolf, to Elaine "he was just Uncle Bo and he was buying her beautiful things." Elaine didn't even realize that others saw anything wrong in her relationship with her "Uncle Bo," though she must have been puzzled by what those others did at times.

Bill and Joe Louis, the two biggest heroes of the black community, were very good friends. They often appeared at benefits together, and Bill made huge bets whenever Joe went into the ring—$25,000 on the Brescia fight, $10,000 on the bout with Carnera.[14] They and their wives saw each other socially. By the time *The Hot Mikado* moved out to Flushing Meadow Park, Joe's wife, Marva, had begun to suspect what was going on with Elaine, and she did not like it. According to Rae Samuels, "They didn't get along too good because Bo was romancing Elaine." Lillian Alpert Wolf was backstage one night. Bill and Elaine were in Bill's dressing room. Lillian saw Fannie and Marva arrive and rushed to tell Bill: "Bo, Little Bo and Marva are coming in. We have to get Elaine out." Elaine escaped out the dressing room window. Thanks to such machinations, Fannie remained unsuspicious about her husband's relationship with Elaine for several years.

August 25, 1939, was Bill Robinson Day at the fair. A local cash-register company wanted him to do a dance on the giant machine that showed the daily attendance, and Bill thought that was a fine idea. However, the insurance company that held a thirty thousand dollar policy on his legs forbade his doing the stunt.[15] He did give one of his backward-running exhibitions—seventy-five yards against local college athletes running one hundred yards forward. He never considered such exhibitions undignified, for himself or other talented runners. He had followed the career of black track star Jesse Owens with great interest and had urged Marty Forkins to manage Owens's post-Olympics career. According to Rae, "After Owens won the Olympics in Germany, on the boat, on the way back to the States, Bill wired him and said he'd got him a manager. It was Marty. Forkins booked him. He booked him in Cuba and he ran against a horse."

Jesse Owens's exhibition races against horses were later regarded as evidence of his degradation as a black athlete in American society; and Marty Forkins was viewed as someone who had used Owens. Patrick Forkins, Marty Forkins's son, disputes this portrayal of his father. He points out that it was Bill Robinson who initiated the contact between Forkins and Owens after the latter returned from the 1936 Olympic Games. Patrick Forkins was then eleven years old.

"When Jesse returned to this country after his legendary performance in the Berlin 1936 Olympics there was quite a lot of praise heaped on him. Here he was met, cheered, and feted by many political and theatrical figures. Among the latter was Bill 'Bojangles' Robinson. Within the next few days they became close friends and Jesse confided to Bill that all this was great and he appreciated it a lot, but he needed to make some money to pay bills and provide for his family. 'Bojangles' said he would fix Jesse up; he put him in his Duesenberg and drove him to my father's office on Broadway. Bill asked Jesse to wait in the outer office for a few minutes while he went in Dad's inner office. In there, Bill announced, 'Mr. Marty, I got outside Jesse Owens, and while he appreciates the fuss being made over him, it ain't helping him none and he needs "walking-around" money, and he wants to start doing something to make money for his family. What can we do for this nice fella?' Then he brought Jesse inside and the three sat and talked for a while to see what could be done to help Jesse." In the meantime, Forkins arranged for Owens to stay at the

Paramount Hotel (he and Robinson footed the bill) and provided a man named Charlie Wellman to stay with Owens to shield him from annoyance. According to Patrick Forkins, "He also, with the assistance of Bill Robinson, provided Jesse with 'walking around money,' which, knowing my father, he never asked to have returned."[16]

Within a few days, Forkins had come up with a scheme. According to Patrick Forkins, "Dad worked a deal with the Cuban government [of Fulgencio Battista] and the Havana racetrack for Jesse to race against a horse that was locally popular, called Julio Caw, on the upcoming New Year's Day. It was set up that Jesse was to be on the inside lane and the race would be run around a curve where a horse normally bears out but a man sticks to the rail, thus giving Jesse every possible chance to win. Other than that, the race was to be run legitimately. Also, Dad would accompany Jesse to Havana to see that accommodations were suitable and the rules of the race were complied with." Patrick Forkins recalled that his father's travel and accommodation expenses were taken care of by the Battista government and he took no commission, for in this way Owens would get more money. Later, Forkins put together a band for Owens to front in a revue that was booked all over the country. Owens was thankful for how Bill tried to help. Later, Owens presented Bill with one of his gold medals as a way of saying "Thanks."

The World's Fair edition of *The Hot Mikado* closed in late October 1939. Mike Todd's press department reported, among other statistics, that Bill had worn out twelve pairs of forty-dollar gold trousers since the show opened seven months earlier. The *Mikado* went on tour a week later, and Bill ordered three more pairs.

Elaine did not go on tour with the company. "I didn't go because I still couldn't leave home. I was supposed to go back to school, but I didn't go. I think Rosetta went on the road with him. We used to be glad when he went because he treated us all like children. He wanted to know where we went between shows—where we went and what we did. And some people used to get sick of him because they wanted to go to different bars. But he made you walk the straight line." Bill kept in constant contact with Elaine by telephone. "He was a phone bug. The girls in Central knew him—you couldn't dial direct back then. One night he even asked them all down to the [Club] Zanzibar as his guests."

As a special favor to Bill, his hometown of Richmond was included on the *Mikado* tour, requiring a long jump down from Washington, D.C.–Baltimore, and an even longer jump back up to Pittsburgh. But back in 1938, when Richmond had held its Bill Robinson Day, he had promised to bring the then upcoming musical to Richmond at the first opportunity. By the time the show reached Chicago in early January, Bill, who had been urged to see a doctor before undertaking his first extended tour in several years, had added an afterpiece to each performance: twenty minutes of dancing and patter reminiscent of the old vaudeville days. From Chicago the show went to Hollywood, then back East to Boston. When the tour ended in mid-April, it had been unquestionably the most successful all-black show since *Shuffle Along* (though the orchestra for the *Mikado* was all white). Bill's next show, it was announced in May, would be all white, with one exception—him.

Marty Forkins and Nat Karson, who had done the costumes for *The Hot Mikado,* had hoped to stage a musical version of *Uncle Tom's Cabin* next, but they couldn't get the necessary financing. Entertainment tastes were changing, and the public was now less receptive to all-black shows. Even Lew Leslie, who had made his fame and enjoyed his biggest success with black revues, saw the handwriting on the wall. After *Blackbirds of 1939,* which starred a young singer named Lena Horne, closed on Broadway after eight nights, he turned to white shows. Unfortunately, however, he had no success with them. According to U. S. Thompson, "He spent a lot of money trying to get a hit, but he never got one. I don't know what it was. He had two or three ventures in white theater, but he never had much success. He had one revue in England with a lot of stars in it called *Whitebirds,* but that didn't make it either." When Leslie died in 1963, Ida Forsyne, one of the original Topsys in *Uncle Tom's Cabin,* who achieved her fame in Europe, commented, "Leslie met his Waterloo when he started playing white international revues." Before he died, Leslie had returned to the form he knew best. "He was trying to promote a show with Ethel Waters called *Black Rhapsody* or *Rhapsody in Black,*" Thompson recalled. "He was broke and needed money, so I gave him a hundred dollars. I didn't have too much money to spare, but he was good to me and Florence. He died owing me that hundred dollars."

Nor did the Cotton Club survive the public's changing tastes; it closed its doors for good on June 10,

1940. The last time Bill played the club was in a brief in-between revue in September 1939. The show, which also starred Louis Armstrong, was a filler between the summer's World's Fair edition of the club's Parade and the new fall show. A variety of problems contributed to the Cotton Club's demise, not the least of which were an indictment for income-tax evasion in the summer of 1939, which had led to a tight federal watch on the club's accounts, higher labor costs, and a stronger musician's union, which demanded one day off per week for its members.[17] Less tangible reasons were the fall from favor of lavish Ziegfeld Follies–type shows and a new interest in the swing jazz of white orchestras led by Benny Goodman, Tommy Dorsey, and Artie Shaw. The larger public responding to jazz found Duke Ellington's style, for example, less exciting. The Duke was upstaged in commercial popularity by Goodman, "The King of Swing."

Blacks in general, and blacks in entertainment in particular, were regarded with suspicion by whites as the decade of the 1930s ended. During the Depression, American Communists had gained a greater foothold, especially among artists and intellectuals, and their widely publicized stand against racial discrimination had not endeared them, or blacks, to the majority population. The WPA Federal Theater Project was among the first casualties of the increasingly rampant anti-Communism in the country. The project became the subject of hearings by the newly formed House UnAmerican Activities Committee, and saw all its funds cut off by Congress in 1939, barely four years after its establishment. In the course of the HUAC hearings, representatives of more than 150 black organizations signed an affidavit attesting that blacks in the project had received equal treatment with whites. But in the view of the committee's chairman, Martin Dies of Texas, that was exactly the point: "Racial equality forms a vital part of communistic teachings and practices."[18]

As the forties began, there were only a handful of black roles to be had either in Hollywood or on Broadway, and these were in otherwise white productions. The actors who got those parts counted themselves lucky. Bill Robinson was among them.

Bojangles was probably the only black performer to graduate from the ranks of pickaninnies to star in a duet in vaudeville, then as a vaudeville single, then to go on Broadway, perform in Hollywood, and appear on radio.

For those who could afford a set, radio guaranteed *free* top national entertainers in the privacy of one's home. Radio was a great way to relieve a starving and depressed nation. Bo and Forkins knew the power of radio, and they grabbed it by the horns. This was no small accomplishment. Unlike its supposedly racially advanced counterpart, film, the radio business had still not decided that blacks were good enough to portray themselves. Shows such as the original *Amos 'n' Andy* only demonstrated that some white radio producers and sponsors were willing to try to get away with old minstrel-show practices. Other white radio producers and sponsors were smarter. They let talent speak for itself on their programs, which were often transplanted vaudeville-style shows. The placard and fanfare were replaced by a musical logo, a fanfare, and a new American breed, the radio announcer. The greatest difference between vaudeville and radio was that instead of playing eight to ten minutes for a few hundred people in a live audience, you were playing to one hundred live audience members, and a microphone hooked you up instantly to a few million listeners on the national radio network.

As far back as 1936, Bill was reaching audiences that had never seen him dance in vaudeville, on Broadway, or in films. Some would never see him, but they loved the distinct sound of his taps. He was akin to a terpsichorean percussionist. His taps were his instrument, though not his only one. He was still using his old vaudeville gag of making funny sounds with his lips (a trombone, a mosquito, or a car) and his ever-endearing deep-throated chuckles. The same qualities that had made him successful in vaudeville were now making him successful in radio. He was one of the few black American citizens who had the ear of the nation. And that ol' publicity hound knew how to use it. Vaudeville, though it was dead or dying on the road, was alive and well on coast-to-coast broadcasts. Most white vaudeville stars found the transition easy, while most black performers found radio just like early vaudeville—difficult to impossible to break into.

In a way, since Bojangles did so few records, Bill Robinson's radio performances were an archives of his talent and performing history. You heard his vaudeville jokes, vaudeville songs and dances ("Grand Opera with the Bunions," "When the Bluebirds and the Blackbirds Got Together," "Old National," and "Swanee River"), the asides he gave while dancing on the stairs, new Cotton Club songs ("Suzi Q," "Truckin'," "Tall, Tan and Terrific," "The Old Man Routine," "That's Why They

Call Me Shine," "The Harlem Bolero," "Going to Ballyhoo," "Copper Colored Girl of Mine," and "The Bill Robinson Walk"), his performance in *The Hot Mikado,* and some of his bond-raising efforts during World War II. Fortunately, many Bill Robinson radio performances were recorded, so his talent will never be lost. (Bert Williams and Florence Mills weren't as lucky. Williams [of Williams and Walker] only made it to Edison cylinders and a few 78-rpm records. Florence's fate was worse. Her talent was never reproduced on records. Her voice and image were recorded only once during a film audition of an Irving Berlin song—and that film is now lost.)

At least once in every radio show you would hear Bo use one of his favorite expressions: "I haven't been this proud since I was colored"; "Ooh, them bunions is running wild tonight!"; what he said to Charlie McCarthy, "Boy, if you get me angry, I'll carve you into a flight of stairs and do a tap routine down your backbone!"; or the way he would call out, "Everything is copasetic!" or "Shoot me while I'm happy! I don't care what happens now!"

In addition to one-liners, he often told stories—a throwback to his Cooper and Robinson days. "Funny thing happened the other day. A colored boy from Harlem walked into Pennsylvania Station and said, 'I'd like to have a job.' They said, 'Sorry. We haven't got any.' He worried the stationmaster so that the master said, 'We'll have to give you a job. Can you grease switches?' He said, 'I can do anything.' The master said, 'Be here tomorrow morning at five A.M. and we'll give you a job.' He goes back to Harlem and says, 'Honey, I got a job greasing switches and I start work tomorrow morning.' In the morning he goes down to the station and they start him out greasing switches. That night at six o'clock he didn't show up. Wednesday he was still missing. Thursday they got kind of worried. But Saturday afternoon they got a telegram: 'I'm in Atlanta, Georgia, but I've run out of grease!'"

And his old vaudeville standard, "Funny thing. Down South when you die, they call it 'sitting up.' Up North, they call it 'a wake.' There was a fellow laying stretched out in a casket and everybody was singing and praying. There was a friend of his sitting behind a stove, laughing. So, one big old sister got up and said, 'Son, you should be ashamed of yourself—laughing at the boy layin' there dead.' He said, 'I'm not laughing at him 'cause he's layin' there dead. I'm laughing at what he said the night before. The night before he died.' She said, 'What was that?' He said, 'We was all over in the poolroom arguing. He said he didn't believe there was no heaven and he didn't believe there was no hell. I'm just laughing at him layin' there all dressed up with no place to go.'"

And just as in vaudeville, Bill always said hello to his friends out there in the audience. Once, Rudy Vallee had just finished giving Bill one of his big buildups and a fanfare. Bill walked onto the stage and up to the microphone. Bo said, "Thank you, Mr. Rudy. That was very copasetic. I just hope my little protégée, Shirley Temple, is listening in tonight. Which she always do. And while speaking of Shirley, ladies and gentlemen, I want to pay thanks to the man who I think is the greatest dancer of all times—and that is Fred Astaire. And Fred, I want to thank you for the lovely things you said about me last week. Folks, do you see these shoes? I bought them especially for tonight. They cost fifty bucks. So lead me into action, professor, and let symphony be kin to sin. Everything is copasetic!"[19]

10

Uncle Bo

It might have been the ideal time for Bill Robinson to retire from the commercial stage. As a dancer, he was at the top of his form. As a professional, he had no peer. If he had announced that he was retiring because Hollywood and Broadway had turned their backs on blacks, his statement would have made headlines, would have been applauded by black activist organizations like the NAACP, and might have caused at least a few Hollywood and Broadway producers to rethink their attitudes. But Bill was in no position to take such a stand. For one thing, he needed the money he earned from performing. It was estimated that in his career in show business he had earned upward of four million dollars. But, as Bill was widely quoted saying on the occasion of his sixty-first birthday, "Mistah, this is the hand that threw away two million bucks that these old dancin' feet have earned. Oh, them dice."[1] Gambling, expensive tastes, expensive gifts, extensive generosity, income taxes, the house in California—all these steadily drained his income. Thanks to Fannie, he did have some equity besides his various insurance policies, but it was not the kind of equity that would support him in retirement. In fact, having no such equity, he was worth far more dead than alive. Since he had no intention of dying anytime soon, he had to keep working to support his life-style.

Even if he had been comfortably fixed for his old age, it is unlikely that Bill would have retired. He *had* to keep working. He needed that stimulus as much as he needed to gamble. He did not know how to relax; for him, relaxing was dancing when he was so tired that his feet went about their business automatically. According to Elaine, "When the reporters asked him when he was going to retire, I don't think they meant that he was getting old. I think they meant, when are you going to stop and have a good time? But to him, working was a good time. I remember him always saying, 'This is fun for me. This isn't work.' And I believe, all through life, that was the way it was for him. The only thing that could get him out of a crap game was work. Even a young bride couldn't get him out of that game." Bill needed to be active, and after fifty-plus years, that meant spending a good portion of his day onstage, any stage. He would have preferred it to be with a black company, and no doubt he approached Forkins with the idea of forming another touring company along the lines of *Goin' to Town*. But Forkins always kept one ear to the show business ground, and he realized that if he couldn't capitalize his musical version of *Uncle Tom's*

Cabin he would have no success finding investors for a Bill Robinson revue. In years past, he could have taken the concept to one of the big vaudeville circuits, but by 1940 they were no longer the powers they had once been. One by one, the major vaudeville houses had changed their presentations from live entertainment to movies; the celluloid medium offered variety shows without the expenses of weekly salaries, sets, or wear-and-tear on the stage. The smart vaudeville managers had turned to film distribution, or formed con-glomerates with filmmakers. In these labyrinthine cor-porate structures, there was no longer a Mr. Keith or a Mr. Albee with whom one could deal directly; or, if such managers were still accessible, they no longer had the power they once wielded.

Vaudeville was alive and well in diminishing numbers of theaters in cities across the nation. It was especially vital in theaters that catered to blacks, but with the ex-ception of the Apollo in Harlem, the Standard in Phila-delphia, the Howard in Washington, D.C., and a few other major black theaters, they could not afford Bill Robinson. And the major white theaters that still of-fered variety shows had followed the change in taste of the majority—they offered what the public wanted, and the public wanted white.

In the middle of October 1940, Bill began rehearsing with the otherwise all-white cast of *All in Fun*. Phil Baker and Leonard Sillman co-starred and co-produced. Bill, along with Imogene Coca, Pert Kelton, Rosita Moreno, Red Marshall, Hope Manning, Nancy Noil, Ben Less, and others, would be seen in specialty num-bers. Representing an investment in the neighborhood of $125,000, the show counted among its backers Tyrone Power and Jack Benny; but a lot of money did not guarantee success. During the out-of-town tryouts, *All in Fun* proved to be anything but: Critics judged it "scattered and mediocre." It lost money in New Haven. In Boston Phil Baker quit both as co-producer and co-star. The show didn't even bother to go on to Philadelphia. Instead, Sillman, now the sole producer, concentrated on changing the show to give it some of the freshness it lacked. By special arrangement with Actors Equity, Sillman was granted an additional rehearsal period in the pre-Christmas layoff. He had to agree to guarantee the cast two weeks' employment from the date of the Broadway premiere—play or pay. By the time the show premiered on December 27 at the Majestic Theater, Sillman was no longer performing, and Bill Robinson was the star—the first time a black had achieved that status in an otherwise all-white production. He stood out in other ways, too, according to the critics. Wrote Brooks Atkinson in *The New York Times,* December 28, 1940, "To begin at the top: Bill Robinson. He is the star . . . and no wonder, for the Hot Mikado of Harlem has tapped his dogs so long that the language they speak is music in everyone's ears. In the third number of the current potpourri Bill comes gleaming on in a white sailor suit and starts dancing like an aristocrat—his back wonderfully straight, his eyes rolling in delight, his head wagging a little from side to side and his feet tapping lightly and crisply a rhythm all his own.

"Everyone knows Bojangles Bill and is devoted to him, and nearly everyone has seen his stair dance, which is repeated here with gaudy stage elaborations that do not improve it. But this department never ceases admiring the genius of this magnetic master of the taps who treats his feet kindly and has preserved all these years the springy step, the impeccable taste of the instinctive artist and the gusto of an honest showman. The rhythm has become so much a part of him that even when he is standing still you feel that he is dancing.

"This notice begins brightly with the good things in *All in Fun,* because most of the show is routine according to old patterns. It reveals little talent and no freshness."[2]

Bill could not save *All in Fun.* It opened on a Friday night and closed Saturday night, having been presented exactly four times, one of which had been a preview. Total receipts amounted to $6,900, which didn't even cover the two weeks' salary for the cast of sixty-four which Sillman had been forced to guarantee. For many in the cast, the failure of the show was disastrous; for Bill, it was a minor setback. He went right into the Versailles, the first time he had ever played an East Side nightclub.

Even when he was not starring in a show, Bill had an uncanny knack of making headlines. At the end of January he played local hero again by trying to run down another purse-snatcher, though this time he did not pull his gold-plated revolver. It was night, and Bill was driving in lower Manhattan. He parked at the intersection of Lafayette and Kenmare streets and saw a teenager reach into the window of the car parked in front of him, grab a woman's purse, and run. Bill swung his car out and around the woman's car and pursued the boy for two blocks before a truck cut him off, and the youth, who looked about fifteen, disappeared. Ironically, just a few days later, Bill shared headlines with another teenager in trouble, this time as his benefactor.

Jay Gould Cotton of Savannah, Georgia, had been arrested in Brooklyn as a fugitive from justice. The previous September he and a friend had robbed a Savannah grocery store of fifty dollars, and both had been arrested. Cotton had been brought to trial first and sentenced to serve ten to twenty years at hard labor. Somehow, he had managed to escape from a Chatham County chain gang and hitchhike to Brooklyn, where he found work as a janitor before being arrested as a fugitive. How Bill became involved with the youth is not known, though it is quite possible that he learned of the boy's plight during one of his regular visits to the police station near Elaine's home. He visited Elaine's family quite frequently and, as was his habit, had made friends with the local police. He put up the boy's $1,500 bail and personally guaranteed that Cotton would be present at the hearing scheduled two weeks hence. In the interim, he bought the boy a new wardrobe. While Cotton stayed with his court-appointed attorney, Lennie L. George, he arrived at the hearing in Bill's car.

It is possible that Jay Cotton did not stay with Bill and Fannie because he had to remain in Brooklyn under the terms of his bail. It is also possible that Bill and Fannie did not have room for him. Roy Wright may have been living with them at the time. Back in 1938 Bill had helped Wright, a former "Scottsboro Boy," who had been arrested in 1931 with eight others on charges of raping two white women, Ruby Bates and Victoria Price, on a train in Alabama. Originally sentenced to die in the electric chair, along with seven of the others, Wright had, through the efforts of the International Labor Defense, the NAACP, and the U.S. Supreme Court, eventually won a new trial in 1937 and, along with Eugene Williams, Olin Montgomery, and Willie Roberson, been released. In August 1938 the four appeared at the Apollo Theater as a "Special Added Attraction," and Bill had taken an interest in Wright. He paid for a vocational training course for him and helped him in other ways—and would have mourned deeply had he lived to know that in 1959 Wright stabbed his wife in a jealous rage and then committed suicide.

In spite of Bill Robinson's fame and wide professional experience, his money and ability to gratify most of his desires, and his *comparative* insulation from the degradation of being black in America, there were two things basic to the majority of human beings that Bill Robinson had not enjoyed—a nuclear family and children. By 1938, when he was sixty years old, he had begun to "acquire" children, and it is probably no coincidence that this urge to care for much younger people had begun to assert itself after meeting and working with Shirley Temple. After Shirley, whose Uncle Billy he would be to the end of his life, there was Roy Wright, then Jay Gould Cotton. In December 1941, he became the wartime foster father of a twelve-year-old girl whose parents, though alive, could not care for her and had turned her over to an organization called Foster-Parent Plan for War Children, which maintained forty-one children's colonies in England. And then there was Elaine, whom he was calling "E" by now (she still called him "Uncle Bo").

At Bill's insistence, they spent a considerable amount of time together, often in Bill's dressing room when he was playing in New York. Although she felt more comfortable with him than she had at first, Elaine was still very much intimidated by him. "He was very strict. He made half hour for every show and expected everyone else to make half hour. He was very neat. He had a trunk for his suits, a trunk for his shoes. And everything was covered when it was packed. And in his dressing room, if you moved one thing from this way to that, while he's talking to you he'd go and put it back the way it was. Everything had to have its right place. Opening day in a new theater, he'd be dusting in there like a porter. Dusting the poles where the clothes would be hung. [According to Rae Samuels, her husband, Marty, who smoked like a chimney, was the only person Bill would allow to smoke in his dressing room.] He used to dust every spot in that dressing room before anything would come out of his trunks. He was spotless. Then he had special cloths. One was embroidered. He would put that on the table with his pictures [most of them of Shirley Temple] and his brush and comb. He would dust the closets and hang up special sheets in the back before he hung his suits. Then he had another cloth that would go over the clothes. Then, in the morning, he would undo all that, fold them up, then put them in a drawer. Then at night, go put them all back again."

Elaine didn't dare touch a thing in Bill's dressing

room. But he seemed to want her there, and she complied. He gave her expensive presents, and to a timid kid from Brooklyn, he was the epitome of wealth and sophistication, if something of a pain in the neck. He was always lecturing her about the company she favored, the places she went, the hours she kept. But he also told her frequently that he would help her with her career.

No doubt he presented the idea of his own club to her in the hope that she might perform there. Certainly, he shared with her his dream of opening a club of his own in Harlem. It had bothered Bill when the lights went out in Harlem, when the Cotton Club moved downtown, when other clubs either moved or closed, and Harlem ceased to be a nightlife center. He had been talking about reviving that Harlem for several years, and in February 1941 he opened the Mimo Professional Club, 2337 Seventh Avenue at 132nd Street. It was a basement nightspot featuring an all-black show at midnight and at 2:00 A.M.; the first shows featured Carol Wright, Charley Bristol, Claudia McNeil, Limegouse Brown, and others, as well as a brown-skinned chorus line. Bill himself performed whenever he could. Clarence Robinson, who had staged many of the Cotton Club shows, did the staging. In the club's short existence, Eddie Barefield, Frankie Newton, and Sidney Bechet led their own bands there.

Unfortunately, Bill was not a businessman. Perhaps he didn't put enough capital into the club in the first place. Recalling the time that Bill needed $750 and asked her to pawn his jewelry to get it, Lillian Alpert Wolf stated that he told her he needed the money "for some club." By 1942 the club was under new management and, known as the Murrain Restaurant, Cabaret, and Lounge, it was in business until 1945.

The Mimo Club might have been more successful if Bill had devoted more time to it. But in a little more than a month after its opening, he was headlining the revue at the Apollo Theater. He enjoyed playing the Apollo, not only because the audiences there were reputed to be the toughest in the world but because there was constant gambling going on backstage. The Apollo was also a forum for new talent, and Bill enjoyed being around youngsters. Sammy Davis, Jr., remembers being taught three tap steps by Bill at the Apollo.

That spring and summer of 1941, Bill threw himself into the war effort, entertaining at war-bond rallies and at local military posts like Camp Dix in New Jersey. At an I Am an American Day celebration in New York in May, he announced that if Hitler ever started for Harlem he personally guaranteed that the Führer would never get past Yankee Stadium.

In the late summer and early fall, Bill appeared in a revival of *The Hot Mikado,* which played a variety of East Coast theaters. Then he was booked as a solo act in theaters in and around New York City. Meanwhile, he did benefits and performed for the war effort. He was not idle, by any means, but it had been some time since he had starred in a major show, revue, or film. And he was not enamored of television. "No one really understood television," Elaine recalled. "He didn't. I remember him doing some closed-circuit show, for one of the colleges. Someone played something that didn't sound right to him when he was dancing toward the steps. He stopped them. He said, 'Wait a minute.' All the fellas said, 'Bill, go ahead, you're on. You can't stop, keep going, keep going.' After turning around and saying something to the piano player, he smiled and there was a whole change when he found out he was actually on." The trouble with live television was that it was hard to know when you were on. And you couldn't improvise or start over if something wasn't right. Even if Bill had understood the medium, he would have had to come up with more new routines than he cared to create. He was well known for having just a few numbers, though he did them to perfection. As George Burns, who was successful in making the transition from vaudeville to television, once said, "If you had fifteen minutes of material [in vaudeville] you could go seven or eight years without repeating a theater. Your fifteen minutes lasted a lifetime. On TV, you need a new joke every night."

Thus, Bill was willing to listen when Twentieth Century-Fox called him to appear in a new film to be called *Stormy Weather*.

Hollywood had recently shown renewed interest in all-black films, and black actors and actresses were too overjoyed to question why. An article in *The New York Times* in February 1943 would shed some light on the matter: "Two major studios, Metro-Goldwyn-Mayer and Twentieth Century-Fox, in producing pictures with all-Negro casts, are following the desires of Washington in making such films at this time. Decisions to produce the pictures, it is stated, followed official expression that the Administration felt that its program for increased employment of Negro citizens in certain heretofore re-

stricted fields of industry would be helped by a general
distribution of important pictures in which Negroes
played a major part." The administration in this case
was Franklin D. Roosevelt's, and no doubt this is one
reason why Bill liked Roosevelt so much.

Lena Horne had already benefited from this govern-
mental pressure on the film industry—she had recently
completed filming *Cabin in the Sky* for MGM, which
also starred Ethel Waters and Dooley Wilson. Now
MGM had agreed to loan her to Fox for *Stormy
Weather*. Cab Calloway and his orchestra were also featured in the film.

Bill and Fannie moved out to their Los Angeles home,
1194 West Thirty-sixth Place, while Bill worked on
Stormy Weather. Lillian Alpert Wolf visited Fannie
while the Robinsons were out there. "She was dressed
in a flowered dress with two different-colored shoes—
one was red and the other was blue. The house was
furnished magnificently. Her bedroom was like a blue-
berry and white. His bedroom was done in brown. We
were sitting there having a drink, a Coke or something,
and I looked at her and I said, 'Little Bo, am I mistaken
or are those glasses on a slant?' She said, 'No, Lillian,
you're supposed to sit and drink until those glasses are
straight.' Then she brought out her dog named Mickey,
a wirehaired terrier. She said to the dog, 'Ethel Waters!'
and that dog growled. Bo and Ethel Waters weren't getting along too well at the time, and Bo had trained his
dog to growl at her name."

Wolf and the Forkinses were in Los Angeles at that
time because Marty had decided to exploit Bill's being

on the West Coast by getting him into a revue produced by Sid Grauman called *Born Happy*. According to Rae, "Bill had just finished the picture *Stormy Weather*, with Lena Horne. Forkins put a little revue together and they played only on the Coast. We had some fellows in there that turned out to be great—the Deep River Boys. We had a real great show. Elaine was with us in *Born Happy*."

When Elaine arrived in California to be in *Born Happy*, Fannie realized at last that Elaine was more to Bill than a protégée. It is likely she had suspected as much for some time, but perhaps Elaine's presence caused her to feel that now she had to act. She confronted Bill and demanded a divorce. Rae Samuels believes that Fannie made a tragic mistake: "Fannie never dreamed he was going to let her get the divorce. *I can tell you that*. She never thought he would let her go through with the divorce, the fool. If she had shut up and done nothing about it, maybe he wouldn't have married that little girl. But when she said to him, 'I'm going to sue for divorce,' he was tickled to death. When they separated, he said, 'I'll give you three hundred fifty dollars a week. Is that fair enough?' Well, whoever heard of getting three hundred fifty dollars a week? But he paid it. He paid it for some time. There were some weeks he missed and then she'd be at him again."

Most people, even those within the special inner circle who were close to Bill and Fannie, were not aware of their impending divorce. It was a shock—to all except Big Bo and Little Bo. They saw it coming. And the reason wasn't money, Elaine, or Fannie. Bo had probably wanted the divorce for a long time—even though he still loved Fannie. But he would never be the one to mention it. He had a binding commitment to Fannie, just as he'd had a commitment to Forkins when they first shook hands to bind their association.

Big Bo and Little Bo remembered the many arguments they had when she tried to convince him to slow down. Little Bo, the former pharmacy school student, was no fool. She knew why Bill was gasping for breath in his sleep and why he felt pains down his arm and in his chest. Bill tried to conceal his doctor's reports, but Fannie didn't need them. She knew he had to retire, or at least slow down to a tolerable pace before he danced himself to death. But if there is such a thing as a "dance-aholic," that's what Bill Robinson was. He would give up everything else, even his own life, before he would give up dancing. Every attempt at showing her love by trying to take care of him only prompted another argument. Pleading with him to reduce his schedule of twelve shows a day had the same result. Telling him to take his medicine and vitamins, to get enough sleep, to do anything to help himself live longer, became irritating reminders of his mortality. He felt she was loving him to death. And if he *had* to die, he wanted to die dancing. Whenever Fannie tried to show her love for him it was enough to give him the needed strength to give up his commitment to her, to Little Bo, the woman he loved most in his life. It was history repeating itself in his mind. He had had to make the same choice as a youngster—stay in Richmond with Granny, or run away to dance. He opted to dance then, and he did again in 1943. Rae Samuels was absolutely correct. They would never have been divorced if Fannie hadn't given him the opportunity by demanding it. But don't think for a moment that Fannie didn't know what she was doing. At the time, she thought it was her last act of loving him.

Bill Robinson was free, free to marry Elaine. He was so sure that it was the right thing for both of them that he didn't bother to consult her. "It wasn't like a proposal," said Elaine Robinson of Bill's decision, "it was more like a statement of fact. He just told some people that it was going to happen. Then, when they asked me, I didn't want them to think that he was a liar, so I just went along with the program. Anyway, he wasn't that kind of person: I can't imagine him saying anything like 'Will you marry me?' He wouldn't walk around saying, 'I love you.' He just wasn't that kind of person." So, it was not actually stated between Bill and Elaine, but understood, that after an appropriate waiting period following Fannie's filing for divorce, the two of them would marry.

Fannie Robinson obtained a divorce from Bill Robinson in Reno, Nevada, on June 19, 1943. By all accounts, it was amicable. Fannie got the house in Los Angeles; Bill kept the apartment in Harlem. Fannie was to continue receiving $350 per week until such time as she remarried. There was no animosity between Fannie and Elaine; Elaine continued to refer to Fannie as "Little Bo," despite the emotional baggage attendant to that name. Fannie did not resent Elaine. According to Elaine, the press—and others—tried to create animosity between them, but it was not really there.

A few days after the divorce, *Stormy Weather* opened at theaters across the northern half of the country. Coming so soon after *Cabin in the Sky,* it was naturally compared with the MGM film, and it suffered from the comparison. In the *New York Sun* of July 22, 1943, the reviewer contrasted the two films and wrote that *Stormy Weather* "keeps away from the earthy, from the poignant, from the imaginative. This picture is Broadway and Hollywood and Harlem, all shiny and expensive and dependent on routines rather than heart. The acting is dull indeed."

While *Cabin in the Sky* had a fairly intricate plot, *Stormy Weather* builds its basically revue format around scenes of Bill relating his character's life story to a group of children. He plays a hoofer who decides to become a professional dancer when he falls in love with a cabaret singer, played by Lena Horne. In that context, he gets several chances to dance, and Lena to sing. In fact, both the film and the song established Lena Horne as a star. Despite its poor critical reception, *Stormy Weather* did well at the box office. It did not pretend to depth, was lively and happy, and, according to black film historian Donald Bogle in *Toms, Coons, Mulattoes, Mammies and Bucks,* represented "wartime escapist entertainment at its peak." The film did not do much for the career of Bill Robinson; by now he was an institution and didn't need any career boosts. The most beloved black entertainer in the country, he had transcended the boundaries of fickle public taste. The fact that his dance routines were well known worked to his favor; in a world turned upside down by the war, he was a comfortable constant in the American entertainment world. Just watching him perform gave people a sense of security, a sense that there were some things that did not change.

Meanwhile, he was undergoing great changes in his personal life. Having been divorced from his wife of twenty years in June 1943, he married young Elaine Plaines six months later. Consistent with his past history, however, he married her while on the road. He was on tour with *Born Happy* in Columbus, Ohio (Elaine was with him and was described in the press as his secretary–dancing partner). They got married at St. Paul's Methodist Church in that city on January 27, 1944. It was a simple ceremony, but anything Bill Robinson did still garnered press coverage, especially when reporters could find a human-interest angle. Bill gave it to them as usual. He put the ring on Elaine's little finger at first, then had to remove it and put it on her ring finger. BOJANGLES JUGGLES RING ran the headline in *The New York Times* on January 28, 1944.

He did not "juggle" much of anything else. When it came to professionalism, he was still a perfectionist. Elaine recalled that not just he, but all the old-timers, were like that. "Sophie Tucker, all of them demanded that respect. Bill would say, 'Only out here twenty minutes to half hour, give me that much respect.' And he also demanded that you be on time. Oh, yes, half hour, better be there. 'Don't just run out of the house, hair not combed and everything. Walk through the streets looking and acting right. If anything happens to you, they're *not* gonna say Sam Brown did this or that, they'll say, "A member of Bill Robinson's show."'"

Nor did he fumble when he was traveling. "Oh, he knew everybody," Elaine recalled. "Every redcap. The waiters. The porters who got the beds. I was always afraid to come out of the room. I only went down to the dining car to eat. But Bill would be out all the time. While the cooks were getting the next meal ready, Bill would sit out there and talk with them. Most of the time he would just listen to the porters on the train. Or passengers would come into the drawing room and come to see him. He never sat still. He was always going."

But in actuality Bill was settling down—at the age of sixty-five, he finally had a family. He may have legally married Elaine that day; but in effect he married her family. He maintained the apartment at the Dunbar in Harlem, but his homebase had now shifted to Brooklyn, where Mrs. Anne Plaines was. "The mother used to bathe his feet," according to Rae Samuels. "That whole family adored him. The mother would have done anything for Bo. He bought her a home over there in Brooklyn and he was wonderful to them. They could have had his heart. It was nice for him to have a family. He didn't have any family."

He called Elaine's mother "Mother," and not just out of politeness. He took a keen interest in the lives of Elaine's sister and brother. Elaine recalled, "My sister was pregnant and we were playing cooncan one night, and the next morning she went to the hospital to have her baby. He said to my mother, 'Mother, we were just playing cards last night. I can't believe it.' He was never close to that kind of thing, and this was so amazing to him. He was probably never around anyone who'd had a baby before."

Home was still Brooklyn for Elaine. "People would come up to the house [the apartment in Harlem] and have dinner just for the night. But that was the only social thing. I don't know about with Fannie, but that was how it was with us. And when he went out I would get right on the train and head back to Mama. I was always heading back to Mama."

On one such occasion, about a year and a half after the marriage, Bill and Marty Forkins attended a baseball game, then returned to Bill's Harlem apartment for dinner. Rae Samuels recalled, "An automobile comes up with Fannie and this undertaker and some politician or judge—could have been Judge Goldstein. Anyway, Goldstein says to Bill and Marty, 'I think congratulations are in order.' They both look at each other, and Goldstein says, 'This is Fannie and her new husband.' Bill stood up and took a bow clear to the ground, like that. He said that was the prettiest damn wedding couple he ever did see. He was so glad that he didn't have to pay the three hundred fifty dollars a week to Fannie anymore."

Bill played Philadelphia, Newark, Pittsburgh, Boston. In between, he went back to Brooklyn. There, every Monday morning when he could manage it, he went down to the local police station and sat in on the lineup. If he saw a youngster or someone else who he felt should not be there, he would bail him out. Elaine went with him once. "It wasn't very enjoyable, but it was very enlightening. They bring these men out who have been accused. This one man, he looked very tough. He was chewing gum, and he kept on chewing it as they said, 'Turn this way,' 'Turn that way,' 'Stand up straight,' 'Take your hat off.' The policeman finally said, 'Take that gum out of your mouth. Is that what you stuck the bank up with?' I will always remember that. Everything was scary to me."

Elaine said that she never saw Bill in a gambling game. But she knew that gambling was a "big part" of his life. Sixty-five years old and he was still outrunning suckers. "I remember one time in California. He had this group of men who gamble there and Bill had won . . . forty thousand dollars. It was a lot of money. Bill had to get back to New York and they didn't want him to leave. Bill got on the train and they followed him in two cars. They were all arrested because in those times gas was rationed. Someone had called the police, I think it was somewhere around Denver. And the police wanted to know how these men made it from California to Denver on the gas that was allotted.

"Then there was the time he was at Yankee Stadium. I was very embarrassed, but I came from a quiet little life. Bill was betting some man a hundred dollars that someone would hit a home run. This big man in the back yelled, 'Oh, sit down. We don't want to touch your dirty money.' And Bill couldn't believe that the man had said that. He yelled back, 'Dirty money? Yeah, pretty, white Shirley Temple money. That's where I got it. Teachin' white Shirley. It's filthy, dirty money!'"

Bill Robinson wasn't bowing to racism anymore—he was too old. And he enjoyed enough respect in the white community to get away with it—even in Miami, where in the 1940s there were no mixed audiences. Rae Samuels Forkins recalled a time when she and Marty had gone to Florida for a vacation, stopping first in Fort Lauderdale and then going on to Miami. Bill decided that he and Elaine should go down there and join them in Miami. "He didn't know anything about down there," according to Rae. "He knew about Richmond, Virginia, but Richmond, Virginia, was high-class in comparison. So, he went down to Miami. He got into a car with Marty, and in those days they didn't allow the colored people downtown at night; they had to be home by eight o'clock. And he wasn't in town more than a couple of hours before he had promoted a benefit in a ball park. Well, you should have seen that."

Bill organized the benefit with Harry Richmond. It was the first all-white show ever to play in Miami for the benefit of underprivileged black children. All the money raised was to be administered by the local chapter of the NAACP, and Bill insisted that blacks be allowed to attend. The mayor of Miami agreed. The blacks had to sit in the back, but they were still allowed to attend, and that was a revolutionary occurrence in Miami. Rae Samuels recalled that the event was memorable in other ways: "He took the mayor's daughter—she couldn't dance at all—and taught her a couple of steps and made her look like she was doing great. The mayor was all puffed up and the place was packed. The poor colored people had to sit in the back. The musicians were all colored and they weren't very good, but Bill didn't want to hurt them or make them look bad. He said to them, 'What's the matter with you fellows? Play out. You're not in Georgia now. Play out.' And all the colored people in the back nearly died. Bo was no Uncle Tom."

By the early 1950s black entertainers like Lena Horne were able to play clubs in Miami. Bill Robinson had helped to blaze the trail.

Bill had initially gone to Florida for a vacation, and that signaled a marked change in his life-style. With Fannie, he had rarely taken a vacation. By 1946, at least according to press reports, Elaine had persuaded him to stop working at the point where he made sixty thousand dollars in any one year, since whatever he earned in excess of that amount would just go to the government. (We suspect that Elaine's mother was the real source of that financial wisdom, not Elaine.) But he was still one of the busiest people alive. He played vaudeville houses, primarily on the East Coast, throughout 1944, and in December of that year he played the Club Zanzibar in Manhattan for the first time. Earl Wilson visited Bill in his dressing room and wondered, to Bill at the time and later in print, how Bill managed to seem so ageless. Bill had no answer. Wilson pronounced that Bill "as of today is copasetic."

"Funny 'bout that word," Wilson quoted Bill saying. "The dictionary write all over the world askin' where did they get that word copasetic, and everybody give me credit in the dictionary. It's a word I started myself when I was three or four down in Richmond. Nobody give it to me, I started it, to mean everything was all right. Nobody else. Jes' myself."[3]

As the new year dawned, everything was all right with Bill. He had a young wife whom he adored, a family at last, and a new Broadway musical revue in the offing. Fannie divorced her undertaker, and moved back into the Dunbar to be close to Bill. *Memphis Bound,* originally titled *Send Me a Sailor,* was a John Wildberg production and an attempt to bring the all-black revue back to Broadway. Also starring Avon Long, a star in later Cotton Club shows, Ada Brown, and Georgette Harvey, *Memphis Bound* was a takeoff on Gilbert and Sullivan's *H.M.S. Pinafore,* first produced some sixty-seven years earlier. In fact, *Memphis Bound* was due to open on Broadway on the eve of Bill's sixty-seventh birthday, and the coincidence was probably no coincidence. After tryouts in Boston, the show opened on Broadway on May 24, 1945. Bill got excellent reviews. The show didn't. It closed in a month.

Bill remained in New York for the baseball season. By November he was back in vaudeville and rehearsing a new revue, featuring Ada Brown, which played in the West through the winter. By mid-March he was back in New York, starring in a revue at the Club Zanzibar, which seems to have taken over from the Cotton Club in its exploitation of various Bill Robinson life and career benchmarks. In May the Zanzibar saluted Bill on his sixtieth year in show business. "Pearl Bailey was there," according to Rae Samuels. "Someone sent him a big horseshoe of flowers, and Bo said, 'Oh, I hope they don't think that I'm dead.'" By this time the celebrations were beginning to take on the atmosphere of memorials.

Bill tried not to regard them that way. He danced along Times Square to benefit the fight against cancer. He participated in a tribute to Jackie Robinson at Ebbets Field. He played an occasional theater date. But he was anxious to be back on the stage regularly, and so Marty Forkins had agreed to produce another Bill Robinson Concert Revue in 1946. It featured the Deep River Boys, who had played with Bill on the West Coast when he was filming *Stormy Weather*; Olivette

Miller, a concert harpist and singer; and Frances Palm, a contralto. Rae Samuels said that her husband, Marty, gave up his other clients in order to produce and travel with Bill's revue, and it is likely that Forkins realized that it would be the last revue he and his old friend would ever do together. For his part, Forkins was afflicted with stomach ulcers and had been cutting back his client roster of late. Theirs was "a beautiful relationship," according to Elaine Robinson. "They really loved each other. Never had a contract—when one promised something to the other, it was done. There was such a closeness, but it was misinterpreted. People didn't think that Bill was his own man, but he was." Elaine recalled a time when she was with Bill in his dressing room and the theater manager came back to say, "I have your money, I'll be back. I'll give it to Marty." According to Elaine, Bill really "blessed that man out." He said, "You give that damn money to me, not to Marty. I'm my own man. I take my own money. I pay him. Was he the man out there working onstage?"

Bill probably needed the money for gambling, or to pay a gambling debt. He was gambling more than ever now that he wasn't so busy working. He frequented the poolhalls from Brooklyn to Times Square to Harlem. "I'm careful," he had told Earl Wilson in 1944. "I know jes' what flat to go in in Harlem and when to come out."

In the same article in which he reported that statement, Earl Wilson wrote that Bill was a "Catholic convert" and noted that Bill had religious tokens in his dressing room along with his Shirley Temple pictures. As there are no references to Bill's being religious before this time, it is possible that he had begun to "get religion" as he grew older. Based on a recollection of Elaine's, however, Bill's attitude toward organized religion was still skeptical. "Some church in Brooklyn had asked him to come over. He went. I knew that he and the Church were so far apart, and I said I hoped he watched himself. I was always so scared. He said, 'First of all, I'm gonna take this handkerchief.' He took it out and he tied his feet up. He told the people in the church, 'These fools [his feet] don't know they're in church. They might break out dancin' any minute. So I'm tying them up to make sure they behave!' And the church just died laughin'. He knew how to get to people. He just said what he felt, no matter where, no matter who he was with. I was so nervous. I told my mother what he said and how nervous I was, and she said, 'What the hell you nervous about? That man's been on the stage for sixty years! He's been before kings and queens. Where have you been?' But I was scared. And it was in Brooklyn, too. If he said anything wrong, my name would be mud in Brooklyn. We were so opposite."

While Elaine worried about her reputation in Brooklyn, Bill had begun to worry about his health. He had developed cataracts and had to undergo an operation; offstage, he had to wear thick glasses, but he would not wear them onstage or in public if he could help it. He did not need them onstage, for he knew a stage—any stage—as if it were part of him. There were few stages in the country on which he had not danced, and when confronted with a new one, all he needed to do was study it thoroughly beforehand and ask questions about the relative position of the orchestra and the type of surface in order to know how to master it. And then he shared that information with his feet, and when they went on they knew just what to do. He could control his feet. But he could not control his heart.

He began to suffer mild heart attacks, though Elaine did not realize what they were. Ironically, it was at a benefit at the Copacabana for the American Heart Association that Bill suffered his first major heart attack, and it came as a shock to everyone, except Bill and Fannie, who saw him perform that night at the star-studded gala. Bill was at the top of his form.

The Copacabana was packed. Ethel Merman, Milton Berle, Louis Prima, Henny Youngman, "Bugs" Baer, Phil Silvers, Sid Caesar, Hildegarde, Cornel Wilde, Ed Sullivan, and Irving Berlin enjoyed encore after encore before Bill even appeared. Then, according to Louise Baer in the *Saturday Home Magazine* of April 24, 1948, "a bolt of ebony flitted across the night club floor and Bill 'Bojangles' Robinson took command. He tapped to cheers, he strutted to thunderous applause, his soft shoe routines brought down the house. Bill Robinson, the grand old man of dance, had done it again. There were whistles and shouts and calling him by name as Milton Berle rushed to the center of the floor and pointing to the frail, graceful, bowing figure—shouted 'seventy years old—how about that? Seventy years old!' Now there was no stopping the applause until Robinson, taking Berle by the arm, did a whirling, strutting, bouncing finish that sent Berle in an exhausted heap while Robinson continued the strenuous bouncing until he disappeared from view."[4]

Backstage, he collapsed and was rushed to the hospital. The doctor who treated Bill immediately took an EKG. "When did he have his first heart attack?" he asked Elaine. "He never had a heart attack!" she responded. "But the X ray shows scar tissue that's healed from an attack," the doctor told her. Then she began to think back. "Sometime he would complain that his shoulder hurt, or that all down his arm it felt numb," she recalled years later. "How did I know that that meant heart? I didn't know from nothing, and I didn't tell anyone. And I remember once when we were on our way to Yankee Stadium. The Dunbar was only a short walk over the bridge to Yankee Stadium and we stopped on the bridge and he said he had to stand there and rest awhile. I said, 'What do we have to stop for?' He didn't say he didn't feel good; he was just holding onto the wall and resting. When Bill said 'attack,' I thought he meant indigestion. It never dawned on me that he was having a heart attack. So he must have been having a few milder ones during those years."

The doctor advised Bill to stop performing, and Bill looked at the doctor as if he hadn't heard him correctly. "But doctor, you don't seem to understand," he protested. "When I walk, I get short of breath. When I talk, I get tired. I even cough and choke when I tries to lie down. But doctor, when I dance I feel wonderful."[5] That was in the third week of April 1948. By the first week in May, he was in Washington, D.C., accepting from President Truman a National Health Assembly citation for his work on behalf of health improvements. On May 24, one month after his heart attack, he hosted three hundred friends at a seventieth birthday celebration aboard the steamship *Bojangles,* an excursion boat that would run from 131st Street at the Hudson River to Coney Island. The boat was forty minutes late being launched because Bill was waiting for "Mother." Finally, the ship had to leave. As it was pulling away from the pier, a policeman ashore shouted that Mrs. Plaines had just arrived, so Bill ordered the ship back to the pier. "Bet nobody ever seen a boat back up for a mother-in-law," Bill joked. He said he knew he was seventy, but he felt more like twenty.[6]

When it came to gambling, he was still acting as if he were twenty. Elaine never realized just how serious his gambling passion was, or how much trouble he could get into because of it. He told her that his habit of borrowing money was just a game, and she believed him. "Another funny thing he used to do," said Elaine in 1974, "he would say, 'It's funny if people think you have money, they are always going to let you borrow money.' It was a game with him, to show that people would give him money." But Bill was protecting her. He needed the money. He may have "psyched out" the people he asked to help him out, but he needed the money nevertheless. And sometimes his life still depended on his getting it.

In August 1948, according to Walter White, who was then executive director of the NAACP, Bill telephoned him and then went to his house with the plea to lend him two hundred dollars. As White later explained in a letter to Marty Forkins, "He told me that he had to pay 1,000.00 by nine o'clock the next morning or else 'something will happen' to him." Bill had eight hundred dollars and called in a favor from Walter White by asking him for the other two hundred. White felt sorry for him and gave in "provided he repaid it by September."7 The money was savings White had laid aside for his son's tuition and he made Bill promise the money wouldn't be returned late.

Bill did not repay the loan by September. By the following September, he still had not paid it back. In October 1949 he received a letter from Walter White addressed to him in care of the Negro Actors Guild of America. White wrote that he was surprised Bill hadn't returned the money, nor had he answered any of White's communications. "It would be most painful for me to be forced to institute legal action to effect repayment," White wrote. He also suggested that Bill send the money and "Thereby save us both unnecessary trouble and unpleasantness."8

Bill never paid White, though it must have bothered him a little not to have done so. He chose instead to use whatever money he had to pursue his gambling habit and to provide for Elaine and her family. Elaine never knew that Bill was in trouble over money. To her, he was still as openhanded as he had always been. "I can remember when he—just like he would get from someone who had, he would give to someone who didn't have," Elaine recalled in 1974. "I guess he was robbing the rich to give to the poor. I never thought of him as a 'Robin Hood' but I guess he was. I know I saw him give away so much money. I used to see kids standing around—and priests. He loved priests. Kids and priests." (Elaine's recollection of Bill's liking for priests supports Earl Wilson's statement that he was a Catholic convert, but since there are no records of Bill's conversion, it may have been an informal one only.)

Whatever Bill's reason for worry—his gambling debts or his heart—he had begun to think seriously about his own mortality. "I sure will be grieved if nobody makes a movie of my life," he told George Tucker of the *Hollywood Citizen-News* in January 1949. "Jolson, Pasteur, Moss Hart, Chopin—[they've made movies about] everyone but me."

He may also have been worried about his finances and his ability to provide for Elaine and her family. Now that he was not working regularly, he was not bringing in much money. Yet Elaine had become accustomed to the lavish life-style he had fostered upon her.

In early February, Elaine and her mother were watching Ted Mack's *Amateur Hour* on television when they were surprised to see Bill appear on the screen. "They had a kid who was imitating him and winning, and when they introduced him to the kid, he cried. It shocked the people on the show, and it shocked us, because that was a sure sign that he was a very sick man. He was not the type of man who would break down into tears. He looked tired. He looked sick. And even though he was crying, he really spoke to that kid. He said, 'Remember, your behavior up here on this stage is fine, but off this stage, out in the street talking with people . . . You can go further up here if you know how to act out there.' It looked like he was remembering back when he was a kid, and it was like he was a tired old man handing over his crown, telling the kid what paths to take and giving him his little bits of knowledge. It was like him saying,

'This is my good-bye,' and it was. You could just see it. He was not scheduled to be on that show. I think he just walked in. And that was the last time we ever saw him on television.

"He came home to Brooklyn from that show. We were all excited, saying, 'We didn't know you were going to be on that show.' But he just sat down and said, 'Mother, I don't think I can go on further.' He put his head down on the kitchen table and I think he was crying. My mother said, 'You've entertained a lot of people and made them happy. You don't have to anymore. Rest. Go on vacation and take care of yourself. Let people entertain you.' He said, 'Mother, I was very touched. I think I actually cried up there.' She said, 'That's okay, Bo. It takes a man to cry. It doesn't make you any less of a man to cry. It shows you have heart. That you're human.' I just sat there in the kitchen. I didn't say anything at all. He almost never left the house in Brooklyn after that."

When he did leave the house, it was to go see his doctor. "He danced up the steps to the doctor's house," according to Elaine. "Just to have any kind of audience, he could pull himself together." He said it was more strenuous to walk up the steps; if he danced, he could get up there quickly and feel a little lighter. Within a month, he was in Columbia Presbyterian Hospital. He had had another heart attack, and when Mrs. Plaines called the heart specialist, Dr. Robert Levy, he said Bill should be taken to the hospital. Elaine's brother drove them all from Brooklyn to Manhattan. "We were two or three blocks from the bridge, and he started to cry," Elaine recalled. "I said, 'What's wrong?' and he said, 'I gotta find a quarter for the bridge.' So I said, 'What do you need a quarter for now? We have practically another half hour before we get there.' He was afraid my brother would have to pay, he never wanted anyone to pay for him. Sometimes he didn't have a dime himself, but he always wanted to be the one. I was scared and worried. Thank God for my mother. He's getting the quarter out and my mother said, 'That's fine.' To me she said, 'How dumb can you be?'"

Bill entered Harkness Pavilion at Columbia Presbyterian Hospital on the evening of November 14. Dr. Levy described his condition as "serious" and hoped that his amazing "native energy" would pull him through. Elaine believed that he would get better, for he was a fighter and was receiving excellent care. "There was one man who came up to us and said that he had arranged for Bill to have nurses around the clock and that he was going to take care of the whole thing. The man said that Bill had done him a favor once, and that he could repay him by paying for the nurses." The press carried frequent bulletins from the hospital—Bill was "resting comfortably," "weaker," "in critical condition," "no significant change in his condition." Thanksgiving Day came, and Bill was still holding on. That morning, Elaine was sitting in the hospital waiting room, listening to the radio. "It was Margaret Mary O'Brien, or somebody, who came on the air and said, 'We're playing this today as Bill Robinson lies dying in the hospital.' That was the first time I thought about him dying. I was really shocked."

Bill knew that he was dying. "We were up there with him," Rae Samuels recalled. "Bill was in an oxygen tent and he kept pushing his hand out underneath the thing [wanting Marty Forkins to take his hand]. Marty kept saying, 'No, Bill, no. Now you've got that all wrong.' I said, 'Marty dear, don't do that. Take the boy's hand.' He said, 'Mother, be still. You don't know.' He was trying to tell him then that he was going. Bo wanted to shake hands with Dad. Marty was trying to say, 'No, no, you've got that all wrong. That isn't so.' But he was going. He lived for a few hours after that."

"It was seven twenty-eight that night," Elaine recalled. "My sister and I were in the waiting room downstairs when the nurse came down and said that he was going. We went up to the room. I touched his hands and they were very cool. They asked us to leave the room. Then, the next time they asked us back in—it was maybe three minutes later—she said he was gone. I remember how he laid there so stiff with a blank expression. I said, 'What do you mean, "He's gone"? His feet are still moving.'

"The next thing I knew, Ed Sullivan, Noble Sissle, and people like that were all around telling me how they were going to handle the funeral and things like that. My mother said, 'It's right. He was a public man and the public deserves him now.'"

Bill's friends and admirers paid for his funeral, using funds collected at a tribute to Bill Robinson held in early December, which had been in the planning stages since soon after his admittance to the hospital. Bill's estate, when probated, consisted of a mere $24,169.43, representing life-insurance policies of which Elaine was the sole beneficiary. She gave his guns to the 135th

Street police station in Harlem, with the exception of the famous gold-plated, pearl-handled revolver. Her cousin, who was then a detective with the police department, wanted that gun, and the precinct captain let him purchase it from Elaine for five dollars. A pair of Bill's dancing shoes was bronzed and presented to the Museum of the City of New York. Another pair went to the Grand Street Boys' Club, where it was displayed. There was talk of establishing a clinic in his name at Mount Morris Hospital in Harlem, but nothing came of it.

Elaine Robinson returned to the stage for a time. In May 1950 she appeared with Cab Calloway and others in a revue at the Earle Theater in Philadelphia. She later married a man named Robert Bushnell, settled in Queens, and had a daughter, Robin, named after Bill Robinson. Shy and timid throughout her life, Elaine studiously avoided interviewers, and until Marty Forkins's death, depended on him to handle all questions regarding Bill Robinson.

Fannie Robinson sent Elaine a gift when her daughter, Robin, was born, but they were not in close contact. Fannie had attended Bill's funeral. Afterward she had talked with Elaine and complained about her second marriage. "The papers said that Little Bo and I had had a fight [at the funeral]," Elaine said, "but that wasn't true. The *Amsterdam News* had printed something that was so untrue, and Little Bo called my mother and wanted to apologize to me. Everyone seemed to try to build up some animosity between us. But there never was. Never." Fannie at one time was reported to be writing a book about her life with Bill

Robinson; but all that came of it was an article for *Ebony* magazine titled "I Remember Bojangles." In that article she stated that she was trying to have a park in Harlem named for Bill, but she was unsuccessful.

Marty Forkins essentially retired from show business after Bill died. "My husband was heartbroken," Rae said. "He wept real tears when that man died. He gave up his whole business at the finish, he gave up all his acts to take him on a concert tour." For the next few years Forkins was involved in various memorials that were held on the occasion of Bill's birthday and on the anniversary of his death. He took care of matters like the letter from Walter White about the loan that Bill had never repaid. He shielded the Plaines family from the numerous inquiries about Bill, and he assisted in planning a variety of stage and film biographies of Bill, none of which ever became reality.

Many people think that the song "Mr. Bojangles" is a tribute to Bill, but it has nothing to do with him. The name "Bojangles" is also a Southern term for a mischief-maker, and that is what the name in the song means.

In 1976 the AMAS Repertory Theatre, far off-Broadway, presented a musical version of Bill's life written by N. R. Mitgang.

The public may have deserved Bill Robinson, as his mother-in-law said, but it did not do much to preserve his memory. More than thirty-five years after Bill's death, most people have heard of him, but few know very much about him—"Oh, the man in the song . . . the dancer." He was so much more than that.

NOTES

Chapter 1. "Everything Is Copasetic!"

1. Sullivan's remarks, and those of Adam Powell, are a compilation of various news accounts of the public funeral service, including a special news radio broadcast and newspaper accounts.

2. Ibid.

3. Rachel, William M. E., "The Capitol Disaster, April 27, 1870," *Virginia Magazine of History and Biography,* Vol. 68, 1960, pp. 193–197.

4. There is no documentation of Bill's birth date or family. Jane M. Piro, Assistant State Archivist, Commonwealth of Virginia, provided the following information after checking the statewide index of births, 1870–1879, a Richmond

City birth register for 1878, and an 1880 Virginia federal census index for Henrico County and Richmond City: A Luther Robinson was born November 17, 1877, to William and Adeline Robinson in Richmond City, and a Luther was born May 22, 1876, to N. and E. T. Robinson in Richmond City. In 1880 there resided in Richmond City a Maria Lawson, black female, aged thirty-seven, washerwoman; a son, Charles Parker, aged twenty, a worker in a tobacco business; a daughter, Mary E. Robinson, aged five; and a son, William H. Robinson, aged three. During his lifetime, Bill gave conflicting information about his age. In 1908 he said he was twenty-three, though he was probably closer to thirty. In 1939 he celebrated his sixty-first birthday. The date we use, 1878, is usually accepted.

5. Haskins, James, *Black Theater in America* (New York: Thomas Y. Crowell, 1982), p. 22.

6. Wittke, Carl, *Tambo and Bones* (Durham, S.C.: Duke University Press, 1930), pp. 245–246.

7. *New York Daily Mirror,* October 28, 1935.

8. According to Toney (in his self-published autobiography, *What a Life*), who later took the stage name of Eddie Leonard, he and Bill left Richmond in 1898, after the Spanish-American War. However, all the Robinson sources give the date as 1887 or 1888. In 1898, Bill would have been twenty years old. Leonard, who enjoyed a long and successful career in vaudeville, was in the habit of fudging his age in his later years. When he died in 1941, he claimed to be sixty-five, but the doctor who treated him stated that he was probably over seventy. We believe that he had advanced his age by ten or eleven years by the time he and Robinson left Richmond together. Another less probable explanation is that Bill left Richmond twice, once alone around 1887 and once again with Leonard around 1898.

9. Ibid.

10. Stearns, Marshall, and Jean Stearns, *Jazz Dance: The Story of American Vernacular Dance* (New York: The Macmillan Company, 1968), p. 180.

11. Ibid., p. 81.

Chapter 2. BOJANGLES

1. Osofsky, Gilbert, *Harlem: The Making of a Ghetto* (New York: Harper & Row, 1968), pp. 12–13.

2. Stearns, Marshall, and Jean Stearns, *Jazz Dance: The Story of American Vernacular Dance* (New York: The Macmillan Company, 1968), p. 75.

3. Kimball, Robert, and William Bolcom, *Reminiscing with Sissle and Blake* (New York: The Viking Press, 1973), p. 43.

4. Stearns and Stearns, p. 75.

5. Ibid., p. 76.

6. Fletcher, Tom, *The Tom Fletcher Story—One Hundred Years of the Negro in Show Business* (New York: Burdge & Company, Ltd., 1954), p. 291.

7. Ibid., p. 291.

8. Albee, Edward F., "The Future of the Show Business," *The Billboard*, December 19, 1914.

9. Ibid.

10. Hering, Doris, ed., *Twenty-Five Years of American Dance* (Rudolf Orthwine), p. 51.

11. This and all other court documents cited or quoted in Chapters 2 and 3 are from the New York City Municipal Archives.

12. According to most other sources, he would have been twenty-nine years old in March 1908. In the next chapter we suggest a possible explanation for his giving an incorrect age.

Chapter 3. BILL ROBINSON ON TRIAL

1. The report of Martin Wright's confusion is contained in an unidentified newspaper article, December 24, 1908 (Lester Sweyd Collection, Schomburg Center for Research in Black Culture, New York).

2. Ibid.

3. Unidentified newspaper article (Lester Sweyd Collection, Schomburg Center for Research in Black Culture, New York).

4. Ibid.

Chapter 4. SHUFFLING ALONG

1. Letter from H. B. Branton in Bill Robinson Scrapbook (N. R. Mitgang Collection).

2. Bricktop, with James Haskins, *Bricktop* (New York: Atheneum, 1983), p. 55.

3. McKelway, St. Clair, "Bojangles I," *The New Yorker,* October 6, 1934, p. 31.

4. Letter from J. Reger, War Department, in Bill Robinson Scrapbook (N. R. Mitgang Collection).

5. Stearns, Marshall, and Jean Stearns, *Jazz Dance: The Story of American Vernacular Dance* (New York: The Macmillan Company, 1968), p. 179.

6. Ibid., p. 180.

7. Letter from F. W. Vincent in Bill Robinson Scrapbook (N. R. Mitgang Collection).

8. Letter from E. F. Albee in Bill Robinson Scrapbook (N. R. Mitgang Collection).

9. Letter from Henry Chesterfield in Bill Robinson Scrapbook (N. R. Mitgang Collection).

10. Bricktop, with James Haskins, pp. 78–79.

Chapter 5. BELOW THE HEADLINES

1. Osofsky, Gilbert, *Harlem: The Making of a Ghetto* (New York: Harper & Row, 1968), pp. 108–113.

2. McKelway, St. Clair, "Bojangles II," *The New Yorker,* October 13, 1934, p. 31.

3. Unidentified Omaha article in Bill Robinson Scrapbook (N. R. Mitgang Collection).

4. *L.A. Daily Times,* July 25, 1922.

5. Unidentified ad in Bill Robinson Scrapbook (N. R. Mitgang Collection).

6. *Variety,* July 21, 1922.

7. *L.A. Evening Express,* July 22, 1922.

8. Letter from John Steel in Bill Robinson Scrapbook (N. R. Mitgang Collection).

9. Ibid.

10. *Variety,* August 23, 1919.

11. *Oakland Tribune,* November 17, 1922.

12. *Fresno Morning Republican,* December 1, 1923.

13. Telegram from Edward F. Albee in Bill Robinson Scrapbook (N. R. Mitgang Collection).

Chapter 6. TIDES AND TIMES KEEP CHANGING

1. *New York Daily News,* April 23, 1946.

2. Based on interviews with Ed Sullivan and Lillian Alpert Wolf.

3. *Zit's Weekly Newspaper,* May 11, 1923.

4. *The New York Clipper,* 1923.

5. The *Chicago Defender,* October 8, 1932.

6. *Variety,* March 19, 1924.

7. Myers, Joe, *Denver Express,* 1924.

8. *Zit's Weekly Newspaper,* May 11, 1923.

9. Unidentified ad in Bill Robinson Scrapbook (N. R. Mitgang Collection).

10. Letter from Rogers and Roberts in Bill Robinson Scrapbook (N. R. Mitgang Collection).

11. From Carl Van Vechten papers, Yale University, New Haven, Conn.

12. Ibid.

Chapter 7. Bo on Broadway

1. Telegram from Louis Schurr in Bill Robinson Scrapbook (N. R. Mitgang Collection).

2. Haskins, Jim, *The Cotton Club* (New York: New American Library, 1984), pp. 48–49, 67.

3. Ewen, David, *The New Complete Book of the American Music Theater* (New York: Holt, Rinehart & Winston, 1970), pp. 43–44.

4. Stearns, Marshall, and Jean Stearns, *Jazz Dance: The Story of American Vernacular Dance* (New York: The Macmillan Company, 1968), p. 156.

5. Ibee, *Variety,* May 18, 1928.

6. Stearns and Stearns, p. 182.

7. Fox, Ted, *Showtime at the Apollo* (New York: Holt, Rinehart & Winston, 1983), p. 10.

8. Barnum, Bushrod, "Bojangles," *Cue,* August 14, 1937.

9. Lewis, David Levering, *When Harlem Was in Vogue* (New York: Alfred A. Knopf, 1981), p. 218.

10. *The New York Times,* May 8, 1930.

11. *The New York Times,* May 14, 1930.

12. Tutt-Whitney, Salem, *The Chicago Defender,* November 1, 1930, in Bill Robinson Scrapbook (N. R. Mitgang Collection).

13. Stearns and Stearns, p. 159.

Chapter 8. MAYOR OF HARLEM

1. *The New York Times,* February 13, 1932.

2. Spritzer, Marian, *The Palace* (New York: Atheneum, 1969), pp. 185–186.

3. Marty Forkins papers (N. R. Mitgang Collection).

4. Meehan, James, "Bojangles of Richmond," *Virginia Cavalcade* (Winter 1978), p. 110.

5. McKelway, St. Clair, "Bojangles I," *The New Yorker,* October 6, 1934, p. 26.

6. Strouse, Richard, *The New York Times,* May 23, 1948.

7. *Virginia Cavalcade,* p. 110.

8. McKelway, St. Clair, "Bojangles II," *The New Yorker,* October 13, 1934, p. 33.

9. Barnum, Bushrod, "Bojangles," *Cue,* August 14, 1937.

10. *New York World Telegram,* June 28, 1934.

11. Undated Bill Robinson concert revue (The New York Public Library at Lincoln Center).

12. Bogle, Donald, *Toms, Coons, Mulattoes, Mammies and Bucks* (New York: The Viking Press, 1973), p. 46.

13. Undated concert revue in Bill Robinson Scrapbook (N. R. Mitgang Collection).

14. Galligan, David, "Eleanor Powell: Born to Dance," *The Advocate,* June 11, 1981.

15. Telegram from Shirley Temple in Bill Robinson Scrapbook (N. R. Mitgang Collection).

Chapter 9. THE HOT MIKADO

1.   Haskins, Jim, *The Cotton Club* (New York: New American Library, 1984), p. 109.

2. Undated Bill Robinson concert revue (The New York Public Library at Lincoln Center).

3. *New York Daily Mirror,* December 15, 1936.

4. Ibid. September 11, 1938.

5. Undated Bill Robinson concert revue (The New York Public Library at Lincoln Center).

6. *New York Herald Tribune,* January 9, 1938.

7. *Richmond News Leader,* June 21, 1938.

8. *The New York Post,* September 21, 1938; *New York Daily News,* September 29, 1938.

9. Undated Bill Robinson concert revue (The New York Public Library at Lincoln Center).

10. Ibid. Undated Bill Robinson concert revue (The New York Public Library at Lincoln Center).

11. Ibid. Undated Bill Robinson concert revue (The New York Public Library at Lincoln Center).

12. Walter, Stewart, "Beloved Ebony," *New York World Telegram,* February 6, 1937.

13. *Richmond News Leader,* November 25, 1939.

14. Barnum, Bushrod, "Bojangles," *Cue,* August 14, 1937.

15. *Richmond News Leader,* November 25, 1939.

16. Edited typescript of an unpublished article, 1984; draft of a letter from Pat Forkins to Paramount Pictures, protesting the portrayal of his father in the TV movie *The Jesse Owens Story.*

17. Haskins, Jim, *The Cotton Club,* pp. 156–157.

18. Haskins, James, *Black Theater in America* (New York: Thomas Y. Crowell, 1982), p. 106.

19. *NBC Royal Gelatin Hour,* September 24, 1936.

Chapter 10. UNCLE BO

1. *The New York Sun,* May 25, 1939.

2. Atkinson, Brooks, *The New York Times,* December 28, 1940.

3. *New York Post,* December 5, 1944.

4. Baer, Louise, *Saturday Home Magazine,* April 24, 1948.

5. Ibid.

6. Schumach, Murray, *The New York Times,* May 26, 1948.

7. Letter from Walter White to Marty Forkins, August 1948, Yale University, New Haven, Conn.

8. Letter from Walter White to Bill Robinson, October 1949, Yale University, New Haven, Conn.

ACKNOWLEDGMENTS

Jim Haskins is grateful to Kathleen Maloney, the late Eunice Reidel, and Randy Ladenheim for beliving in this project, and to Ann Kalkhoff, Ann Jefferies, and Kathy Benson for their help.

There are many who have contributed to the writing of this book. N. R. Mitgang would like to thank the following for their inspiration, expertise, and spirit:

Bill "Bojangles" Robinson
Fannie Clay Robinson
Rosetta LeNoire
Elaine Robinson Bushnell
Robert Bushnell
Dot Smalls

Ulysses S. "Slow Kid" Thompson
NBC
William Paley
Bill Bryant
Phil Cappice

Ernest LeoGrande
Marty Forkins
Rae Samuels, "The Blue
   Streak of Vaudeville"
Part Forkins
Lillian Alpert Wolf
Curt Davis
Gwenn Mapp
Idilio Garcia Pena
Monty Arnold
Joe Scandore
Eubie Blake
Dave Chertock
Shields and Yarnell
Cab Calloway
Dan Foley
Bee Freeman
Kenn Freeman
Garson Kanin
The New York Public
   Library at Lincoln Center
Museum of the City of
   New York
Lester Sweyd Collection,
   Schomburg Center for
   Research in Black Culture
Negro Actors Guild
   (Executive Board)
Fred O'Neil
Charles "Honi" Coles
"Sandman" Simms
Bob Markel
Tharon Raines
Aaron Priest
Billy Rowe

Richard Eder
James J. Kriegsmann
James C. Bland
Murray Butchen
Gene Bell
Charles Silver
Museum of Modern Art
Sammy Davis, Jr.
Vernel Bagneris
Billie Allen
Tom Mallow
Chuck Selber
AMAS Repertory Theatre
Gary Halcott
Jerry Lapidus
Ernestine Allen
Pepsi Bethel
James Moody
William T. Deibel
Bertha Case
Alfred Cobbs
Dramatists Guild
Donald Epstein
Joe Franklin
Anita Freeman
Eddie Hunter
Robert Lantz
National Urban League
Molly Moon
Lorenzo Tucker
Al Vigale
Sharon Zinker
Yale Music Library
Lyndon Hart
Screen Actors Guild

Herbert Sydney
Allan Seif
Ed Sullivan
Leigh Whipper
Emmett "Babe" Wallace
Kathryn Barton
Emory Evans
Mr. & Mrs. Jack Mitgang
Ira Cirker
Randy Ladenheim

Shirley Temple Black
Virginia State Library
Lemmuel V. "Eggie"
    Eggleston
New York City Archives
Marion Held
Bert Goldblatt
Bruce Levinson
Dr. Helen Johnson

From the New York City Archives.

Sussman v. *Robinson* trial (March–December 1908). Photostats were acquired by N. R. Mitgang of the following documents:

1. Indictment of William Robinson for the charge of robbery in the first degree, four counts
2. Deposition by Sussman and plea by Robinson
3. Abstract of testimony and guilty verdict
4. Sentencing of Robinson to eleven to fifteen years at Sing Sing
5. Motion for new trial
6. Notice of motion for new trial. Section includes jurors' report and addidavits by:

Percy G. Williams   Bert Williams
Philip F. Nash   David E. Tobias
Edward F. Albee   Samuel McKee
Samuel K. Hodgdon   Charles Hall

William Hammerstein	Martin Wright
F. F. Proctor, Jr.	Henry Rogers
Martin Beck	James Burris
George Walker	George W. Cooper

7. Memorandum in opposition to motion for new trial, submitted by William Travers Jerome, District Attorney

8. Memorandum on motion for new trial, submitted by Karlin and Busch, Defense Attorneys

9. Order and notice of new trial, signed by the Honorable James T. Malone, Judge

New York City Archives collection of letters and telegrams:

Date	To:	From:
10/31/34	Mayor La Guardia	E. Stone
11/7/34	Mayor La Guardia	Bill Robinson
12/15/36	Bill Robinson	Stanley Howe
12/3/37	Mayor La Guardia	Bill Robinson
11/30/37	Bill Robinson	Stanley Howe
11/30/37	Bill Robinson	Mayor La Guardia
4/10/39	Stanley Howe	Bill Robinson
5/12/39	Bill Robinson	Stanley Howe
5/25/39	Bill Robinson	Mayor La Guardia
5/25/39	Bill Robinson	Stanley Howe
11/30/39	Bill Robinson	Mayor La Guardia

Thanks to Bill and Fannie Robinson for creating the Bojangles scrapbooks of newspaper clippings, personal letters, telegrams, and artifacts covering the years 1915–1925. And special thanks to Rae Samuels Forkins and to Pat Forkins for contributing those articles to this book.

PERMISSIONS

From Schirmer Books, A Division of Macmillan Publishing Company, permission to reprint excerpts from *Jazz Dance: The Story of American Vernacular Dance* by Marshall Stearns and Jean Stearns, New York, 1968.

From Viking Penguin, Inc., permission to reprint an excerpt from *Reminiscing with Sissie and Blake* by Robert Kimball and William Bolcom, New York, 1973.

From *The Billboard*, permission to reprint a quotation from Edward F. Albee, December 19, 1914.

From Da Capo Press, Inc., permission to reprint an excerpt from *The Tom Fletcher Story—One Hundred Years of the Negro in Show Business* (New York: Burdge and Company, Ltd., 1954).

From Atheneum Publishers, an imprint of Macmillan Publishing Company, permission to reprint an excerpt from *Bricktop* by Ada Smith and James Haskins, 1983.

From *The New Yorker* magazine, permission to reprint excerpts from "Bojangles 1" and "Bojangles 2" by St. Clair Mckelway, October 6 and October 13, 1934.

From *Variety*, permission to reprint excerpts from advertisements from the following issues: August 23, 1919, July 21, 1922, March 19, 1924, and May 18, 1928.

From *Cue*, courtesy of *New York* magazine, permission to reprint excerpts from "Bojangles" by Bushrod Barnum, August 14, 1937.

From *The* (Oakland) *Tribune*, permission to reprint excerpt from an article of November 17, 1922.

From *The New York Times*, permission to reprint excerpts from articles in the following issues: May 14, 1930, May 18, 1930, February 13, 1932, and May 23, 1948.

From Shirley Temple Black, permission to reprint a telegram from July 29, 1936.

From the New York City Municipal Archives, permission to reprint excerpts from court documents involving Bill Robinson.

From *The Richmond News Leader,* permission to reprint excerpts from articles from the following issues: June 21, 1938, and November 25, 1939.

From the "NBC—Royal Gelatin Hour," permission to reprint excerpts from the transcript of the program of September 24, 1936.

Index